Volcano Escape!

Kathleen Weidner Zoehfeld

RANDOM HOUSE 🏠 NEW YORK

p. i © Greg Vaughn/Alamy Stock Photo; p. 8 © USGS; p. 9 © Sailorr/Shutterstock; p. 10 © Wead/ Shutterstock; p. 11 © servickuz/Shutterstock; p. 12 © S-F/Shutterstock; p. 15 © BlueRingMedia/ Shutterstock; p. 16 © honglouwawa/Shutterstock; p. 17 © Tyler Boyes/Shutterstock; p. 18–19 © www.sandatlas.org/Shutterstock; p. 20 © Brian Overcast/Alamy Stock Photo; p. 21 © Jesús Eloy Ramos Lara/Dreamstime; p. 22 © USGS; p. 25 © Vitoriano Junior/Shutterstock; p. 26 © Pierre Leclerc/Shutterstock; p. 28–29 © Greg Vaughn/Alamy Stock Photo; p. 30 © USGS; p. 31 © Daxiao Productions/Shutterstock; p. 32 © Stocktrek Images, Inc./Alamy Stock Photo; p. 33 © N.Minton/Shutterstock; p. 34 © neelsky/ Shutterstock; p. 35 © Alexey Kamenskiy/Shutterstock; p. 36 © Marisa Estivill/Shutterstock; p. 37 (top) © Sekar B/Shutterstock; p. 37 (bottom) © bierchen/Shutterstock; p. 38 © Krishna.Wu/Shutterstock; p. 39 © Nina B/Shutterstock; p. 40 © Jim West/Alamy Stock Photo; p. 41 © USGS; p. 42 © robertharding/ Alamy Stock Photo; p. 44 © Matyas Rehak/Shutterstock; p. 45 © Reuters/CORBIS; p. 47 © Rat007/ Shutterstock; p. 48 © ZinaidaSopina/Shutterstock; p. 49 © Zach Holmes/Alamy Stock Photo; p. 51 © National Geographic Creative/Alamy Stock Photo; p. 52 © USGS; p. 53 © USGS; p. 55 © Boris Sosnovyy/ Shutterstock; p. 56 (top) © www.sandatlas.org/Shutterstock; p. 56 (bottom) Tom Grundy/Shutterstock; p. 57 © www.sandatlas.org/Shutterstock; p. 58 © Leene/Shutterstock; p. 59 (top left) © ronnybas/ Shutterstock; p. 59 (top right) © Bill Perry/Shutterstock; p. 59 (bottom) © ermess/Shutterstock; p. 60 © Vladislav Gajic/Shutterstock; p. 61 (granite) © Gyvafoto/Shutterstock; p. 61 (limestone) © michal812/ Shutterstock; p. 61 (sandstone) © Alexlukin/Shutterstock; p. 61 (basalt, gneiss, marble, phyllite, quartzite, schist, slate) © Tyler Boyes/Shutterstock; p. 63 © godrick/Shutterstock; p. 64–65 (bottom), 65 (top), 66 (top), 66 (bottom), 68 courtesy of NASA; p. 69 (top) © Art Directors & TRIP/Alamy Stock Photo; p. 69 (bottom) courtesy of NASA/JPL-Caltech

Published in the United States by Random House Children's Books, a division of Penguin Random House LLC, New York.

Random House and the colophon are registered trademarks of Penguin Random House LLC.

Visit us on the Web! randomhousekids.com

Educators and librarians, for a variety of teaching tools, visit us at RHTeachersLibrarians.com

Library of Congress Cataloging-in-Publication Data
Zoehfeld, Kathleen Weidner, author.
School of dragons : volcano escape! / Kathleen Weidner Zoehfeld.
p. cm. — (School of dragons)
Audience: Ages 7–10.
Audience: Grades 2 to 5.
ISBN 978-1-101-93337-4 (trade) — ISBN 978-1-101-93338-1 (lib. bdg.) —
ISBN 978-1-101-93339-8 (ebook)
1. Volcanoes—Juvenile literature. I. Title. II. Title: Volcano escape!
QE521.3.Z64 2016 551.21—dc23 2015030597

Printed in the United States of America 10 9 8 7 6 5 4 3 2 1

Contents

Note to Readers

What do dragons have to do with real-life science and history?
More than you might think!

For thousands of years, cultures all over the world have told stories about dragons, just as they told fanciful tales about unicorns, fairies, mermaids, ogres, and other mythical creatures. People made up these and other legends for many reasons: to explain the natural world, to give their lives deeper meaning, sometimes even just for fun! Stories passed down from generation to generation began to change over time. In many cases, fact (what's true) and fiction (what's made up) blended together to create a rich legacy of storytelling.

So even though you don't see them flying overhead, dragons are all around us! They are a part of our history and culture, bridging the gap between the past and the present — what's real and what's born of our limitless imaginations. This makes the *DreamWorks Dragons* Dragon Riders ideal candidates to teach us about our world!

Think of the School of Dragons series as your treasure map to a land of fascinating facts about science, history, mythology, culture, innovation, and more! You can read the books cover to cover or skip around to sections that most interest you. There's no right or wrong way when it comes to learning.

And that's not all! When you're done reading the books, you can go online to schoolofdragons.com to play the interactive School of Dragons video games from JumpStart. There's no end to what you can discover. Be sure to check out the inside back cover of this book for a special game code that will allow you access to super-secret adventures!

All ready? Hold on tight, dragon trainers! Here we go . . .

Meet the Characters

Astrid

Hiccup

Snotlout

Fishlegs

Stoick the Vast

Gobber

Ruffnut & Tuffnut

5

Meet the Dragons

Toothless
Species: Night Fury

Barf & Belch
Species: Hideous Zippleback

Hookfang
Species: Monstrous Nightmare

Meatlug
Species: Gronckle

Stormfly
Species: Deadly Nadder

Understanding Volcanoes

Most people go through their whole lives without expecting a nearby mountain to explode. They don't worry about avalanches of fiery hot rock and ash. They don't wonder if their houses and schools will be buried. . . .

But in some places, the ground shakes and the mountains roar! Places where super-hot rock comes up from deep inside the Earth are called **volcanoes.** When a volcano erupts, tons of hot rock and ash come crashing down. They destroy everything in their path.

Volcanoes are even more powerful than dragons!

Mount Vesuvius in Italy

People who live near volcanoes sometimes get scared. Why do mountains explode? What can people do to keep safe?

Since ancient times, people have tried to understand volcanoes. The Romans had many myths that helped them make sense of the world around them. The word *volcano* comes from one of these stories. In Roman mythology, Vulcan was the god of fire. Vulcan was said to live under a very violent volcano named Mount Etna.

On August 24, 79 CE, something strange was going on with the Roman mountain **Vesuvius.** The ground around it was shaking, but this was nothing new. There were lots of earthquakes in this area. But this time, the mountain was rumbling, and a very odd cloud was forming over

Mount Vesuvius and ruins from Pompeii, Italy

the mountain's peak. The cloud was narrow at the bottom, like a tree trunk, but it rose up high and spread out wide.

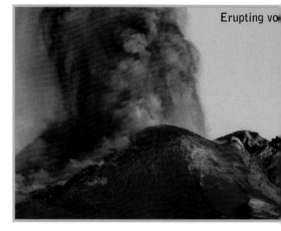

Erupting vo

A leader in the Roman navy, Pliny the Elder, came out of his house to take a look. He was one of the world's **naturalists,** which means he studied the natural world all around him. Pliny was not impressed by stories of gods under mountains. He wanted to know the truth. He ordered his men to get the boats ready. They were going to row as close to the mountain as possible.

Sometimes solving problems takes brains and brawn.

Meanwhile, the ground near Vesuvius began to shake violently. Nearby towns could hear a booming worse than thunder. They were showered with rock and ash. The terrible sounds got louder by the minute. The volcanic cloud grew so thick it blotted out the sun. The day became as dark as night. Lightning struck the mountaintop. Ash and rock rained down from above.

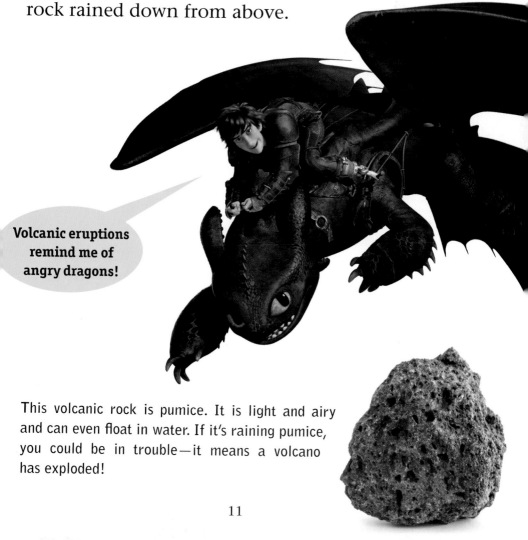

Volcanic eruptions remind me of angry dragons!

This volcanic rock is pumice. It is light and airy and can even float in water. If it's raining pumice, you could be in trouble—it means a volcano has exploded!

Pliny took notes during the eruption. When it was over, Pliny's nephew, Pliny the Younger, put together his uncle's notes and his own observations. He shared his work with a friend who was an historian so that others could learn about the volcano, too. His description of the eruption was so precise that explosive eruptions like this are now known as **Plinian eruptions.**

Pompeii was a town near Vesuvius in 79 CE. During the eruption, roofs were pounded by falling **pumice!** A deep layer of ash filled the streets, blocking doors and windows. People who stayed indoors were trapped. Outside, people

Towns like Pompeii were buried right up over the tallest rooftops. Today you can visit Pompeii and see what happened for yourself!

tied pillows on their heads to protect themselves from the falling rocks. They tried to run to safety through the chest-deep ash. They held cloths over their faces to keep from choking on the dust and smoke. But there was no escaping their fate.

What could the people in these towns have done differently? First, they should have left the area as soon as they heard explosions and saw the strange cloud. They may have escaped in time.

We have come a long way since Pliny the Younger's first account of volcanoes. Scientists continue to study volcanoes, hoping to understand them better and find ways to keep people safe when they do erupt.

We need to find out what's going on in our Hatchery!

Inside the Earth

Since ancient times, humans have wondered where volcanic ash and melted rock come from. For many years, **geologists**—scientists who study the Earth—thought that the Earth had a huge fiery center and that melted rock came up through underground tunnels. It was hard to be sure. Geologists could not see inside the Earth!

Then, in the 1800s, scientists invented a tool called a **seismometer.** When an earthquake strikes or a volcano erupts, the ground moves and shakes. Seismometers measure and record movements deep inside the Earth. Geologists set up seismometers all around the world. This gave them

Seismometer

frame

wire

weight

rotating drum

vibrations

base

information about what Earth is like beneath the surface.

Today, we know that there are no volcanic tunnels underground. We also know that Earth does not have a fiery center (although it is very hot there!).

Sometimes we feel the ground shake near the Hatchery!

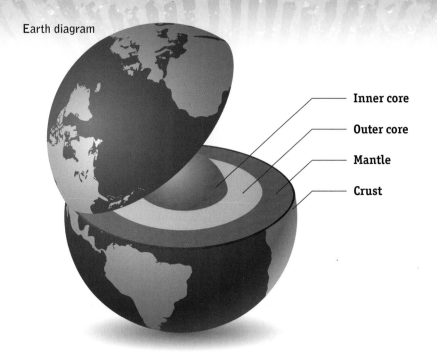

Earth diagram

Inner core

Outer core

Mantle

Crust

Earth is made up of several layers. At the center is the **inner core.** The inner core is a solid ball made up of two metals: iron and nickel. The temperature in this layer is close to 9,000 degrees Fahrenheit (5,000 degrees Celsius). That's as hot as the surface of the sun! That much heat should melt the inner core, but there is so much pressure that it stays solid.

Around the inner core, there is an **outer core** of hot liquid metal. Around the outer core is a thick layer of super-hot rock: the **mantle.**

The outermost layer of Earth is called the **crust.** This is the layer we live on. Compared to the size of Earth's other layers, the crust is very thin. Under the oceans, the crust is around four miles (seven kilometers) thick. On land, it can be more than thirty-seven miles (sixty kilometers) thick!

The deepest anyone has ever drilled is only around seven and a half miles (twelve kilometers). So you can forget about digging a hole to the center of the Earth. That hole would have to be 4,000 miles (6,370 kilometers) deep!

The crust under the oceans is thin, but it is made up of very dense, heavy rock, which forms when erupting lava cools very quickly. This rock, called **basalt,** makes up most of the Earth's crust.

The heat inside the Hatchery keeps our dragon eggs warm.

Volcanoes come from natural holes or cracks in the crust. In some areas, the hot rock of the mantle begins to melt. The melted rock is called **magma.** Deep under Earth's surface, magma pools form in pockets called **magma chambers.** Magma is lighter than the

Lava flow in Hawaii

solid rock around it, and this makes it float. Where there are cracks or weak spots in the crust, the magma keeps rising. If there is a crack in the surface, the melted rock escapes, and a volcano forms!

The hot, melted rock that erupts from a volcano is known as **lava.** If lava and ash keep escaping, a hill or mountain builds up. This can happen quickly, or it can take thousands of years.

Just how fast can a volcano form? Imagine this: In 1943, in central Mexico, a farmer was out plowing his field. Suddenly he heard a noise like thunder. He looked up, but there wasn't a cloud in the sky. He felt the ground begin to shake beneath his feet. A crack opened up in his field!

Six feet high is almost as big as a Gronckle!

He shouted for his wife to come quickly. When he turned back to look at the crack, it had changed. The ground around it had swollen up. It was now a mound about six feet (two meters) high!

A spray of fine gray ash shot up through the hole. The farmer heard a loud hiss and noticed a smell like rotten eggs. The farmer and his family ran away from the farm. They were smart!

The explosions became more and more violent. By the end of the week, the mound had turned

Parícutin volcano in Mexico

into a volcanic cone. It was nearly 500 feet (150 meters) high! Two months later, it was twice as tall. The volcano was named Parícutin after a nearby village.

After about a year, Parícutin slowed down. For the next nine years, it only erupted once in a while, until it finally stopped. By then, the volcano was a small, 1,400-foot (424-meter) mountain!

The town of Parícutin was buried in lava and ash, but everyone got away safely.

Should you worry about a volcano erupting in your backyard? No! Volcanoes only appear where there are weak spots in Earth's crust.

Cathedral ruins in Parícutin

Here in Berk, we're ready for anything.

Where Do Volcanoes Form?

If you wanted to see a volcano for yourself, where could you find one? Many of Earth's volcanoes are around the Pacific Ocean. A long chain of volcanoes runs along the western coasts of North and South America, continuing all the way to the islands of Japan, Indonesia, and New Zealand. Altogether, there are more than 450 volcanoes in this chain! They form a huge circle around the ocean called the **Ring of Fire.**

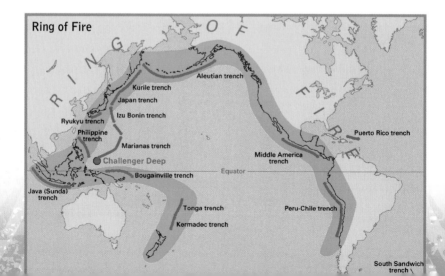

Ring of Fire

RING OF FIRE

Aleutian trench

Kurile trench

Japan trench

Izu Bonin trench

Ryukyu trench

Philippine trench

Marianas trench

Challenger Deep

Puerto Rico trench

Middle America trench

Bougainville trench

Equator

Java (Sunda) trench

Tonga trench

Peru-Chile trench

Kermadec trench

South Sandwich trench

Why are there so many volcanoes in this area? To find out, geologists look at Earth's layers. The crust and top layer of the mantle together make up the **lithosphere.** Think of it as a hard shell around the Earth. But this shell isn't just one piece of solid rock—it's broken up into huge chunks known as **plates.** There are about a dozen major plates and several smaller ones—all of which are always moving! The layer of super-hot rock below them is soft and mushy. The plates drift very slowly, like rafts, over this softer layer of rock.

When scientists come to a conclusion based on their observations, it is known as a **theory.** The idea of plate movement is called the **theory of plate tectonics.**

When Vikings find a new dragon species, we get to name it! The names usually come from the characteristics of the dragon.

Volcanoes almost always happen at the edges of plates. In some places, plates are moving away from each other. In other areas, plates are slowly moving toward each other. In the Ring of Fire, most of the volcanoes form where plates are moving together. When a plate under the ocean moves toward a plate covered by land, the oceanic plate slowly sinks under the land, or continental, plate. This process is called **subduction,** and it happens because oceanic crust is heavier than continental crust.

As the oceanic plate slides down, water gets carried with it. The water makes the hot rock of the mantle melt fast and magma forms. At the same time, cracks open up in the continental crust. The magma rises through the weak spots. It keeps moving higher and higher until a volcano erupts!

All along the Ring of Fire, oceanic plates are sinking under continental plates. It's no wonder that three-quarters of all Earth's volcanoes are in the Ring of Fire. The edges of the oceanic crust

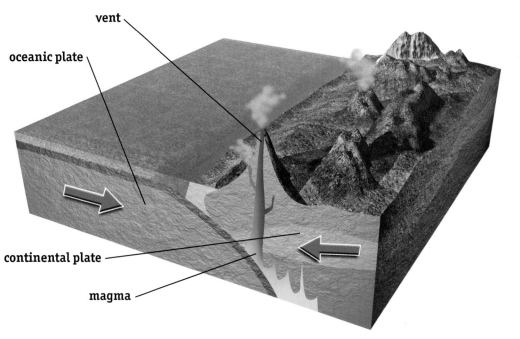

Subduction

vent

oceanic plate

continental plate

magma

become part of the mantle, and volcanoes form as the continental crust crumples and cracks.

The volcanoes you've heard of are probably all on land. But volcanoes even erupt underwater! Most underwater volcanoes happen in areas where plates are moving apart. **Rifting** is the term used when plates separate. In rifting, long, deep cracks called **rifts** open up. Magma from the mantle rises, and lava spills out. The lava hardens and builds up on both sides of the rift. This lava becomes new oceanic crust.

Geologists have spent years studying the Ring of Fire, but they still have some volcano mysteries to solve. Sometimes a volcano erupts away from the edge of a plate, and geologists are not sure why. The volcanoes that make up the island chain of Hawaii are an example.

Kauai island in Hawaii

Berk has its own volcano.

The Hawaiian Islands are right in the middle of the Pacific Plate, and scientists think there may be a tall column of very hot rock, called a **mantle plume,** below them. These plumes are sometimes known as hot spots.

The oldest Hawaiian island likely formed over a plume about twenty-eight million years ago. The Pacific Plate is slowly moving toward the northwest. If the plume stayed in the same place, the first island would have been carried away in that direction. Eventually, another volcanic island would have formed over the plume. And then another and another. Because of the arrangement of Hawaii's islands, it looks like that's exactly what happened!

Today, eight major islands make up the state of Hawaii, along with almost 130 smaller islands. The island of Hawaii is the biggest and youngest of all. It was built up from five volcanoes. Another island, Loihi, is forming right now! The top of the island is still more than a half mile under the ocean's surface . . . but someday, it may rise high enough for people to live on!

Hawaii Volcanoes National Park

Different Types of Eruptions

In some ways, volcanoes are just like dragons: a little fiery, a little unpredictable . . . and no two look the same! If you want to learn more about the different types of volcanic eruptions, you should look at the kind of magma involved. Volcanoes have magma that's thick and sticky or thin and runny.

Where magma is thick, like in the Ring of Fire, volcanoes have violent eruptions. This is because the gloppy magma clogs up the volcanoes' vents. At first, the magma is

Tungurahua volcano in Ecuador

If my dragon, Stormfly, gets red-hot mad . . . watch out!

trapped underground, and pressure builds up. Then it breaks through the blocked-up vent. Super-hot water and gases bubble up and escape. Picture a bottle of soda. When you shake the bottle, bubbles fizz and pressure builds up. Quickly take off the cap and—*BOOM!* The soda explodes out of the opening!

When the volcano vent opens up, lava shoots out. The gases that escape make the sticky lava explode. The tiny pieces of lava are what make up **volcanic ash.** The ash goes flying into the air.

Anak Krakatau volcano in Indonesia

Volcanic ash can make a huge mess—and be very deadly. But even more dangerous things can come zooming out of volcanoes. Sometimes great blobs of lava fly up, cool off in flight, and get rounded in shape. Nearby rocks get broken up, too. Large chunks go flying. These blobs and chunks can be huge—sometimes as big as a house! Scientists have given them a very fitting name: **volcanic bombs**! And they are thrown through the air with *a lot* of force.

Once the explosion stops, the lava and rocks lose power. Everything falls back to Earth. But that's just the beginning! Hot ash, poisonous gases, and rock bombs tumble down the side of the volcano.

Pyroclastic f

They can fall as fast as 250 miles per hour (400 kilometers per hour). These volcanic avalanches are named **pyroclastic flows.** When one comes crashing down, nothing is safe. No living thing can escape its path of destruction!

Lava, ash, and chunks of rock pile up. Over the course of many eruptions, this buildup creates the most familiar shape for a volcano: a volcanic cone.

Volcanic cone of Ngauruhoe volcano in New Zealand

After an eruption is finished, any lava that hasn't shot out usually sinks back down into the vent and turns solid. That leaves a bowl-shaped **crater** at the top of the volcano.

A steep hill made of cooled lava—that definitely sounds like our Hatchery!

Mount St. Helens National Volcanic Monument

Mount St. Helens is a famous volcano in the Ring of Fire. In 1980, the whole northern side of the mountain began to bulge and crack. For many days, the bulge grew bigger and bigger. The magma under the mountain was rising. Then, one morning, an earthquake shook the area, and the bulge gave way. A huge wall of rock plunged down the mountain.

This released a lot of pressure from the magma chamber. The magma frothed up, and the top of the mountain exploded! Smoke and ash darkened the skies for miles around. A pyroclastic flow destroyed a big patch of forest below.

Sometimes the rocks and ash from an eruption mix with a lot of water. This creates a volcanic mudflow, known as a **lahar.** Lahars can cover vast areas in a thick, sticky layer of mud. Some lahars run deep and fast, and when that happens, watch out! They can quickly flatten villages, burying thousands of people.

In some hot spots, like Hawaii, eruptions are not explosive. They are gentler and last longer. This is because the magma is thin and runny. For example, Mauna Loa has been gently erupting over and over again for about a million years. Lava oozes from the volcano's vent, and streams of lava flow down the sides.

A Hawaiian volcano erupting lava into the Pacific Ocean

Mauna Kea summit overlooking Mauna Loa in the distance

Mauna Loa is a **shield volcano.** It is built up of thousands of layers of lava. This gives it a wider, flatter shape, which makes it look like a warrior's shield. Mauna Loa is the largest shield volcano on Earth. If you measure it from the seafloor to its top, it's taller than Mount Everest!

Shield volcanoes do not have pyroclastic flows. Instead, they have slower lava flows. The molten lava glows red hot, and as it cools, it gets thicker and gooier. When it has cooled completely, the lava turns hard and dark in color.

As lava flows down the side of a volcano, it takes on interesting shapes. These shapes are named after

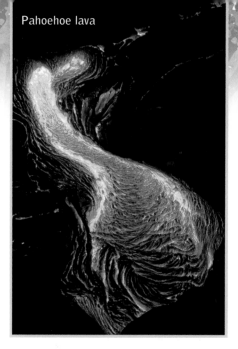
Pahoehoe lava

Hawaiian words. **Pahoehoe** (pah-HOE-eh-hoe-eh) forms from thin, fast-flowing lava. The lava spreads out in sheets. The surface layer cools, but under the surface, molten lava keeps moving. This twists and folds the thin surface layer into smooth, ropy shapes.

A'a (AH-ah) forms as lava cools and grows thicker. The surface layer gets a rough texture. Under the surface, lava keeps flowing, and the surface breaks into chunky blocks. Even if lava flows are slow, they can be very dangerous. A large lava flow can bury a whole town!

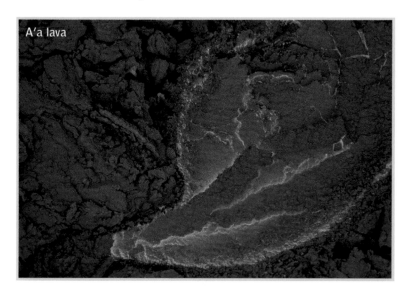
A'a lava

We now know that different volcanoes erupt in different ways. But sometimes even the same volcano changes its mind! Mount Fuji and Mount Vesuvius have both had explosive *and* gentle eruptions.

A volcano made from many layers of lava, rock, and ash is called a **stratovolcano.** *Strato* is a Latin word that means "layer."

Sometimes a "hot spot" can create another type of volcano: a **supervolcano.** Supervolcanoes are never gentle! In these areas, heat from the mantle melts a big area of crust. A lot of very sticky magma builds up in a huge shallow chamber. Thinner, runnier magma continues to pool even deeper below. The runnier magma rises in places, and gases bubble up. The pressure on the sticky magma chamber above grows and grows. When

Even dragons can be of two minds. Barf and Belch rarely agree with each other!

the pressure becomes too great, a massive eruption can occur!

One example of a supervolcano is the Yellowstone supervolcano. This supervolcano has erupted at least three times in the past. The last time was 640,000 years ago. Once a supervolcano erupts, it doesn't leave behind a cone. Instead, ash and rocks are shot out over thousands of square miles. The magma chamber sinks, leaving behind a wide, shallow hole called a **caldera.**

Yellowstone National Park in Wyoming

At the Ashfall Fossil Beds State Historical Park in Nebraska, you will see fossils of rhinos, camels, and other prehistoric beasts that were buried in ash. This happened when the Yellowstone hot spot erupted twelve million years ago. The red tags you see here are used by scientists for identification purposes.

The Yellowstone supervolcano has a caldera that is larger than the state of Rhode Island!

Supervolcanoes may be big, but they do not make the biggest volcanic eruptions. The largest ones are under the oceans, where plates are moving apart. The narrow undersea rifts can run for thousands of miles. The eruptions are usually slow and gentle, but they release tons of hot lava. When the lava hits the cold seawater, it cools quickly. This creates **mid-ocean ridges.** An example of this is the Mid-Atlantic Ridge, which has been building up for more than 200 million years.

World Distribution of Mid-Ocean Ridges

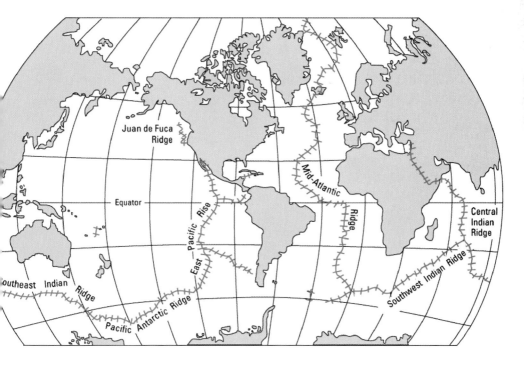

When Will It Erupt?

If you live next to a volcano, you probably want to know if or when it will erupt! The answer could be *very soon!* But it could also be *never.* Volcanoes can be **active, dormant,** or **extinct.** A dormant volcano is one that has not erupted for a very long time. Nearby towns are probably safe. An active volcano, on the other hand, is one that has

Mount Visoke in Africa

erupted within the past few hundred years, or is showing signs that it may erupt soon. Around the world, more than fifty volcanoes erupt each year.

Volcanoes become extinct when they are completely cut off from their source of magma. Extinct volcanoes are the only safe volcanoes. All active volcanoes can be dangerous. And even dormant volcanoes can quickly pose a threat. Do you remember Mount Vesuvius? Before it erupted in 79 CE, it had been quiet for eight hundred years. You never know when a sleeping volcano will wake up.

Berk's volcano hasn't erupted for a long time . . . but we should still be careful!

Mount Vesuvius towering over Naples in Italy

It might be hard to imagine that people would want to live near such a danger. But more than two million people live near Mount Vesuvius today. Because so many people live there, scientists consider it one of the most dangerous volcanoes on the planet! Vesuvius has erupted many times since 79 CE. It could erupt again at any time. That would mean big trouble for those who live nearby, as most of its eruptions have been explosive.

If you're going to live near an explosive mountain, you need smart, prepared people to help protect you. **Volcanologists** are geologists who study volcanoes. They keep a close watch over active volcanoes like Mount Vesuvius. Today, scientists know more about volcanoes and have better tools than they did in ancient times. They are better able to predict when a volcano might erupt.

What are some key signs that an eruption is about to take place? Tiny earthquakes are a very common clue. When it looks like an old volcano is becoming restless, volcanologists move in fast. They place seismometers all around the volcano. The seismometers can pick up very faint vibrations—even ones that might be too small for people to feel.

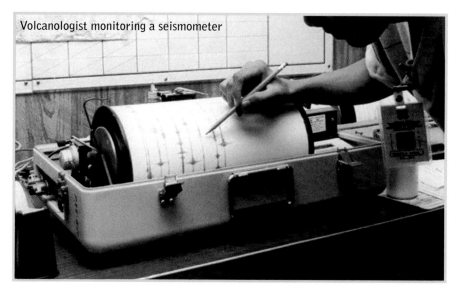

Volcanologist monitoring a seismometer

When magma begins to rise up through a volcano's vent, it makes the whole mountain shake. The seismometers record these vibrations, and volcanologists study them. These vibrations are like a code, and different patterns tell volcanologists what might be happening. Certain patterns usually happen before an eruption. When scientists start to see them, they go on high alert. There is no way to be sure *exactly* when a volcano will erupt, so they must study the mountain carefully, looking at every clue.

Volcanologists look at the rock and ash from old eruptions. Understanding a volcano's past helps them create **hazard maps.** Hazard maps show which areas around the mountain could

My dad, Stoick the Vast, is our fearless leader. It's his job to make big decisions. If the volcano erupts, Stoick will know what to do.

The Hideous Zippleback dragon knows all about deadly gases.

One head shoots out a thick green gas . . . and the other creates a spark to set the gas on fire!

be in the most danger. If the signs get worse, the people who live in these areas will be the first to move out.

If a volcano is about to erupt, it may also begin to give off steam or poisonous gases. These gases may come from the central vent or from smaller cracks in the volcano's sides.

Kawah Ijen volcano in Indonesia

Fumarole on Mutnovsky volcano in Russia

Small cracks in the side of a volcano are called **fumaroles.** Volcanologists watch these very carefully. They even use special detectors to keep track of the gas. Volcanologists look for even the tiniest of changes, as they could be a sign that something is about to happen. For example, what happens if the gas has a little more sulfur dioxide? For one thing, it will get very stinky! This chemical has a rotten-egg smell!

I love the smell of rotten eggs! Every Viking worth his or her salt has a little stench.

But more importantly, this would tell a volcanologist that magma is on the move.

Volcanologists also keep an eye on the shape of the mountain. If they see any bulges or cracks, they can tell that an eruption may be near. Volcanologists depend on modern technology for such an important job. From out in space, satellites help them watch for changes. Satellites can detect even the smallest crack or bulge!

Satellites can also warn volcanologists about changes in heat. As magma rises, the ground around a volcano often becomes warmer, and special satellites can pick up on changes in ground temperatures.

All these clues help volca-nologists predict what a volcano might do next. If the signs look bad, they warn the local towns and help them prepare for disaster. People in these areas must have a plan in place for getting out fast.

A volcanologist's gear:

• **Protective suit:** Many volcanologists get dangerously close to lava flows. Along with heavy boots and thick gloves, a protective suit can keep scientists safe from the extreme heat.

• **Gas mask:** Tiny, sharp grains of volcanic ash can harm lungs. A gas mask keeps out these particles. It can also lower the risk of breathing in poisonous gases.

• **Thermometer:** Lava temperatures can be as high as 2,200 degrees Fahrenheit (1,200 degrees Celsius). Hot lava would melt an ordinary glass thermometer. Volcanologists use an electric thermometer made of metal.

• **A pen and notebook:** Of course!

volcanologist ascends the rim of Mount Nyiragongo in the Democratic Republic of the Congo.

The United States Geological Survey (USGS) aids people in need. They have a Volcano Disaster Assistance Program (VDAP). If any country is worried about a particular volcano, VDAP's team of volcanologists is ready to go. They help local scientists figure out if the volcano will erupt soon and how big that eruption might be. This gives people the information they need to decide if and when to leave the area.

VDAP experts are always working to make better tools to observe volcanoes. They also train scientists in many areas around the world.

A USGS scientist monitors a Global Positioning Station on Mount St. He

Volcanic Explosivity Index

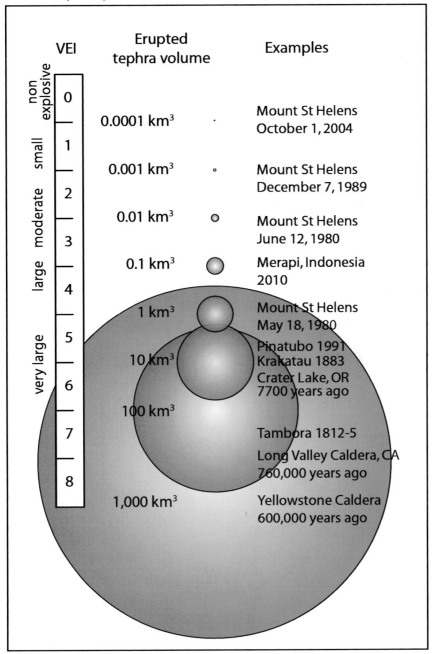

VEI		Erupted tephra volume		Examples
non explosive	0			
		0.0001 km³	·	Mount St Helens October 1, 2004
small	1			
		0.001 km³	∘	Mount St Helens December 7, 1989
	2			
moderate		0.01 km³	○	Mount St Helens June 12, 1980
	3			
large		0.1 km³		Merapi, Indonesia 2010
	4			
		1 km³		Mount St Helens May 18, 1980
very large	5			
		10 km³		Pinatubo 1991 Krakatau 1883 Crater Lake, OR 7700 years ago
	6			
		100 km³		
	7			Tambora 1812-5 Long Valley Caldera, CA 760,000 years ago
	8			
		1,000 km³		Yellowstone Caldera 600,000 years ago

Volcanoes Rock!

Volcanoes can be scary and dangerous. But they can do plenty of good, too! As soon as hot molten lava comes out of a volcano, it begins to cool. It gets thicker and harder. When the lava hardens completely, it becomes brand-new rock!

The rocks on Berk were used to build the training grounds and School of Dragons lab!

Rocks are just about everywhere you look. People use them in many different ways. A **rock** is a solid material made up of one or more minerals. **Minerals** are substances that are formed in nature.

Each mineral has its own color and hardness, and its own special structure or shape. Geologists call this shape the mineral's **crystal** structure.

There are three types of rock: **igneous, sedimentary,** and **metamorphic.** The rocks on Earth are always changing (sometimes very slowly). This process is known as the **rock cycle.** Volcanoes have an important part to play in this process.

Amethyst

Rock that forms when lava or magma cools is igneous rock. Even though **igneous** rocks may come from the same super-hot liquid, they can look and feel very different. This is because of how slowly or quickly they cool. When lava cools quickly, the crystals in the rock are small. Sometimes they are so small that they are hard to see. This gives the rock a smooth texture.

Obsidian
(volcanic glass)

What about when the magma cools slowly underground? This allows the rock's crystals time to grow bigger, which gives the rock a rougher texture. It's easy to see and feel the crystals in these rocks. **Granite** is an example of igneous rock that has cooled slowly. This strong rock may be easy to recognize since it's used in many buildings.

Pink granite

Types of Igneous Rocks

Igneous comes from the Latin word ignis, which means "fire."

Basalt is made up of quartz and feldspar that cooled quickly.

Granite is made up of crystals of quartz, feldspar, and biotite that cooled slowly underground.

Rhyolite is made up of crystals of quartz, feldspar, and biotite that cooled quickly aboveground.

Gabbro is made up of crystals of pyroxene, olivine, and feldspar that cooled slowly underground.

Gabbro

Volcanoes make new igneous rock. But almost as soon as new rock forms, it begins to break down. Over time, this forms **sedimentary** rock. First, the forces of weather slowly grind the rock into tiny grains of **sediment.** Giant rocks might not be so easy to move, but tiny bits of sediment are moveable. Flowing water sweeps up sediment and carries it away. Eventually, the stream of water slows down. Then the sediment sinks and settles, and layers of it build up.

All those layers of sediment press down on top of each other. The grains of sediment get squeezed closer together. As the water dries up, it leaves minerals behind. These minerals bond the grains together. They have made a brand-new kind of rock from tiny pieces of older ones!

Sedimentary rock cliffs

Sand and mud are two kinds of sediment. Grains of sand are bonded together to form **sandstone**. Mud turns into **mudstone**.

Sandstone

Mudstone

As sediment layers form on top of each other, they can bury some amazing secrets . . . like fossil bones! After a bone gets stuck in a layer of sediment, minerals fill in all its tiny pores. This can **preserve,** or save, the bones for hundreds of millions of years.

...ehistoric fish fossil in ...dimentary rock

Sometimes we find fossil bones when we go exploring!

The third kind of rock, **metamorphic** rock, is made from heat and pressure deep inside the Earth. Sometimes it is formed by the heat of a volcano. Igneous rock is created from cooling magma or lava. But under the surface, any rock that is near the rising magma gets heated like bread dough in an oven. The baking process changes the rock.

Marble is a type of metamorphic rock formed when limestone is squeezed and folded.

Metamorphic rock can also form where tectonic plates collide. One plate slides under the other, and great pressure and heat build up. The rock here is squeezed, stretched, and folded—and ultimately changed forever.

Tremendous heat and pressure slowly change the crystal structures of rock, turning them into new kinds of rock.

With heat and pressure, igneous and sedimentary rock can turn into metamorphic rock. Likewise, older metamorphic rock can change into different kinds of metamorphic rock. Check out the chart below and see if you can spot the differences!

 Granite turns into **gneiss.**

Basalt turns into **schist.**

Limestone turns into **marble.**

Sandstone turns into **quartzite.**

Slate turns into **phyllite.**

No wonder we have so much farming on Berk. The minerals in our soil help us hungry Vikings grow nutrient-rich food.

Volcanic ash is rock that has exploded. Like all rock, it is made up of minerals. When ash falls to the ground, minerals make the soil better for growing crops. That's one reason why many people live near volcanoes, in spite of the dangers.

All types of rocks are useful for people. We use them to build houses, schools, and libraries. We use rock to pave roads and sidewalks, and to create beautiful sculptures. The minerals in rocks give us the rich soil we need to grow our food. In these ways, volcanoes can be very useful!

Volcanoes in Space

If you could take a trip across the solar system, you'd notice something amazing. Earth is not the only place with volcanoes!

Look up at the full moon at night. Do you see the dark craters? Some say they look like the face of the "Man in the Moon." They are really huge fields of hardened lava.

The Moon

The first eruptions on the Moon happened between three and four billion years ago. Back then, the Moon was bombarded with giant meteorites. Every time a meteorite crashed into the Moon, the heat and force of impact cracked open its outer shell, and molten lava poured out.

Can you imagine the Moon covered in lines of fire-red lava? That sounds out of this world! You won't see any eruptions if you look up at the night sky these days. The Moon's last major volcanic eruptions were about one billion years ago.

A robotic spacecraft that orbits the Moon has sent back images of much smaller volcanoes that may have been erupting until as recently as 50 million years ago. But today, the Moon is probably too cool to erupt again, and collisions with meteorites are very rare.

If Earth and its moon have volcanoes, what about the other planets in our solar system?

View of Earth from the Moon

Venus has even more volcanoes than Earth does! But there is no Ring of Fire on Venus. Instead, its volcanoes have formed all over the surface. Unlike Earth, Venus does not have giant shifting plates. Venus has a thin crust, with many mantle plumes, or hot spots.

Space probes have also shown great fields of lava on Venus. They have seen groups of low "pancake domes" that have been pushed up by magma. And there are many wide calderas where domes have collapsed.

Some of Venus's volcanoes could still be active! Space probes have detected bright flashes near a giant shield volcano named Maat Mons. These could be signs of a fresh lava flow or an active hot spot.

Earth and Venus have some extra-large volcanoes, but the most gigantic volcano in the solar system is on Mars. It's known as Olympus Mons.

Olympus Mons on Mars

Olympus Mons has the shape of a shield volcano and spreads across an area as big as the state of Arizona. Its slopes are gentle, but it rises almost sixteen miles (twenty-five kilometers) above its base. That's like stacking three Mount Everests on top of one another!

Some of Mars's volcanoes, like Olympus Mons, formed from mantle plumes, or hot spots. Others, like Alba Mons, were probably caused by meteorites.

Alba Mons is one of the biggest lava fields in the solar system. Just how big is it? It's as wide as the entire United States! That's more than twenty times bigger than the largest lava flow on Earth.

All of Mars's volcanoes have been quiet for the past 500 million years. But scientists think some of them could become active again.

It wasn't until 1979 that humans first saw a volcano erupting in space. As the *Voyager 1* spacecraft flew past Jupiter, it sent back images of Io, one of the planet's larger moons. The images showed a big volcanic cloud. It looked like a giant

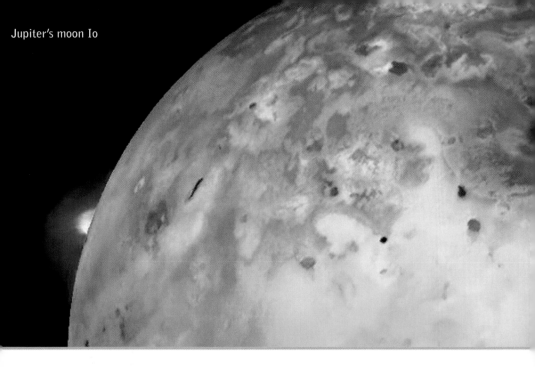

umbrella popping open into space! A little later, *Voyager 2* spotted several more volcanic clouds. Since then, scientists have counted more than one hundred active volcanoes on that moon alone!

More recently, scientists found something strange on Enceladus, one of Saturn's moons. They saw what looked like a huge geyser, shooting up hundreds of miles from the surface. On Earth, geysers erupt with scalding-hot water. But the upper layers of this moon are mostly made of ice! Could this weird geyser be a sign of volcanic activity? Yes! But there is no molten rock. Only water and gases erupt from volcanoes on ice worlds.

Ever wonder why Saturn has rings? Ice crystals and gases from volcanoes on Enceladus helped create at least one of them!

Saturn's moon Enceladus

rock core

rust of ice

water/ice mantle

Aren't volcanoes supposed to be hot? How can volcanoes erupt on ice worlds? The ice in the mantle of these worlds may get warmed in certain places. If cracks or weak spots appear in the icy crust, pressure is suddenly released. Water vapor and other gases shoot out. These are **cryovolcanoes.**

Other space probes have seen volcanoes erupting even farther out in space. There are volcanoes on one of Neptune's moons, Triton. That's billions of miles away from Earth! Triton's volcanoes are the most distant ones we've ever seen. But as we continue to explore the solar system and beyond, who knows what we may find? Perhaps there are different kinds of volcanoes erupting *everywhere* in the universe!

Glossary

a'a: A lava flow with a rough, rubbly surface.

active: Moving about or doing something. An active volcano is one that has erupted within the past few hundred years and is likely to erupt again.

basalt: A type of fine-grained igneous rock that can form when lava cools quickly.

caldera: A large volcanic crater. A caldera often forms after a volcano erupts, when the center of the volcano collapses into the empty magma chamber below.

crater: A steep, bowl-shaped hollow in the ground. A crater can form at the top of a volcano, or at the site where a large meteorite crashes into the surface of the Earth or another planet.

crust: The rock that makes up the outer layer of the Earth.

cryovolcano: An ice volcano. A cryovolcano erupts water and other gases rather than lava. There are no known cryovolcanoes on Earth.

crystal: A solid whose atoms are arranged in a particular shape, such as a cube or pyramid. Different minerals each have their own special crystal shape and color.

dormant: Resting, or inactive. A dormant volcano is one

that has not erupted for hundreds or thousands of years, but which may erupt again in the future.

extinct: No longer active. An extinct volcano is one that has erupted in the past but will not erupt again.

fumarole: A crack or hole in the Earth near a volcano, where volcanic gases leak out.

geologist: A scientist who studies rocks and minerals and the ways in which the Earth has changed over millions of years.

granite: A type of coarse-grained igneous rock that can form when magma cools slowly.

hazard map: A map of an area highlighting places where volcanic activity, such as lava flows and pyroclastic flows, have been most destructive in the past.

igneous rock: Rock that forms when hot molten lava or magma cools and becomes solid.

inner core: The hot, dense, ball-shaped center of the Earth. The inner core is made up mostly of iron and nickel.

lahar: A volcanic mudflow made up of volcanic rocks and ash mixed with water.

lava: Hot molten rock that has flowed out onto the Earth's surface.

lithosphere: The rigid outer layer of the Earth. The lithosphere is made up of the Earth's crust plus the upper layer of the mantle.

magma: Hot molten rock below the Earth's surface.

magma chamber: A space belowground filled with magma.

mantle: The thick layer of hot rock below Earth's crust and above the core.

metamorphic rock: A type of rock that forms when already-existing rock is changed by heat or pressure deep within the Earth.

mid-ocean ridge: An undersea mountain chain that forms where two oceanic plates are moving apart.

mineral: A solid substance found in the ground that does not come from living things. Each type of mineral has its own chemical makeup and crystal form.

mudstone: A blocky, fine-grained sedimentary rock formed when tiny particles of mud are pressed together and bonded, or cemented.

naturalist: A scientist who studies the plants, animals, minerals, and other things found in nature.

outer core: The layer of Earth's core that surrounds the inner core. The outer core is made up of hot liquid metal, mostly iron and nickel.

pahoehoe: A lava flow that has a smooth, ropy surface. It forms from thin, fast-flowing lava.

plate: One of the huge blocks, many miles thick and hundreds or thousands of miles wide and long, that make up the Earth's lithosphere.

Plinian eruption: Any huge volcanic eruption that is similar to the eruption of Vesuvius in 79 CE. The name honors Pliny the Younger, who wrote an accurate description of the eruption.

plume: A tall column of very hot rock that rises up from deep within the mantle. These are also sometimes referred to as hot spots.

preserve: To save something or make it last a long time. The remains of living things are sometimes preserved in sedimentary rock as fossils.

pumice: A light igneous rock that forms from frothy, or bubbly, lava.

pyroclastic flow: A fast-moving avalanche of hot volcanic rock, dust, and ash mixed with air that rolls down the side of an erupting volcano.

rift: A very long, deep crack that appears in the Earth's crust where two plates are moving apart.

rifting: In plate tectonics, the process of two plates moving apart.

Ring of Fire: A nickname for the long, nearly circular arrangement of active volcanoes that occur around the edge of the Pacific Plate.

rock: A naturally occurring solid, made up of one or more minerals.

rock cycle: The set of natural processes that change rocks of each of the three types—igneous, sedimentary, and metamorphic—into the other two types.

sandstone: A coarse-grained sedimentary rock formed when grains of sand are pressed together and bonded, or cemented.

sediment: A collection of loose mineral grains, such as sand, mud, or pebbles, which are not bonded, or cemented, together.

sedimentary rock: Any rock that forms when sand, mud, pebbles, or other pieces broken off from already-existing rocks are pressed and bonded, or cemented, together.

seismometer: A tool that can measure the shaking of the Earth that happens during an earthquake or volcanic eruption.

shield volcano: A volcano with a broad, gentle dome.

stratovolcano: A large, cone-shaped volcano with alternating layers of lava and material from pyroclastic flows.

subduction: The process through which one tectonic plate sinks down and pushes under another plate.

supervolcano: An immense volcano that shoots out more than 240 cubic miles (1,000 cubic kilometers) of lava, dust, and ash in one eruption. No supervolcanoes have erupted in recorded human history.

theory: An explanation based on experiments and observations of how or why something happens. Theories help predict future events and are supported by a great deal of evidence.

theory of plate tectonics: The idea that the outer layer of the Earth, the lithosphere, is made up of several separate plates that move slowly over the mantle.

Vesuvius: An active volcano near Naples, Italy.

volcano: An opening or vent in Earth's crust through which lava, ash, and hot gases flow during an eruption. A volcano can be described as active, dormant, or extinct.

volcanic ash: Tiny bits and pieces of minerals and glass that form when hot lava explodes and cools quickly in the air.

volcanic bomb: A large chunk of rock or blob of sticky lava thrown into the air during a volcanic eruption.

volcanic cone: A shape that many volcanoes form when lava, ash, and chunks of rock pile up over time.

volcanologist: A geologist who studies volcanoes.

INDEX

Practice Perfect Baseball

AMERICAN BASEBALL COACHES ASSOCIATION

Bob Bennett, Editor

Human Kinetics

Library of Congress Cataloging-in-Publication Data

American Baseball Coaches Association.
  Practice perfect baseball / American Baseball Coaches Association, Bob
Bennett, editor.
     p. cm.
  Includes index.
  ISBN-13: 978-0-7360-8713-1 (soft cover)
  ISBN-10: 0-7360-8713-3 (soft cover)
  1. Baseball--Coaching. I. Bennett, Bob, 1933- II. Title.
  GV875.5.A46 2010
  796.357077--dc22

                         2009037684

  ISBN-10: 0-7360-8713-3 (print)
  ISBN-13: 978-0-7360-8713-1 (print)

Developmental Editor: Cynthia McEntire; **Assistant Editor:** Scott Hawkins; **Copyeditor:** Patrick Connolly; **Indexer:** Dan Connolly; **Permission Manager:** Martha Gullo; **Graphic Designer and Graphic Artist:** Kim McFarland; **Cover Designer:** Keith Blomberg; **Photographer (cover):** © Human Kinetics; **Photographers (interior):** chapter 7 Tim Jamieson; chapter 13 Sean McNally; **Photo Production Manager:** Jason Allen; **Art Manager:** Kelly Hendren; **Associate Art Manager:** Alan L. Wilborn; **Illustrator:** TwoJay!; **Printer:** United Graphics

Human Kinetics books are available at special discounts for bulk purchase. Special editions or book excerpts can also be created to specification. For details, contact the Special Sales Manager at Human Kinetics.

Printed in the United States of America   10   9   8   7   6   5   4   3   2   1

The paper in this book is certified under a sustainable forestry program.

Human Kinetics
Web site: www.HumanKinetics.com

United States: Human Kinetics
P.O. Box 5076
Champaign, IL 61825-5076
800-747-4457
e-mail: humank@hkusa.com

Canada: Human Kinetics
475 Devonshire Road Unit 100
Windsor, ON N8Y 2L5
800-465-7301 (in Canada only)
e-mail: info@hkcanada.com

Europe: Human Kinetics
107 Bradford Road
Stanningley
Leeds LS28 6AT, United Kingdom
+44 (0) 113 255 5665
e-mail: hk@hkeurope.com

Australia: Human Kinetics
57A Price Avenue
Lower Mitcham, South Australia 5062
08 8372 0999
e-mail: info@hkaustralia.com

New Zealand: Human Kinetics
P.O. Box 80
Torrens Park, South Australia 5062
0800 222 062
e-mail: info@hknewzealand.com

E4959

Practice
Perfect
Baseball

contents

Practice is one of the most important things coaches and players do. *Practice Perfect Baseball* was written with that in mind. No matter the level of competition, both coaches and players will find the information in this book useful for developing sound practice habits. Each chapter has been carefully written to be applicable to players and coaches at all levels. Inexperienced coaches will profit greatly from those who have already traveled the path they are pursuing. Veteran coaches will have their practice methods affirmed or uncover new ways to improve practice procedures.

A lot has been written about position play, pitching, and all aspects of hitting and fielding, but not much has been written on practice and practice schedules. This book fills that void. Some of the most successful and respected coaches in the United States have come together to produce a book that deals with every aspect of practice.

Every coach and player will benefit from the expertise of these authors. By following the advice of these expert coaches, the reader will walk away with a better understanding of all aspects of practice. Because baseball has so many facets, both offensively and defensively, practice organization is sometimes difficult. *Practice Perfect Baseball* teaches coaches how to organize practice, get the most out of players, best use the allotted time, and assess talent and evaluate practices and games. The scope is broad, spanning how to organize an indoor practice to how to get the most out of each individual practice session.

Each author was selected based on his expertise on the specific topic of his chapter. The knowledge and passion of each author leaps from the pages, and the information in each chapter has stood the test of time.

Any coach or player looking to develop and execute a single practice session, a series of practices, or a season of practices will be able to find the answers in *Practice Perfect Baseball*.

key to diagrams

P	Pitcher
C	Catcher
CO	Coach
1B	1st base player
2B	2nd base player
3B	3rd base player
SS	Shortstop
LF	Left fielder
CF	Center fielder
RF	Right fielder
OF	Outfielder
IF	Infielder
B	Batter
R	Runner
X	Any player, if position isn't applicable
⟶	Path of player
- - ➔	Path of ball
▯	Batting tee
✢	Batting tee or hitting sock screen
Ⓜ	Pitching machine

chapter 1

Establishing a Practice Work Ethic

ED CHEFF

Practice—To perform repeatedly in order to acquire or enhance a skill and to execute skill performances in conjunction with game strategies.

Work—Physical or mental effort to reach a specific condition through repeated effort.

Ethic—A principle of right or good conduct or a body of such principles.

A baseball coach needs to develop a team philosophy that will establish a positive work ethic in the practice environment. The initial process of doing this should focus on defining the body of knowledge to be taught as well as the appropriate methodology that will be used in the teaching process.

Coaches can acquire a wealth of baseball knowledge in a number of ways, beginning with their own personal playing experiences. They can also gain knowledge by attending coaching clinics, studying the strategies of respected managers, observing and performing video analysis of skills and techniques being performed by elite players, and consulting the hundreds of articles and books written about the game.

However, coaches should always remember that baseball is a rather simple game. Sparky Anderson, one of baseball's all-time most respected managers, said it best: "There ain't no genius ever managed in this game." Sparky's hall of fame second baseman Joe Morgan summed up Anderson's influence on his Cincinnati Reds teams with this statement: "Sparky pointed us in the right direction to win." Defining the "right direction to win" in the practice environment is what this chapter is about.

The emphasis is on defining a work ethic for practices that stresses the characteristics of the style of play expected from the players. All of the behavioral traits that a coach encourages his players to project in the practice environment cannot just be a wish list—rather, they must be a set of principles perceived by players as statements of fact. These are the absolutes of practice behavior put forth by a coach, and they should be communicated to players in an emphatic and passionate manner. As in any group endeavor, openness and clarity of communication are essential. In our program, the overall goal of our preparation is to ultimately raise the skill level of our players as expediently as possible while always striving to make sure that the team's competitive level is in line with the talent level. Teams earn the right to compete for a championship based on the legitimacy of their practices.

"Vision without execution is hallucination."

Thomas Edison

Earning Respect

Much has been written and spoken about the importance of coaches gaining respect from their players. I have always believed that it's a major mistake for coaches to demand respect from their players as opposed to earning that respect.

I want to emphasize the word *earning* when discussing the process of obtaining the team's respect. Respect cannot be successfully demanded from a player just because of a coach's position of power. Too often resentment and resistance toward the coach become part of the team's chemistry. Even worse are coaches who in various ways ask for a player's respect and then put themselves in a compromising situation, the implications of which are obvious.

Because the individual players on the team change from year to year, so does the challenge of ensuring that the entire coaching staff earns the respect of the players. The coaches must have a plan for earning respect, and all staff members must stick to that plan. As a coach, I've always been very adamant about defining principles relating to all facets of our program. These are the principles that we emphatically believe in and try to live by.

All coaches on the staff must demonstrate the ability to communicate effectively with every player—regardless of position—about all aspects of every offensive and defensive strategy employed in the program. All the coaches need to have a consistent and definitive understanding of our methodology for skill development at all positions. In other words, members of the staff always speak the same language. This is not to say that the staff should believe in cloning player skills—the coaches should not have a closed mind to the variances that may be seen in the optimum performance of biomechanical skills such as hitting, pitching, fielding, and so on. An open-minded staff has more options available to push the right kinetic button when teaching. Helping players adjust their execution of a skill should be subtle and based on a player's inability to execute. Often a very minor mechanical adjustment can serve as a placebo for a confidence issue. However, we believe in certain cognitive processes associated with pitching, hitting, throwing, and catching—and these processes are instituted without exception. This is also true for the expected levels of intensity and emotional control.

All on-field communication from coaches to players will be in a baseball context, never a personal one. Criticism of a player's failure to perform or respond in a manner deemed acceptable may be pointed and forceful, but that criticism is never meant to be given or taken personally. When the coaching staff challenges players to maximize mental or physical effort, some players may display the "I did my best" mentality; this is especially common among players who are new to the program. Because developing players often do not have a good perspective of what their best really is, the players' perception of this is often inaccurate. Players must trust that the coach is the best judge of a player's potential level of play. A coach should never demand more than a player is capable of giving and should never accept less than the player's best. Coaches need to exhibit a sincere off-field care and concern for their players, and players need to understand that the player–coach relationship in the practice environment is not always the same as in other environments. This enables the coaches and players to come to a better understanding. Management through fear, humiliation, and intimidation has short-term results and provides no long-term behavioral changes in the way players approach the game.

The coaching staff should consistently demonstrate the same practice ethic demanded from players. Hypocrisy can be a cancer in a baseball program, and no greater hypocrisy exists than coaches constantly challenging players to reach their full potential while failing to do so themselves. Players will recognize effort and commitment from their coaches in practices; therefore, the coaches should be sure to demonstrate these things every day.

Motivating Players to Adopt a Team Work Ethic

Once the team's style of play is defined, we need to ensure that all players conform their individual style of play to the prescribed team style of play. There is not much latitude for individual styles.

The motivation to make this happen doesn't need to be very complex or something that requires a behavioral psychologist to figure out. Every player has an intrinsic desire and need to be respected by his peers. Extrinsically, every player knows that he has to earn the respect of his teammates if he is going to play.

Because of immaturity and pampered backgrounds, some players have a tough time consistently committing to building a strong legacy. These players confuse words for actions. They have a difficult time understanding the difference between what they think they are and what their actions say they are. They avoid making critical judgments about themselves and are more apt to make excuses. In short, they establish a loser's legacy. They don't understand that critical judgments are necessary to identify problems—and that excuses simply disguise problems by transferring responsibility.

For purposes of motivation, the concept of respect can be developed and sustained by convincing players that their baseball legacy will be the most important thing they will ever build in baseball. To date, one of the best things we've done at Lewis and Clark State is to establish a tradition of emphasizing that legacies are very important. Players are asked to write out their legacies before the season. My most frequent question to players is "How are you going to be remembered?" A player's legacy statement should reflect competency in the following areas:

Displays Mental Toughness

- Player responds in a positive way to adversity.
- Player's desire to win exceeds his fear of failure.
- Player is able to focus under the perception of pressure.

Displays Physical Toughness

- Player doesn't avoid physical discomfort when playing.
- Player plays through minor injuries.
- Player doesn't overreact to pain.

Understands the Game

- Player demonstrates an intellectual appreciation for the execution of skills and strategies.
- Player understands the 27-out, no-clock principle of baseball.

Displays Emotional Stability

- Player never gets too high or too low.
- Player appreciates Skip Bertman's baseball law of averages regarding bad hops, flare fly balls, seeing-eye ground balls, and so on.

Cares About Teammates

- Player projects empathy and understanding in interpersonal relationships.
- Player can share his success with teammates and can feel good for their successes.

Some players inaccurately analyze what they project about themselves to their teammates. For many years, we have used a sociogram to provide feedback to players on the type of teammate they are perceived to be by their teammates.

To develop the team sociogram, we ask each player to evaluate qualities of his teammates in five areas: empathy for teammates, social maturity, baseball talent, work ethic, and mental toughness. Players use a scale of 1 to 5—5 means exceptional, 4 above average, 3 average, 2 poor, and 1 unacceptable. All evaluations in each category are totaled and divided by the number of players doing the sociogram to determine an average ranking for the player. We are also interested in how objective small groups of players are in evaluating close friends as well as individual-to-individual rankings. We administer the socio-gram at the beginning of the season and again at midseason. At midseason, we always find a notable increase in the average scores for the majority of our players; the sociogram seems to serve as a wake-up call for players, especially those who are new to the program. Once a player understands how to earn the trust and respect of his teammates, his self-image grows more positive, and his confidence level rises significantly. It's easy to believe in yourself when your teammates believe in you.

Using Drills and Scrimmages That Include Game Pressure

Our objective is to ensure that our players are prepared to compete against outstanding teams. Our players must be prepared to react to all the elements of baseball that these teams bring. In big games, we will need to compete against teams that have outstanding speed, power, and execution on offense; there-fore, for practices, we design all defensive drills to be effectively realistic and competitive. Competitive teams also offer the challenge of effective pitching staffs that feature a variety of types of pitchers. To prepare for this, we make sure our hitting drills (proficiency and power drills) are always conducted in a highly competitive manner. We need to consistently "win the practice" by outperforming in practice any team we might play during the season. We all realize that pressure can negatively affect skill performance and cause sound offensive and defensive strategy to break down. Therefore, the goal is to develop players who have been exposed in practice to specific game situations that include the pressure to perform. Then, when the players are faced with challenging situations in big games, they can say, "I've been here before many times." Fearing failure and playing not to lose are trademarks of teams that do not simulate game pressure in practice. A coach cannot hand out confidence to players. The players must earn confidence through practice.

Implementing Drills That Fit the Program Philosophy

Determining a starting point for skill development depends on several factors: player expertise, facilities, available staff, and, of course, time. Once these factors have been determined, I subscribe to the concept of simulating the actual skill as opposed to overfractionalizing the biomechanics of hitting, pitching, fielding, throwing, and catching. Breaking skills down into components that are too small can result in mundane, time-killing exercises that fail to truly challenge and measure players' physical toughness, mental toughness, baseball intellect, and emotional stability. Drills should be specifically defined and conducted so that they challenge each player's kinesthetic self-awareness. This will help players analyze and adapt their skills. Skill analysis by the player and coach through DVD replay is critical to visual learning.

Players should accept the responsibility of assisting in their own development by self-teaching themselves the physical skills and mental focus of the game. Players who devote time to teaching younger players to play the game become better players themselves because they have to think through all the physical and mental components of the game. Those who can teach others have a far greater capacity to teach themselves. Players should also perform realistic self-evaluations in regard to their skill progression and intellectual growth. This can create productive mind-sets in players so that they don't depend entirely on a coach's analysis.

Defining Practice Absolutes

A vast spectrum of philosophical approaches may be used to define and measure player effort within the practice environment. Coaches must prioritize elements of the game that they believe are critical to their team's style of play. The coach should then demand that the team fully incorporate those elements in practice. We clearly communicate to players the absolutes of practice protocol that are expected to be followed at all times during every practice. These absolutes certainly do not encompass all modes of practice behavior; rather, they speak to the specific elements that we believe are integral to raising the team's competitive level and defining its style of play.

All position players are timed periodically in all situational baserunning (i.e., home to first, home to second with headfirst slide, and so on). The first-base coach (during scrimmages) or a coach on the field (during drills) records times and compares them to the player's best time. For example, if a player's best time for a run to first on a turn is 4.5 seconds, the player should always run a 4.5 on a turn when a ball he hits leaves the infield.

Along with the defensive aspects, offensive execution can be emphasized during a full-team, on-field batting practice. Defensively, our goal is for infielders to make a play on every playable ball hit in batting practice, always simulating a potential double play up the middle or home to first. When there is more than one defender at a position, the players alternate repetitions.

Infield tempo is always aggressive and quick but never rushed. Whether turning a double play or just getting an out at first base, the goal is to complete the play in 3.9 seconds or less from the time of contact. On double plays, shortstops are expected to get the ball to first base in 1.1 to 1.25 seconds after the first touch on the pivot. The second baseman's time should be 1.25 to 1.35 seconds.

In all drills, scrimmages, and games, infielders are challenged to do the following:

- Maximize every effort to keep high-velocity ground balls hit right at them in the infield by exhibiting a great desire to keep their chest and face perpendicular to the ball.
- Demonstrate a desire to dive for any ball hit beyond the extent of their lateral range, maintaining the full face of the glove to the ball while looking the ball into the glove.
- Square up on all short-hop throws, keeping the chest and glove perpendicular and centered and keeping the face behind the glove.

Infielders must not show any fear of the ball. They must exhibit the mental toughness necessary to perform zero-tolerance fielding actions, causing a positive carryover toward mastering all other aspects of infield play.

Outfielders must always show enthusiasm for making diving catches. They must show no fear of the fence, execute proper routes, and simulate proper footwork and throwing mechanics. An outfielder must also throw to the appropriate base with simulated runners at first and second in a one-out situation.

Catchers catch all bullpen pitches and warm-up pitches during scrimmages from a receiving posture that helps them best receive, block, and throw in a simulated first-and-third defensive situation. Without fail, catchers must block every wild pitch during every bullpen workout. They must simulate proper footwork, ball-glove exchange, and arm action on 30 to 50 percent of bullpen pitches.

To maintain the desired tempo of scrimmages, everything is timed. Players have 25 seconds to assume their defensive positions after the final out of an inning. Between innings, a well-trained fungo hitter follows a specific routine for hitting specific double-play ground balls for 2 minutes. Each infielder has time to field 3 ground balls and start 3 double plays, for a total of 12 double plays every half inning.

Outfielders go to center field for a 2-minute fly-ball drill. The fungo hitter follows a specific routine for the types of fly balls that the outfielders work on. The outfielders should make three tough catches and execute three fundamentally solid throws between innings. There is nothing casual about the work performed between innings—the mood is gamelike, and the effort is always all out.

The maxim for scrimmages is a heightened level of competition that meets or exceeds game level.

Developing Mental Toughness

Mental toughness is a key component in a player's makeup—one that leads the player to have a solid work ethic in practice and game settings. *Mental toughness* is a popular term for coaches to use when discussing an athlete's ability to compete. Ron Polk offers that mental toughness is an athlete's ability to withstand prosperity as well as despair each time his skill is tested—pitch by pitch and game by game. Gary Ward believes that in a mentally tough player, the desire to succeed is greater than the fear of failure. Jerry Kendall emphasizes the player's ability to respond well in high-pressure situations as an indicator of mental toughness. Bobo Brayton looks for an aggressive and positive response with an "all day, every day" attitude. For all four of these esteemed coaches, the definition of mental toughness requires the player to consistently display positive reactions to negative situations.

Adversity can come at an athlete from any direction and can produce a variety of implications. It can test his emotional stability, his ability to function within his baseball intellect, and his physical tolerance. Adversity does not build character; it merely evokes a choice of responses, positive or negative. Our challenge as coaches is to make sure that players make appropriate choices when faced with adversity. Continually heightening the degree of difficulty in practices and holding players responsible for lack of positive response are critical for the players' development. High-pressure, gamelike drills and scrimmages with consequences for failure will expose players to adversity. Coaches and players must recognize that emotional response, baseball intellectual function, and physical tolerance have to be examined separately when building or measuring mental toughness. A player might be able to use his baseball knowledge to conceptualize an acceptable response to an adverse game situation, but the player could deviate from this response because of weak emotional stability.

Finally, players must understand that baseball, like life, is not always fair. Those who dwell on the fact that they've experienced some bad breaks will never find success.

Establishing a Program Identity

The coach must instill in players the idea that they have the opportunity to demonstrate characteristics of a playing style that is respected in the game. Effort is respected. Humility is respected. Teammates who care about and believe in one another are respected. Emotional stability is respected. Mental toughness is respected. Earning respect is what playing baseball should be all about.

chapter 2

Planning Productive Practices

KEITH MADISON

We have all heard the adage "practice makes perfect." Most of us have also heard the more accurate quote "perfect practice makes perfect." Without a plan, the perfection and success that coaches desire will most likely never occur.

Planning, attention to details, and organization are concepts that, quite frankly, have never come easily for me as a coach. Having never played college baseball, I joined the Mississippi State coaching staff after playing five years of minor league baseball and coaching two years at the high school level. My first year as a head coach at the high school level, I entered the season opener in panic mode, having not even come close to covering the many phases of the game. I vowed to never again enter a season unprepared.

Fortunately, at Mississippi State I spent one year as a graduate assistant being mentored by Ron Polk, arguably the most organized coach in all of college baseball. Under Coach Polk, I was quickly introduced to the world of staff meetings and detailed practice schedules that accounted for each minute. That year, I learned much about coaching techniques, coaching philosophy, team discipline, and the game itself. I was able to learn about competing at the college level while working for two of the greatest coaches in the game. Not only was Ron Polk the head coach, but another legendary coach, Mark

Johnson (Texas A&M and Sam Houston), was Ron's top assistant. One of the most important lessons I learned in 1978 was the importance of planning and organizing a productive baseball practice.

Taking time to organize and plan each practice will give you, your staff, and your team a sense of confidence. With a long-range plan and a daily practice schedule, you will be sure to—pardon the pun—have all of the bases covered.

Visualize the Big Picture

While planning productive practices, you should try to visualize the end of the season and all that you want to accomplish. List all the phases of the game that your team needs to work on in order to reach your goals. Table 2.1 is not all-inclusive, but it may serve as a foundation for a master plan for your off-season, preseason, and in-season practice schedules. Consider ranking the various components of the game in order based on their significance to the success of your program; then schedule the appropriate time for each.

As you look at the big picture and list the many phases of the game that need to be covered, remember that your players need to understand your overall baseball philosophy as well as your philosophy in the following areas: team offense, team defense, hitting, pitching, and conditioning and strength training. This will cut down on the number of times you hear the question that so many players ask during practice: "Why are we doing this?"

Set the Tone

The first practice of the year could set the tone for your entire season. Organization, structure, and a positive atmosphere for learning will not only help the team produce wins, but will also earn respect for the coaching staff. Sloppy play, lack of intensity, and distractions cannot be tolerated. Players should never be allowed to walk from station to station.

Punctuality and positive energy are musts for each practice. This should be a major point of emphasis from day one. If a coaching staff is slack in this area early on, by the end of the season, the coaches will be inundated with excuses and lethargic practices. The batting cage, bullpen, field, and dugout are all classrooms. Create a challenging, interesting atmosphere of teaching, competition, and discipline through proper planning and using championship standards each day in practice.

Create the Practice Schedule

A written, well-organized practice schedule is your blueprint for success. It is an essential tool for every coach. Post the practice schedule every day before 10:00 a.m. at the same specific spot on campus. This will reveal to the players

Table 2.1 Phases of Baseball

Strength training and conditioning	Team defense	Pitching	Hitting	Team offense
Philosophy	Philosophy	Philosophy	Philosophy	Philosophy
Off-season conditioning	Bunt defense	Bullpen routines	Two-strike hitting	Sharing knowledge after first time through lineup
Preseason conditioning	First-and-third defense	Pickoff plays	Approach	First-and-third offense
In-season conditioning	Drills	Pickoff moves	Execution (hit-and-run; bunt; man on second, no outs; bases loaded; leading off an inning)	Baserunning (stealing bases, reading down angle, leads, tagging)
	Pregame infield warm-up	Holding base runners to control the running game		
	Rundowns	Tempo	Positive-count hitting	Signs
	Pickoffs	Drills		Communication with base coaches
	Cutoffs and double relays	Long-toss routine		
	Communication among catchers, pitchers, and infielders about picking off and holding runners	Pitching mechanics		
		Deception		
	Double-play footwork	Grips		
	Communication on fly balls and pop-ups	Pitchouts		
	Infield in	Intentional walks		
	Double-play depth	Backing up bases		
	No doubles	Covering home		
	Defending the squeeze play	Pitchers' fielding practice		

how important practice is for the team, and it will help the players mentally prepare for their afternoon or evening on the baseball field. Now that e-mail and other types of technology are available to every high school and college student, coaches can send the practice schedule electronically as well as post it on a bulletin board.

I'm a quote guy. When I was coaching, I always put a quote at the top of the practice schedule, and I often asked the team if they knew the quote of the day. Someone would always repeat it. One day, I forgot to add a quote on the schedule, and several players mentioned during practice that I had forgotten the quote.

Use the schedule as an outline of what you would like to see your team accomplish. Try to stay on time. If you allot 20 minutes to work on rundowns, don't spend an hour if things don't go well. Let your players know that improvement is needed, and work on it again at the next practice. Don't let frustration and lack of progress in one drill destroy the entire practice. We live in a remote-control, microwave, high-tech, fast-paced society. Spending too much time on one drill is counterproductive. Use your schedule and clipboard as a checklist and report card. Make notes and grade each drill or station. This will give you a good idea of what needs improvement in future practices. Post schedules in dugouts, batting cages, bullpens, hitting tunnels, and the locker room.

Have a manager or student assistant help the coaching staff keep track of the time for each station or hitting group. This person should give a two-minute warning to help the coaches and players wrap things up before moving to the next station or assignment.

Arm care is something that many coaches overlook in planning practices. Proper warm-up is needed before each defensive drill. It is wise to schedule each defensive drill immediately after throwing at the beginning of practice. On some days, to emphasize the importance of baserunning, you might plan baserunning drills after stretching at the beginning of practice; the team can then move into throwing and defensive drills.

A typical practice schedule is shown in figure 2.1. Notice that time is allotted for players to arrive early (if their class schedules permit) to hit in the cage, take extra ground balls, and so on. A coach may also use this time for some one-on-one work with a player who may be struggling in a specific phase of his game. During this time, a small group could also work on a specific skill such as turning double plays, fielding bunts or slow rollers, performing pickoff moves, or hitting.

Begin practice with a short meeting on the mound or in the dugout to briefly go over the practice schedule and the progress you want to achieve. You may want to encourage, challenge, or motivate the team at this juncture. After a stressful day of classes or tests, players need to be pumped up a little before practice. I call these quick meetings *motivational minutes.* I might share a story about a player or team that overcame adversity to have a successful season, or perhaps a lesson about a historical hero such as Charles Lindbergh (who overcame many challenges and much negativity to accomplish the first transatlantic solo flight). You could tell stories about people such as former pitcher Jim Abbott, who became an All-American and pitched successfully in the major leagues with one arm. You may want to talk to your team about past teams or about someone in your own program who overcame adversity or left a positive legacy.

After the motivational minute, have the entire team run a couple of laps at three-quarters speed to increase heart rate before a good stretch in the outfield. Stretching should be supervised by a coach, strength coach, or trainer. Horseplay and distractions should not be tolerated during the stretching routine.

After stretching, an incredibly important part of practice occurs—team throwing and catching. Infielders should throw with infielders, catchers with catchers, outfielders with outfielders, and pitchers with pitchers. Coaches should use this time to check four-seam grips, throwing mechanics, and catching techniques. Emphasize throwing accuracy (most errors are throwing errors) and encourage proper footwork. No one, especially infielders, should reach to catch a ball. The feet should be moving, and the player should catch the ball with two hands in the center of the chest. Players should not be talking during this time. Listening to a dozen baseballs popping leather is a beautiful thing.

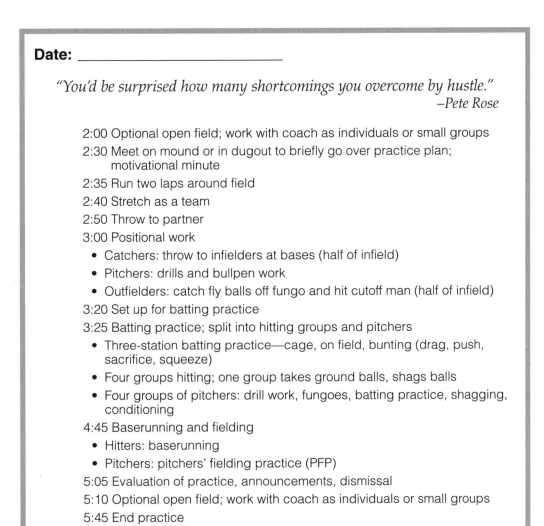

Date: _____

"You'd be surprised how many shortcomings you overcome by hustle."
—*Pete Rose*

2:00 Optional open field; work with coach as individuals or small groups
2:30 Meet on mound or in dugout to briefly go over practice plan; motivational minute
2:35 Run two laps around field
2:40 Stretch as a team
2:50 Throw to partner
3:00 Positional work
- Catchers: throw to infielders at bases (half of infield)
- Pitchers: drills and bullpen work
- Outfielders: catch fly balls off fungo and hit cutoff man (half of infield)

3:20 Set up for batting practice
3:25 Batting practice; split into hitting groups and pitchers
- Three-station batting practice—cage, on field, bunting (drag, push, sacrifice, squeeze)
- Four groups hitting; one group takes ground balls, shags balls
- Four groups of pitchers: drill work, fungoes, batting practice, shagging, conditioning

4:45 Baserunning and fielding
- Hitters: baserunning
- Pitchers: pitchers' fielding practice (PFP)

5:05 Evaluation of practice, announcements, dismissal
5:10 Optional open field; work with coach as individuals or small groups
5:45 End practice

Figure 2.1 Sample practice schedule.

In at least one practice each week, the coach should initiate concentrated throwing drills. During the 10 to 12 minutes allowed for throwing, a coach should count the balls that hit the ground. At the end of practice, the entire team runs a lap for each ball that hit the ground during the concentrated throwing drill. The first time I did this, our team ran 18 laps. At our last practice that same year, the team ran 0 laps. Perfect practice does indeed make perfect. To make this drill more meaningful and challenging, set up cones at 40-foot (12.2 m), 60-foot (18.3 m), and 90-foot (27.4 m) intervals. Players throw and catch from 40 feet for the first 3 minutes, 60 feet for the next 3 minutes, 90 feet for the next 3 minutes, then back to 60 feet for the final 3 minutes. Do not allow lobbing. Demand proper throwing footwork and catching techniques. Competition and pressure are always an integral part of practice.

Defensive drills should follow the throwing segment of practice. At this time, the players' arms are loose. If defensive drills are done later in practice, time is wasted because additional warm-ups are necessary. When players are required to warm up their arms multiple times each practice, this will eventually take its toll with sore arms or even injury.

After the defensive work, players may be allowed a short break of 5 to 10 minutes to help set up the field for batting practice. (More information on batting practice is provided later in this chapter.) After batting practice, the players should move the batting cage and screens and should prepare for the final drills of the day.

At the end of practice, the head coach should give a short evaluation of the day's practice, make any necessary announcements, and dismiss the team. The coaches could schedule more one-on-one or small-group coaching sessions at this time.

The entire practice (not counting the open-field time) was two and a half hours long. Usually, practices should not run any longer than that. Coaches should be able to observe the players' body language to determine whether the next practice should be a short one-hour practice or a challenging two-and-a-half-hour workout. At times, giving a team a day off or rewarding them with a short one-hour practice will give them more energy and enthusiasm for the next practice. During preseason, reserve longer practices for Saturday, and consider holding two practice sessions a day (each session being one and a half to two hours long), one in the morning and the other late in the afternoon. More can be accomplished with two short sessions as opposed to a sluggish, mentally exhausting four-hour practice. It's been said that practice is for coaches and games are for players. If that is true, in order to make practice more challenging, fun, and rewarding for players, we should make each practice as competitive and gamelike as possible while maintaining an atmosphere of learning and growing.

No player is perfect. Therefore, players will not execute perfectly on every drill. Mistakes made with honest effort are well and good, as long as they are corrected. Correcting mistakes is one of the building blocks toward success. Coaches need to have patience.

The times before or after practice for working one on one or with small groups should be more relaxed times of teaching and training. These sessions should include positive dialogue between coach and player.

Organize Batting Practice

Team batting practice is the most time-consuming and perhaps the most challenging part of practice. Depending on the level of play, there could be anywhere from 12 to 22 hitters to supervise. Unless you plan properly, this could be a logistical nightmare and could be boring or dangerous.

Most college programs have a fully funded staff, volunteer coaches, and even student assistants to help manage a baseball practice with multiple stations. When I was a high school coach, the junior varsity coach assisted me on some days, but many times I was on the field alone. Coaches who may be short-handed should spend their off-season recruiting volunteers from the school or community to help in practices. These volunteers can throw batting practice and hit fungoes. Perhaps you could find a retired coach or a former high school or college player who loves baseball and would enjoy contributing or giving back to the game. You should teach these volunteers how to throw good batting practice and how to properly hit fungoes. If volunteers can't be found, you will need to teach a student manager or pitcher (one who doesn't play another position) how to use the fungo bat. And perhaps you can train a backup catcher or outfielder how to throw good batting practice. Throwing good, firm strikes in batting practice is the key to a productive session. Even if you must set aside a few Saturdays to train volunteers or student-athletes, this will reap big dividends throughout the season.

For batting practice, the pitcher should throw from a mound so that hitters see as many pitches as possible from the downward angle. You may move a throw-down plate 4 to 5 feet (122 to 152 cm) in front of the permanent plate, and hitters will still be hitting in the dirt. Many sporting goods equipment companies sell portable mounds that you can move in front of the original mound, or you could build one with plywood. When using the throw-down plate and portable mound, the batting practice pitcher throws from 45 to 50 feet (13.7 to 15.2 m) as opposed to 60 feet (18.3 m). This helps the batting practice pitcher throw more strikes and save his arm. It also firms up the velocity so that a 70- to 75-mile-per-hour fastball appears to the hitter to be a more gamelike 80- to 85-mile-per-hour fastball.

To have an effective multistation batting practice, several pieces of equipment are required:

- Two L-screens, one for the field and one for the batting tunnel
- One portable batting cage for the field
- Two protective screens, one positioned so the first baseman can take throws from infielders and one positioned so the bucket man on the outfield side of second base can retrieve balls from the outfield
- Two throw-down home plates, one for in front of the permanent home plate and one for the batting tunnel
- Two portable mounds, one for in front of the pitching mound on the main field and the other for the batting tunnel

Make sure you use proper protective screens and strong netting with no holes, especially if student-athletes or student managers are helping with batting practice. I almost lost an assistant coach one year during short toss because of a hole in the net portion of the protective L-screen.

During batting practice, each station should be supervised by a coach or at least by a responsible senior leader on the team. The objective of this phase of practice is to get as many good swings as possible in the time allotted. There should be very little standing around. Every player should look at the posted schedule and know his assignment.

Table 2.2 is a sample schedule for a one-hour, four-station batting practice. Groups rotate every 15 or 20 minutes, moving from on-the-field hitting, to the batting tunnel, to baserunning, and then to defense. When coaches are pitching batting practice, the catchers are optional. Infielders are encouraged to spend at least half of their defensive rotation taking live ground balls and the other half taking ground balls from fungo hitters. Outfielders should play shallow and work on live reads off the bat. Pitchers should assist in shagging balls and should stay clear of the outfielders. Pitchers will retrieve balls that get by outfielders and toss the balls to the bucket man. Pitchers alternate between assigned fungo, bucket, or shag stations and conditioning or drill work at the coach's discretion.

The field station in batting practice could be a competitive station if a student manager keeps execution points on a clipboard. The number of strikes thrown by the batting practice pitcher and the readiness and hustle of the hitters in the group determine the number of rounds a group will be able to fit in.

Every swing in every round should have a purpose. For example, in round 1, hitters hit two sacrifice bunts with a runner on first base, two cuts with a runner on second base and no outs, and four hits hard up the middle. In round 2, hitters hit one sacrifice bunt with a runner on second base, two hit-and-runs, and four hits gap to gap. In round 3, hitters hit two squeeze bunts, one safety squeeze, and three hits gap to gap. Finally, in round 4, hitters hit four balls gap to gap. The emphasis is offensive execution. Before or after practice is a great time to work with individual hitters on their strokes; team batting practice is the time to work on execution.

Table 2.2 One-Hour, Four-Station Batting Practice Schedule

	Group 1	Group 2	Group 3	Group 4
Location	Field	Batting tunnel	Field	Field
Assignment	Hitting, batting cage	Hitting, tunnel	Baserunning	Defense
Hitters	Abbott	Tews	Pryor	Morse
	Green	Rhea	Miller	Gonzales
	Jones	Blandford	Keown	Brooks
	Bragga	Young	Hayes	Hindersman
Catcher	Hindersman	Bragga	N/A	N/A
First-base fungo	Downs	Henderson	Reid	Fisher
Third-base fungo	Thompson	Smith	Gibson	Frazier
Bucket	Reid	Froning	Thompson	Henderson

In live batting practice, base runners react to what is going on by reading bunts, recognizing the hit-and-run, and so on. Fungo hitters must be aware of the live hitters when fungo hitting ground balls. Safety and responsibility are paramount. Outfielders, infielders, and base runners should work just as hard during these stations as they do while hitting.

Put a student manager or volunteer coach in charge of awarding a point for each properly executed swing. Reward the winning group by relieving them of the duty of moving screens, cages, and equipment after practice.

A machine can be used in the batting tunnel so hitters can work on hitting the breaking ball. A short-toss station could also be set up in the tunnel. In the tunnel, hitters could rotate from tee work (hitting into the net) to the machine or soft toss.

A coach or manager should use a watch to keep the rotations on time. Issue a two-minute warning across the field to keep the groups rotating in a timely fashion.

To keep batting practice from becoming too long, too routine, and too boring, you may sometimes have two groups hit before team practice and two groups hit after team practice. This is a good way to have a short, crisp team practice on a day that you also want to emphasize hitting.

Make the Most of Time

Why is it that time drags when you want it to pass quickly and flies when you need more of it? Time isn't very cooperative. Time is the great equalizer. We all have the same amount—24 hours in a day, 60 minutes in an hour, and 60 seconds in each minute. Some opponents may be bigger, faster, or more talented, but they have the same amount of time to prepare as you do. Using time effectively may make up for lack of size, talent, or speed. Successful people invest their time; average people spend time; and underachievers waste time. Time is more important than money. Money is a renewable resource, but time is limited. When you give people your money, you've given them something they can replace. But, when you give them your time, you've given them a part of your life.

You have just enough time to fulfill God's purpose (being a coach) in your life. If you can't get everything accomplished that you want, this means one of two things: You are doing things God never intended for you to do, or you are doing the right thing in the wrong way.

To best use your time, you should take notes during each practice on what went well and what needs improving. The next morning, carefully plan the day's practice accordingly. A carefully structured practice will help you, your staff, and your players accomplish more in a shorter amount of time. It will also save mental and physical energy for the next practice or for game day. Poorly structured practices lead to standing around, dead time, and boredom.

Communicate

Baseball fields are large. If your pitchers are in the right-field bullpen, a group of hitters are in the left-field hitting tunnel, and a group of infielders are on the infield, how do you communicate with everyone? I was blessed with a voice that seems to carry very well. It has been said that I learned how to whisper in a sawmill. But even with a loud booming voice, it's difficult to verbally communicate across the field on a windy day.

As a coach, you have several ways to communicate to the entire team during practice:

- Schedule short meetings on the mound or in the dugout at least once at the midpoint of practice.
- Post practice schedules in each dugout, in the hitting tunnel, on the portable batting cage, and in each bullpen.
- Require your student manager to keep a bullhorn available for impromptu team meetings on the infield.
- Use the sound system from the press box by using a wireless microphone on the field.

Team communication on the field can be difficult, sometimes requiring the coach to yell across the field and speak to large groups of players in what my wife describes as a coaching voice. Use the one-on-one and small-group time before and after practice as an opportunity to be more laid back with the players. This will encourage dialogue with players and inspire them to ask questions that they may not feel comfortable asking in a larger team setting. In the individual or small-group setting, coaches can also ask players questions such as "Why do you grip your changeup that way?" and "Have you ever experimented with this grip?" These types of questions will help the coach learn from and teach players.

Communication during practice is essential in helping your team grow and improve. Remember that a crucial part of the communication process is observing body language and picking up on not only what players say but how they say it. Confront negative comments and body language immediately, one on one, and privately. If possible, ask questions and learn as much as you can. You never know what might be going on in a player's life, including issues that may be detrimental to his own personal progress as well as the team's. Nip it in the bud quickly to prevent the loss of an entire team practice. Serious personal problems sometimes manifest themselves on the practice field. At times, it's wise to give a player a day off, follow up with him after practice, and listen to him. As John Wooden often said, "Players don't care how much you know until they know how much you care."

Collaborate With Assistant Coaches

Much of the information in this chapter comes not only from what I learned from mentors (such as Ron Polk and Mark Johnson) but also from what I learned from the assistant coaches who have come through my programs. I tried to surround myself with people who are much smarter and much more organized than I am. Give assistant coaches a voice when planning practices and let them contribute to your overall program. These coaches should not be robots or clones of the head coach; the more responsibility you give assistant coaches, the more they will contribute. They may not teach a skill the same way as you would teach it, but their method may be just as effective—if not better. Spend time talking with your assistant coaches about philosophy and teaching techniques, then trust them. Creativity is stifled when you surround yourself with yes-men. Some players naturally respond more to the assistant coach than to the head coach. Many effective leaders have said, "It's amazing how much can be accomplished when no one cares who gets the credit."

When selecting a staff, whether you have a paid staff or volunteers, you should try to attract people who are gifted in areas where you are not. I have had to work hard to improve my organizational skills. By nature, I'm not a detail-oriented person. The first assistant coach I hired at the University of Kentucky, John Butler, was very detail oriented. I could trust him completely with any detail, from helping to organize practice to making sure that the field was set up perfectly for practice. He also planned team travel, ordered equipment, and mastered a host of other things that would have otherwise been a tremendous burden to me. John was with me for 15 years. Other successful assistants had similar skills: Jim Hinerman (former head coach at Georgetown College), Bob Smith (former assistant at Tennessee, Virginia Commonwealth, and George Washington University), Daron Schoenrock (current head coach at the University of Memphis), Greg Goff (current head coach at Campbell University), and Scott Malone (current head coach at Texas A&M University at Corpus Christi).

Other assistant coaches, such as Jan Weisberg (current head coach at Birmingham-Southern College), had great people and recruiting skills and could throw batting practice for hours. But, like me, Jan had to discipline himself to stay organized. The rewards of friendship, camaraderie among staff, and success are special gifts that come from this great game of baseball.

Assistant coaches and their contributions are very important to the productivity of a baseball practice. Being on the baseball field alone during practice is a huge undertaking. Whether you are able to hire assistants or you recruit volunteers, you need to bring in assistant coaches who are men of character and who have passion for the game. This is critical to the success of your practices, season, and program. "As iron sharpens iron, so one man sharpens another" (Proverbs 27:17).

Check Your Attitude

In practice and games, coaches often focus on the attitude of their players, and rightly so. But, what about your attitude as a coach? Several years ago, Billy Graham stated that the most influential people in America today are coaches. He didn't say politicians, corporate CEOs, or even pastors. He said coaches. What an awesome responsibility coaches have to influence players in a positive way.

The negative attitude of just one coach will result in an unproductive practice. Midway in my career at the University of Kentucky, we were in a heated battle with several other SEC teams for first place. On this particular weekend, we were slated to play the last-place team in the league. If we swept our series and if LSU (the top team at that time) lost their series, we would be only half a game out of first place. That didn't happen. We were rained out of one game and proceeded to lose two games to the last-place team. Meanwhile, LSU swept their opponent.

After a very long bus ride back to Lexington, my attitude became more and more negative. I don't believe I slept more than two hours that night. By the time I began preparing for the next practice, I was in quite a foul mood. My goal for practice that day was to make my team pay for their poor performance from the past weekend.

When I pulled into the parking lot that afternoon for practice, our football coach, Bill Curry, pulled in next to my car on his way to spring football practice. As we both got out of our vehicles, Coach Curry said, "Keith, I was very sorry when I read in the paper this morning about your doubleheader loss. I felt so bad for you. It almost felt like I had lost a football game. I know how important those games were for you."

I mumbled a grumpy "Thanks, Coach" and walked away. He stopped me and said, "Hey, wait a minute. If you go out to your practice looking like you do now, practice will be a disaster. You look terrible!" He went on, "If you go out to your field looking and acting the way you are now, your season may be over. You need to change your attitude in a hurry. Those young men are looking to you for help."

I was stunned by Coach Curry's remarks, but they had a profound effect on me. I changed into my practice gear, and I changed my attitude. We had a great, upbeat practice that day. The following weekend, we swept number one LSU. If Bill Curry had not taken the time to be truthful with me and expose my sorry attitude, our season could have been over. As a coach, you must check your attitude each day before taking the field. Your players are looking to you for leadership and direction. If you want positive results in practice—and I know you do—you must be a positive leader with a dynamic practice plan designed to challenge and improve your team.

chapter 3

Assessing Team Strengths

TERRY ROONEY

For a team to achieve at the highest level, a coach must analyze each individual element of the team and must discover the team's strengths. A systematic approach to evaluation is the best way for a coaching staff to assess their team. The specific plan presented in this chapter is broken down into each position, along with the team component. The chapter provides a detailed description of that plan and the means by which to incorporate it into a daily practice.

The first step a coach must take to develop a winning team is to fully identify the strengths and weaknesses of the team. Then the coach needs to devise a practice plan that will allow players to display their abilities in various scenarios. These practice plans should be sequential and should vary in the types of situations they simulate. After assessing your team, you must put your players in the best position to be successful. The evaluation process is extremely important; without it, you are simply coaching to one single style. The key to being a successful coach is to understand that each individual and team is entirely different. Our job as coaches is to help all of our players and teams reach their full potential.

Identifying Player Strengths

The first step in identifying a team's strengths is to evaluate the basic skills of each prospective player. In determining the criteria for evaluation, the coach must decide which items are the most important to that specific position. The elements determined to be the most significant must be displayed by the player in the evaluation. These aspects are unique to each coach and are best finalized with the input of the entire coaching staff. Although certain skills are required to be successful in baseball, regardless of the playing level, the importance placed on each skill is entirely up to the coach.

Second, the timing of the evaluation is also of great importance. The positional evaluation should be the first portion of the process. A coach must know the physical skill level of a player before putting that player into a competitive situation. This information includes specific statistical data, along with objective grading from the coaching staff. Make sure the prospective player knows why this portion of the evaluation process is occurring. The player should know that this is only a single aspect of the process and will not determine status on the team. Each potential player must get an equal number of repetitions, and each individual must believe that he was given ample opportunity to display his physical tools. The positional breakdowns described in the following sections begin the evaluation phase.

Pitchers

Place the pitcher in the bullpen; the pitcher will throw a sequence of pitches that demonstrate potential command, along with game-type sequences. These sequences are vital for demonstrating what the coaching staff views as the minimum requirements for a pitcher to be successful.

The importance of each area depends on player age and skill level. However, certain absolutes dictate a pitcher's ability to be successful. The key is to determine which of these areas can be improved and the level of that improvement.

Areas to Evaluate
- Arm strength
- Command
- Mechanics
- Poise and presence
- Projectability

Observations to Note
- Arm slot
- Arm action
- Movement on pitches

- Ability to make adjustments
- Effort level on pitches
- Tempo and pace

Stretch Sequence

The pitcher pitches the following sequences from the stretch (for a total of 15 pitches):

- 3-1-2: three fastballs low and away; one fastball up and in; two fastballs low and in
- 2-2: two changeups low and in; two changeups low and away
- 2-2: two breaking balls or sliders low and away; two breaking balls or sliders down and in
- 1: one fastball middle of plate

Windup Sequence

The pitcher pitches the following sequences from the windup (for a total of 15 pitches):

- 3-1-2: three fastballs low and away; one fastball up and in; two fastballs low and in
- 2-2: two changeups low and in; two changeups low and away
- 2-2: two breaking balls or sliders low and away; two breaking balls or sliders down and in
- 1: one fastball middle of plate

Each pitcher brings something positive to the mound. However, the type of pitching staff you have will dictate not only your style of pitching, but also your team defense. While evaluating pitchers, focus on these additional areas to determine the style of your team:

- Movement on the ball. With additional movement on the ball, the pitcher may induce more ground balls.
- Control of the running game. Watch for quickness to the plate, pickoff moves, and tempo. A pitcher who understands these factors is able to keep the double play in order.
- Average velocity. Having only average velocity will not detract from a pitcher's ability to pitch, but more balls will be put in play.

Note if a pitcher has an above-average fastball. The harder a pitcher can throw, the more likely a hitter will swing and miss the pitch. Also note if the pitcher has a below-average command of the strike zone, because this would increase the chance of additional base runners.

During practice, emphasize fielding mechanics, holding runners, and positioning. Use a chart like the one shown in figure 3.1 to make notes and track the stats of pitchers.

Player name and number	Pitching hand	Fastball velocity	Curveball velocity	Slider velocity	Changeup velocity	Move	Comments

Figure 3.1   Sample chart for tracking pitcher statistics.

Catchers

Place the catcher behind home plate in his receiving position. The catcher begins with a series of throws to individual bases and concludes with a set of blocking drills. This serves as an initial evaluation of the prospective catcher's skill level. The player must understand the significance of this position. The introductory evaluation shows only the physical tools of the potential player. To be successful, the catcher must also demonstrate the nonphysical qualities required for this position. These can be viewed in depth during game-type scenarios. However, a catcher must first display the minimum level of physical ability.

Areas to Evaluate
- Arm strength
- Receiving
- Exchange
- Footwork

Observations to Note
- Arm action on backside
- Flight and carry on baseball

- Accuracy in throws to bases
- Replacement of feet
- Posture and core strength

Throwing Sequence

For the throwing sequence, the catcher throws to second and third base (for a total of 12 throws):

- Throws to second base: two warm-ups; four live
- Throws to third base: two warm-ups; four live

Blocking Sequence

The blocking sequence has two parts (for a total of 16 blocks):

- Block and react: four front; two left side; two right side
- Block and recover: four front then throw to second base; four front then throw to third base

Most teams need to have two capable catchers, preferably an offensive catcher and a defensive catcher. This allows the team to focus on a particular area in any given game. An offensive catcher is able to drive the ball consistently and will bat in the middle of the lineup. A defensive catcher has outstanding receiving and throwing skills and is able to communicate well with the pitching staff.

During practice, catchers need daily repetition in both offense and defense. This will allow each catcher to maintain his strengths and improve on his weaknesses. If a team has a balance of both types of catchers, then a daily practice schedule can be followed.

Outfielders

Place the outfielder in right field. The outfielder begins by fielding a series of balls and throwing them to the designated base. The batted balls are a combination of simulated game plays, ground balls, and pop flies. The outfielder should be required to play various types of balls off the bat because each outfielder is being evaluated for three different positions: left field, center field, and right field. Each outfield position presents its own challenges and requires a different way of playing the ball. A player's physical tools largely determine his specific outfield position. These tools are a combination of all baseball-related areas. However, the following provides a basic outline that can be used to view the player's tools and to determine which outfield position will provide the greatest chance of success.

Areas to Evaluate

- Arm strength
- Arm accuracy
- Arm action

Observations to Note

- Flight and carry on baseball
- Footwork
- Angles to baseball
- Speed and agility

Throwing Sequence

The outfielder throws to third base and home plate (for a total of nine throws):

- Fields and throws to third base: two front; one left side; one right side
- Fields and throws to home plate: two front; one left side; one right side; one slow roller

The type of outfielders a team has clearly affects the playing style of the team. In fact, the strengths of the players in this position have the greatest impact on the style of play and the structure of a practice.

Defensively, for example, outfielders with good speed are able to cover more ground and get to a larger percentage of balls. Outfielders with exceptional arm strength are able to keep runners from advancing, and they have a better chance of assisting in an out.

Offensive power can make up for any defensive shortcomings in the outfield. The preference is for two of the three outfielders to be able to hit home runs. This is clearly an asset because the outfielders do not have fielding attempts on a large percentage of plays.

During practice, outfielders should focus on team defense, first-step quickness when fielding fly balls and grounders, positioning, and offensive strengths.

Infielders

Place the infielder at the shortstop position. The infielder will field a series of balls and throw to first or second base. Use the shortstop position regardless of the player's preferred position. This area of the field provides the greatest distance for fielding game-type balls and also provides the longest throw across the diamond. For each of the four infield positions—first base, second base, shortstop, and third base—the coach will determine the value and significance of each tool. Each spot on the infield requires a minimum level of physical ability that can be determined by the following evaluation.

Areas to Evaluate

- Arm strength
- Arm accuracy
- Fielding consistency
- Foot speed in relation to fielding ball (range)

Observations to Note

- Flight and carry on ball
- First-step reaction to batted ball
- Ball-to-throw exchange
- Accuracy of throws to bases

Throwing Sequence

The infielder runs through the following fielding and throwing sequences (for a total of 18 throws):

- Fields and throws to first base: two front; two glove side; two backhand; two slow rollers
- Fields and throws to second base (double-play turns, shortstop to second base to first base): two front; two glove side; one slow roller
- Fields and throws to first base from second base (double-play turns): five pivot turns from second base to first base (all throws received from second base)

Defensively, the infield is the most important aspect of the game. Evaluation must reveal the speed of the game at which infielders can play. This tempo dictates the style and practice of the team. The quicker the tempo, the more defensive the team. For a slower team, the emphasis becomes offensive output.

During practice, infielders should focus on fielding mechanics; ground balls, slow rollers, and backhands; and positioning.

Offensive Evaluation

The final components to the position evaluation are speed and hitting. Because the player's foot speed (both current and future) determines the value of the player's offensive strengths, both areas—foot speed and hitting—must be evaluated with equal consideration.

The speed component is the first phase of the evaluation. Speed can play a vital role in determining what position best suits a potential player. The significance of running speed varies by position. Knowing this information will help you when assessing which position best suits the player.

The speed evaluation consists of a 60-yard (54.9 m) sprint and a run from home to first base. The player should run both distances two or three times to get an accurate time. In many cases, there is a discrepancy between straightaway speed (60-yard sprint) and game speed (home to first base). This difference can be caused by the quickness, or lack thereof, in which the batter gets out of the box. Therefore, assessing both times will give the most accurate reading.

Observations to Note

- Running form
- Stride length

- Quickness of first step
- Comparison of time in 60-yard sprint (straightaway speed) and time in run from home to first base (game speed)

The hitting evaluation is a critical phase of assessing a player's strengths. Because each position has minimum offensive requirements and absolutes, this evaluation will help the coach identify the potential in each position player. This information is also vital in assessing the collective offensive potential of the team. This phase of the evaluation is tremendously significant when determining a potential player for a specific position. Each position on the field is associated with a different type of offensive trait. For example, a coach would prefer to have a power player at a corner position (first base, third base, left field, or right field) and a player with more speed in the middle of the diamond (shortstop, second base, or center field). During the hitting evaluation, you should note these qualities because the strengths of each hitter should coincide with his potential position. Use a chart similar to figure 3.2 to track the results of the hitting evaluation.

Observations to Note

- Bat speed
- Swing path
- Balance

Teamname _____

Player name and number	Position	Statistics	Walks to strikeouts	Bunts	Runs	Power	First pitch	Favorite pitch	Comments

Figure 3.2 Sample chart for tracking hitter statistics.

- Power
- Ability to use all fields

Many aspects besides the physical tools should be considered in order to accurately evaluate the offensive capability of a team. Evaluating these aspects will help coaches make the decision regarding the offensive style that the team will play.

For example, playing a good short game requires a team that is able to sacrifice bunt, drag bunt, and push bunt. This team must also be able to hit the ball anywhere on the field and instinctively steal bases. Playing for the big inning requires a team that is able to hit the ball out of the ballpark and has good awareness of the strike zone (leading to more walks and additional base runners); the players on this team need to be strong physically and have good bat speed, both qualities of players who can hit for power.

Identifying Team Strengths

The second aspect of evaluating a team is to identify team strengths during the competition phase. The timing and structure of this phase are crucial. When you are evaluating an individual player's or a team's ability to compete, each player must believe he has been given every opportunity to display his baseball ability without being required to learn other areas that take away from his ability to focus on competing. This evaluation should take place in a gamelike setting. The competition phase is made up of three parts:

1. **Initial phase.** The emphasis during the initial phase is to allow players to play the game the way they have learned. They should know that they are being evaluated. Do not change anything in the mechanics of a player leading up to this point. You want the player to feel confident in his present abilities. Even if the suggested change is correct, it will cause the player to focus on another area. If a change is made and the player does not experience immediate success, the fault is on somebody other than the player. This is the reason for the competition phase. The focus should be on identifying player strengths, not changing them.

2. **Adjustment phase.** During this phase, you should begin to identify what corrections are needed, and you should implement a routine to solve them. The corrections to be made during this phase should be minimal. Keep the emphasis on game adjustments. These areas will take less time to master but will put the player in the best situation to be successful.

3. **Game phase.** The focus in this phase is the same as in the initial phase. The difference is that the players—both individually and collectively—are being introduced to team-related concepts. The player should understand that the emphasis is still on the competition phase. However, the team concept has come to the forefront. Basic team fundamentals are now being taken into

consideration, and the player's ability to understand and implement this area has a direct effect on the competition. This last phase incorporates the initial and adjustment phases, combining the two elements required for game success.

The format of the competition varies, depending on the coach's preference and the skill level of the players. Four types of competition formats may be used:

1. **Intrasquad games.** For these contests, players are divided evenly into two teams with similar ability levels. The coach makes a lineup based on his evaluation of players.

2. **Controlled intrasquad games.** These contests are controlled by the coaching staff. The staff puts the teams in game situations to emphasize specific areas of execution, whether to benefit the offensive team or the defensive team. By controlling the game, the coaching staff can put the players in situations that will occur during a normal competition.

3. **Coach-pitched intrasquad games.** For these contests, players are also divided evenly into teams. The coaches pitch to the hitters. This is another way the coaching staff can control the game, and it also avoids putting additional innings on your pitching staff.

4. **Outside competition games.** These contests are played against an outside opponent. This is the last type of competition used for evaluation. The only variation is the type of competition that the coach chooses to play.

The competition phase is crucial in the assessment of individual players and the team as a whole. A fundamental key to success is the ability of a player to separate the mechanical elements of his position from competition. For a player or team to focus fully on these efforts, the players must be able to separate the two aspects. A player's focus must be solely on playing the game; he cannot be consumed with external factors. This is where the title *gamer* is earned. In assessing an individual player or team, a coach must understand how to put these individuals in situations where they can demonstrate their abilities to the fullest potential.

Shaping a Style of Play

Based on the evaluation, the coach must develop an outline that coincides with the team strengths. Within this outline are absolutes that are implemented daily; these are the fundamental techniques that must be practiced consistently, regardless of the style of the team. Although these are required activities, they still provide a chance to assess team and individual strengths. The following elements must be worked on daily.

Defensive Play

The throwing session is crucial to a team's success. It also provides a chance to evaluate the abilities of players. This phase of a practice is done daily. Various

Table 3.1 Weekly Throwing Program

Monday	Tuesday	Wednesday	Thursday	Friday	Saturday	Sunday
150 feet	200 feet maximum	150 feet	No throwing	200 feet maximum	150 feet	150 feet
12 to 15 minutes	15 to 20 minutes	12 to 15 minutes	N/A	15 to 20 minutes	12 to 15 minutes	12 to 15 minutes

formats can be used to help players achieve improvement while the coach assesses talent. The traditional way of dividing players into groups of pitchers and positional players is an adequate way for players to prepare their arms for practice. The amount of throwing done by each group is dictated by the weekly schedule (table 3.1).

A throwing session is an additional opportunity for evaluation. All players must throw for distance and duration on a daily basis. The amount of throwing is dictated by the structure of practice. Table 3.1 is a brief outline of a structured throwing program. The distance is the total distance that the player should throw. The time is how long the entire throwing session should last. Following these criteria allows a player to build both arm strength and endurance. These two aspects are essential in improving and maintaining the player's arm stamina throughout a season.

In addition, the daily routine (figure 3.3, page 32) includes position-specific drills. These drills provide an additional opportunity for the coach to evaluate individual players. The following drills are suggestions for each position.

Pitchers

- Rotate late: Emphasize backside rotation with direction in upper body.
- Low lift: Emphasize a slide step or abbreviated lift to be quicker to the plate.
- Balance to power: Emphasize the full leg lift and consistent balance point.
- Pivot lift: Emphasize the pivot portion of the delivery, along with backside stability.

Catchers

- Block: Front, angle left, angle right
- Block and recover: After the block, the catcher throws as quickly as possible.
- Exchange and throw: Emphasize the quickness and mechanics of the ball-to-glove exchange.

Outfielders

- Crow hops: Front, angle left, angle right
- First-step angles: Front, angle left, angle right
- Fence drill: Emphasize playing the ball off the wall as quickly as possible.

Infielders

- Short hops: Front, glove side, backhand
- Ball rolls: Front, glove side, backhand
- Quick hands box drill: Focus on the ball-to-glove exchange with an emphasis on speed.

Defensive Practice Schedule

7:45–8:00 a.m. Team announcements

8:00–8:15 a.m. Dynamic warm-up (left field)

8:15–8:30 a.m.
- Position players (left-field line): throwing program
- Pitchers (right-field line): throwing per pitching coach's schedule

8:30–9:00 a.m.
- Position players: defending against base runners (home to first, primary and secondary leads, steal breaks)
- Pitchers: throwing per pitching coach's schedule

9:00–10:00 a.m. Team defense (communication, pop-up priorities, double cuts)

Figure 3.3   Sample defensive practice schedule.

Offensive Play

The offensive component includes both speed and hitting. Both areas must be evaluated and practiced with equal consideration. Figure 3.4 shows a sample offensive practice schedule.

Work on speed every day. Use the 60-yard sprint and the home-to-first run. Players do both runs two or three times to get an accurate time. The 60-yard sprint trains straightaway speed, while the home-to-first run trains game speed. When evaluating, note the difference between straightaway speed and game speed. For each player, you should evaluate running form, stride length, and first-step quickness.

During hitting practice, evaluate each player's bat speed, swing path, balance, power, and ability to use all fields. Based on the evaluation of each player's individual offensive strengths and the overall strengths of the team, you can determine the best offensive strategy. A team that can bunt, hit anywhere on the field, and consistently steal bases is well designed for playing the short game. A team with a lot of offensive pop and good awareness of the strike zone is better suited for playing for the big inning.

Offensive Practice Schedule

8:45–9:00 a.m. Team announcements

9:00–9:15 a.m. Dynamic warm-up (left field)

9:15–9:30 a.m.

- Position players (left-field line): throwing program
- Pitchers (right-field line): throwing per pitching coach's schedule

9:30–9:55 a.m.

- Position players: bunt routine (drag, push, squeeze), baserunning (secondary leads)
- Pitchers (right-field line): throwing per pitching coach's schedule

9:55–10:45 a.m. Batting practice in groups (see chart)

Position players

Group 1	Group 2	Group 3	Group 4
Name–Hit on field	Name—Second base	Name—Cages	Name—Baserunning
Name–Hit on field	Name—Shortstop	Name—Cages	Name—Baserunning
Name–Hit on field	Name—Right field	Name—Cages	Name—Baserunning
Name–Hit on field	Name—Second base	Name—Cages	Name—Baserunning
Name—Baserunning	Name–Hit on field	Name—Center field	Name—Cages
Name—Baserunning	Name–Hit on field	Name—Second base	Name—Cages
Name—Baserunning	Name–Hit on field	Name—Shortstop	Name—Cages
Name—Baserunning	Name–Hit on field	Name—First base	Name—Cages
Name—Cages	Name—Baserunning	Name–Hit on field	Name—Bullpen
Name—Cages	Name—Baserunning	Name–Hit on field	Name—Bullpen
Name—Cages	Name—Baserunning	Name–Hit on field	Name—Center field
Name—Cages	Name—Baserunning	Name–Hit on field	Name—Left field
Name—First base	Name—Cages	Name—Baserunning	Name–Hit on field
Name—Right field	Name—Cages	Name—Baserunning	Name–Hit on field
Name—Second base	Name—Cages	Name—Baserunning	Name–Hit on field
Name—First base	Name—Cages	Name—Baserunning	Name–Hit on field
Name—Third base	Name—Cages	Name—Baserunning	Name–Hit on field

Figure 3.4   Sample offensive practice schedule.

Putting It Together

Developing a winning team involves many factors. The preliminary stage of evaluation is a key component to success. This initial evaluation provides the basis for formulating a productive practice plan. It guides the coach in determining and developing the strengths of each individual player and the team. Knowing these strengths helps the coach identify the areas of focus for the team.

After the initial evaluation is complete, you should have a better understanding of each player. The individual qualities of each player help mold a successful team. During evaluation and practice, put players in various situations so that you can get a true read on all players' strengths.

The last step is to maintain those strengths—both player and team strengths—while improving weaknesses. The ability to objectively assess a team's strengths is a necessity for being a successful coach. Each team, each player, and each year brings a potentially different style that can be identified and used effectively only if assessed properly. Each individual brings something positive to the field. It is the coach's responsibility to determine if those individual strengths can collectively make the team successful.

chapter 4

Developing and Motivating the Total Player

MARK JOHNSON

With the natural maturation of a player's growth—physically, mentally, and emotionally—talent will certainly also bloom. However, if not cultivated, the development of this talent tends to level off with each growth spurt. Developing individual players requires good coaching, but more important, it requires a player who is motivated to improve and willing to work toward that end.

Motivation is the fuel that enhances the development of the individual player; therefore, motivation must be addressed daily. Human nature tends to adhere to a basic premise of motivation. Folks tend to achieve and reach higher levels when they belong to a group that is working together toward a common goal. Very simply, we all want to belong, to be wanted, to be needed—and we all want to be counted on to produce and to carry our load.

The development of individual players begins with motivation—each player's desire to enhance his talents. Our game is played with a team. Rudyard Kipling declared, "The strength of the wolf is in the pack, and the strength of the pack is in the wolf." This statement stresses the importance of the team assisting the individual's development as well as the individual assisting in the team's development. The team and the individual need each other.

Individual Development for the Team Cause

A family, a church, an army platoon, a city government, a corporation—these all involve teams working together toward a common goal. The team is made up of different parts, shapes, and styles, but all are part of a completed puzzle. Each part is of equal importance, and all parts depend on each other. Each part influences the parts on its immediate sides. The parts are individuals alone but a unit together. If one piece of the puzzle is missing, the unit is incomplete.

It just takes one missing piece—one player who is not there, not prepared, or not ready—to prevent the puzzle from being complete. Developing each individual player is paramount to the success of the team. Motivation is fueled by thousands of different thoughts, circumstances, and responses to the environment surrounding the movement. The competitive desire to win the game should be the overriding motivator, but in the long-range quest to win, motivation must be present at the practice field—in the trenches where individual talents are developed. Chief among all sources of proper, lasting, and consistent motivation is one word: accountability. That means accountability to the cause and accountability to each member of the team; accountability of each player to "carry his load" and to "watch and have his teammates' back"; a trust that grows in each moment of practice, each final repetition in the weight room, each final step in a wind sprint; and a trust that the player's team can count on him.

Getting the Job Done

Accountability is not defined by the age-old cliche "I'm doing my best." That cliche is comforting, but it is no longer in the vocabulary of many achievers. Our best is often so poor that it is not the answer. The answer is "Yes, I will get the job done. I will find a way!"

"My best" is too indefinable and often does not include a sense of urgency or a moment of truth. "Getting the job done" is the mind-set that explains why unbelievable displays of strength happen in times of great duress or desire (such as lifting a car to free a trapped child or running faster when the bear chases you). After performing in a time of urgency, people often say, "I didn't think I could do it, but I did. I had no other choice. I just did it." For a winner, there are no other options, choices, or alternatives. They just do it.

If we agree that attitude is a critical component of action, then we must say that the attitude "I'm doing my best" is not strong enough. "I will get the job done" is the proper attitude. Players with this attitude will do what it takes to knock the ball down, to put the ball in play, or to punch the ball to the right side to move the runner at second base. They just do it.

Winston Churchill, Great Britain's famed leader in World War II, said, "It is not enough that we do our best; sometimes we have to do what is required." Certainly, success does not happen by accident. For a baseball player, the foundation of success is a motivation to get better, to develop individual talents, and to be accountable for getting "his piece of the puzzle in its proper spot."

Everyone Counts

How does a player become accountable? It starts with the realization that his piece of the puzzle is important. Even if he is the least important part of the puzzle, he has a role in completing the puzzle. Everyone counts because everyone brings an attitude, an energy, and an enthusiasm to the team every day, every moment. Attitude, energy, and enthusiasm are contagious. Nelson Mandela said, "As we let our light shine, we unconsciously give others permission to do the same." Each player affects the team's success. Never allow a player to feel as though he does not count. Each player gets the same amount of coaching and the same number of batting practice swings, fungoes, or practice pitches. Each player must feel worthy.

How can a player feel worthy if he is struggling to throw strikes, to hit the ball, or to catch a fly ball? He can (to a large degree) if he knows he is putting an equal amount of sweat in the bucket as the other players. This player is in the trenches with the team. The coach does not ask for equal amounts of talent in the bucket. The coach asks that each player commit and be accountable for bringing all his talents and working as hard as everyone else to develop his individual skills.

Standing Alone

The goal is to win the game. The team deal makes it happen, but it comes down to individuals standing alone—hitter facing pitcher, pitcher facing hitter, defender facing ball, base runner taking a proper turn at the bag to get to the next bag in time (sometimes a hundredth of a second before the ball). The game amounts to individual moments being intertwined with the team unit. Baseball is a team game played in individual moments.

In baseball, developing individual skills is critical. Each player must enhance his competency in running, throwing, fielding, and hitting. Most often, the game does not allow a coach to choose who gets the tough, game-winning defensive play or the critical hitting moment. The coach isn't always in control of who gets to pitch in the critical situation with a 3-2 count, two outs, bases loaded, and a one-run lead. The game does not have a clock. You can't run the clock down. You have to play the game out.

In football, you can give the ball to your best running back every play. In basketball, you can get the ball to the best shooter a high percentage of the time. In baseball, everyone hits in a preset order in a lineup—no skipping or choosing. Your best defender may not have a ball hit to him for the entire game. Your best hitter may not come to bat in a key, critical situation in a game. Each individual will get his moment, not necessarily by choice but by the way the game is structured. Each player's attitude of being accountable, through practice and preparation, must be present every day, every moment.

Competitive Attitude

To develop individual skills, a player's attitude must be solidly entrenched in his goals toward the team's success. *Attitude* is another key word in proper development. Everyone has an attitude: good, bad, soft, intense, and so on. A player has total control of his attitude just as he does his energy and enthusiasm. How does an attitude happen? Look closely at the following statement by an unknown author:

> *Be careful of your thoughts, because they will eventually become your body language.*
> *Be careful of your body language, because it will eventually become words.*
> *Be careful of your words, because they will eventually become your actions.*
> *Be careful of your actions, because they will eventually become your habits.*
> *Be careful of your habits, because they will eventually become your character.*
> *Be careful of your character, because it will eventually become your destiny.*

It all starts with what a person thinks. Mahatma Gandhi said, "A man is but the product of his thoughts. What he thinks, he becomes." And from the Bible, Proverbs 4:23 says, "Be careful how you think, your life is shaped by your thoughts."

Coaches, teammates, parents, and teachers all play a role in influencing an individual. A proper positive attitude—guided by proper thoughts—is critical to developing not only the individual but the team as well.

How is this attitude developed? A noted psychologist once said, "We are not what we think we are, nor are we what others think we are. We are what we think others think we are."

Do we have that much influence on those we encounter? Yes, we do. Tell a young person he is bad enough times, and he will fill that role. Show unswerving confidence and respect in a person, and the person will become trustworthy. If your child knows you expect him to act poorly, he will not disappoint. If a player does not believe that you think he is capable of learning individual skills, the player will probably not develop those skills. We actually influence the attitudes of others. As a coach, you should project a positive attitude of high expectation. Don't let a player pass up his moment because his attitude isn't right.

Life is full of folks who wish they had one more chance. This is true in all walks of life, from parenting, to relationships, to closing a deal at work, to preparing to sell a product. It comes down to your attitude and approach to life.

Some folks love challenges, the beauty of getting out on the edge and going for it. Others shy away from challenges, from responsibilities, and from commitments to reach a goal. Those who choose the latter miss out on the exhilarating moments that life brings us. They just live day by day and do not want to make decisions. Millions of folks live their lives like that. It's an attitude they choose.

On the other hand, a person who chooses the more challenging lifestyle will develop a competitive attitude. This attitude is not necessarily in opposition to someone else, but it is developed within the person's makeup. The person commits himself to success and achievements. As this lifestyle grows and matures, it becomes a normal reflex. A pride grows within that says, "On my watch, it will be done." Some folks call it refusing to lose. Others simply call it an achiever's approach. Whatever you wish to call it, it becomes who you are.

Interestingly enough, the competitive attitude surfaces almost daily in all areas of a person's life. The attitude doesn't just surface during a big moment in life. It occurs everywhere, even in the smaller areas of life. Does this mean that the person will always achieve? Certainly not, but it does mean that as the person continues to aggressively take on challenges, he will develop a resolve, an understanding, and an awareness. He will learn how to achieve in life's journey. He prepares for success without even knowing it.

The game of baseball should never be the most important thing in a player's life. What is important is that a person develops an achiever's attitude. A person's attitude is not necessarily a reflection of achieving worldly materials, trophies, or recognition. The strength of an achiever's attitude is that it can't be bought. Motivation based on material items is short lived and worthless.

Your attitude is who you are. It defines your being. No one but you controls it. It doesn't work for money or materialistic goals. It works only for you. You choose what you will accept and what you will not accept. If you want to be labeled a true competitor, you will develop this in your attitude, and it will automatically rise up on any challenges and on any day. It can't be turned off and on. Consequently, with two strikes and a runner on third base with fewer than two outs, your attitude will determine the outcome far more times than your talent will. And when you are with a group of folks who are combining their talents toward a common goal—and all of these folks have a common, true competitive attitude—anything is possible. Regardless of the outcome, your journey toward the goal will be made up of cherished moments of exhilaration and exhaustion that you will remember the rest of your life.

Big Game Principles

Success in big games—such as playoff games or championships—is often determined more by mental and emotional preparation than by physical preparation. Therefore, coaches must address the need to prepare individual players and the team for the big game. The following 11 principles may help when preparing yourself, the team, and individual players for these special moments:

1. Don't get hung up on the possibility of losing. Get hung up on the possibility of winning. It is easy to get scared when the entire season or a championship is on the line. Being worried or scared is connected to the fear of losing. Focus on the positive. Expect to win, and believe you will win. This belief is a stronger power.

2. Don't get hung up on the illusion of the event. Get hung up on the competitive nature of the next pitch. Big crowds, large venues, lots of media attention—the event can take a team or player out of the game. Focus on the game, the same game you have always played.

3. Don't get hung up on the results. Get caught up in the moment, your moment. Play the game one pitch at a time. The last pitch—whether a strikeout, error, base on balls, or hit—is over. Play for the moment. It may be your moment to make the difference. Play in the now.

4. Don't get hung up on making a mistake. Get hung up on persistently overcoming adversity. Feed on your ability to handle the adversity that the game brings. This separates the winners and losers.

5. Don't get hung up on doubts, questions, and fears. Get hung up on knowing that you are prepared to be comfortable in the uncomfortable. You've practiced. You are ready. Be confident. Do not allow the game to speed up.

6. Don't get hung up on the enormity of your opponent. Get hung up on knowing that your opponent can't claim an edge in the game without your permission. Your opponent may be the big school or the undefeated monster that no one wants to play. Give these thoughts no grounds. The game gives you a hope, a chance. Play every pitch knowing that you can win. Believe.

7. Don't get hung up on the pressure of the game. Get hung up on joyously embracing the risk. This is why you compete. Take in the pressures you can handle and no more. It's not life or death. Go for it. Embrace it. No one wants to play a game that doesn't matter. Enjoy it.

8. Don't get hung up on your shallow breath and rapid heartbeat. Get hung up on taking a deep breath and getting your heartbeat in sync with the one heartbeat of the team—everyone together. Breathe. Calm yourself by taking a deep breath. Feed off the energy of your teammates.

9. Don't get hung up on seeing negatives. Get hung up on visualizing positives. See yourself achieving. Relish the opportunity to live out your positive dreams.

10. Don't get hung up on cursing the darkness of the moment. Get hung up on lighting a candle. The game provides good and bad moments. Encourage your teammates. Don't flinch or buckle during the rough times. Bring your energy and consistent belief to your team. Stay positive. Keep hope alive.

11. Don't get hung up on the waves in the water. Get hung up on bringing in the boat. Sometimes you just have to get the job done. Complaining, blaming others, or yelling at the umpire brings nothing to the goal. Handle the tough times and get the job done.

Attitude Development

Alex Haley, one of the great authors of our time, has a saying: "Find the good and praise it." Perhaps we could add another part to this statement: "Find the good, praise it, and build on it." Praise is the foundation of improvement for all of us. Praise and encouragement are much more effective in helping people attain success than criticism and negativity are. This is proven every day.

Not only can we find the good, praise it, and build on it, but we can also develop, enhance, and enlarge a person's self-image. All of us limit ourselves by setting boundaries about who we think we are and what we think we can achieve. Coaches, parents, teachers, friends, and teammates have a unique opportunity to enhance a person's self-image by encouraging each player to believe he can achieve at a higher level, to believe he is worthy. Self-image is critical in all phases of development and improvement. If a player feels good about himself, he will achieve at a higher rate. People who do not feel good about themselves rarely accomplish great goals. Helping others feel good about themselves is a part of parenting, teaching, coaching, and friendship. It is a part of helping others rise to the next level.

Words alone are often not enough to communicate praise and approval, to help a person develop proper attitudes, or to enhance a person's self-image. Body language plays a critical role as well. Dr. Albert Mehrabian, professor emeritus of psychology at UCLA, says that in communicating feelings and attitudes, 55 percent of communication is done through body language alone. Words are often not enough. Approving body language is critical to affecting a player's self-image.

Realistic Expectations

When there is proper development of individual players within the framework of the team, expectations should rise, not only for each individual player but for the team itself. Long-range and short-range goals should be addressed. The coach should direct and nurture this process.

Inevitably, we all foresee the outcomes we want before we even begin a task. This is human nature. Understandably, we all have high hopes and strong wants. Although that is important, it is not nearly as important as developing realistic expectations about the outcome. Realistic expectations will seldom produce surprises.

How we perceive our actions to be is often how they will be. We need to perceive achievement in order to produce achievement. We need to expect achievement of goals if we are to realistically reach them.

The difference between being good and being a champion is a composite of many little things. This doesn't just happen by accident, however. The conversion from good to champion is initiated by how you perceive yourself, how you think, and how you act. It culminates in your response to adversity and challenges, to the tough times and situations, and to the pressure points in the game. The conversion is related to your respect for your teammates and to the pride you have in yourself and your team.

To become something that you want to become, you must first think and act along those lines. One of the dangers of high expectations is that the fall becomes greater and the hurt bigger. That's why many folks don't achieve what they really should be achieving. Subconsciously, they simply do not want to be let down. They are afraid to step forward and go for it. They are afraid to say, "I am going to be the champion." Consequently, they very seldom enter the winner's circle.

Every endeavor worth striving for has tough and difficult times. When those times hit, the weak minded begin to change what they perceive the outcomes to be. The mentally tough know that the tough times are not stumbling blocks—they are stepping stones. These people emerge from the tough times stronger than they were before adversity hit. They will stand a good chance of being champions. By the time an endeavor is half over, most folks have already determined their fate by how they perceive it to be in their minds.

Your body responds to what your mind tells it. If you are scared or nervous about your ability to achieve, or if you doubt yourself, your body will respond in that manner. If you act as if you will be successful, or if you act confident, you are telling your body that you will achieve. You should avoid acting with despair or disarray in your approach to achieving. Your mind, either consciously or subconsciously, will relay the response to the body. Every person has a chance to control his mind, and consequently, his body.

Think positively and expect to be champions, to be achievers. This is a risk for the weak minded, but not for the mentally tough. Begin by believing you will achieve. Increase the belief to the point where you are expecting to achieve. Imagine yourself in positive achievement roles. As you believe, set realistic expectations, and perceive yourself as a winner; then begin to physically fill the role. Start by acting like a winner. Your belief and expectations should be shown by your actions even before the challenge. Handle yourself with poise, particularly if the achievement does not come immediately. Just confidently keep on keeping on. As you continue to fill the role, success will begin to come. The weak accept their role. Remember, anybody can be average.

Interestingly enough, like so many other things, this approach is contagious to those around you. This is the reason that winning traditions are built. It's the reason why, when surrounded by players with good ability, those with average ability often rise to the higher level. How you handle and conduct yourself will have an effect on those around you.

Everyone in the puzzle can influence another person's attitude, but no one can control how other people individually and collectively believe. No one can control a person's expectations or his power to perceive himself in a positive achievement role. Only each individual can do that. However, if each person is accountable for his own strength of belief, a team together can accomplish huge tasks. It's called *synergy*, when the whole becomes greater than the sum of the parts.

Can a coach guide and empower individuals in the development of their belief? If a player trusts the coach, the coach has a tremendous effect in this area. When the team believes in these expectations of achievement, a *power* is born—a power with a strength far greater than the coach or fans. A demand blossoms within the team, one individual to the next, that everyone must bring all his talents, a positive attitude, an energy, and an enthusiasm to get the job done. Anything less is unacceptable.

Basic Coaching and Teaching Approaches

Handwriting is unique but structured. The personality of each person shows in his handwriting, but he must still follow basic fundamentals in order for the writing to be legible. Handwriting is useless if it does not adhere to the basic structure of the letters in the alphabet. Similarly, a player's performance of a skill will not be successful if the player does not adhere to the basic fundamentals of body mechanics. Each individual player has his own strengths, weaknesses, and uniqueness—his own signature. He must be allowed to exhibit and improve the characteristics he possesses. Placing every player in the same stance or teaching all players the exact same actions would be an injustice to the players and to the team. Certain fundamentals, guidelines, and boundaries are needed; however, if the coach is going to get the maximum from each player, the coach must allow creativity within the basic philosophy of the skill. An old poem has been passed along that illustrates this point. The author is unknown, but the point is clear:

> *There once was a .400 hitter named Krantz*
> *Who had a most unusual stance.*
> *But with the coach's correction*
> *His form is now perfection,*
> *But he can't hit the seat of his pants.*

Too much specialized instruction—whether in painting, pitching, playing music, or kicking a football—can inhibit a person's creative and individual talents in that particular activity. Structure tends to lead to performance without emotion or passion. It can actually stifle a player's skills because the player is trying to perform another person's creative skills. Watch closely for the teachable moment when working with young players who just want to play ball.

Each person has his own individual talents. No two people grow at the same rate. Many of the best ballplayers, painters, and musicians have their own signature style. What may be a fault in one player may be a gold mine for another. Helpful hints in early development are certainly important, but too much coaching can confuse a player.

When teaching any type of physical activity, a coach needs to cover the use of mental pictures. It has been said that what the mind can perceive, the body can achieve. If a player's mind can tune in or picture what the body is supposed to accomplish, the skill is close to being accomplished. The three approaches to teaching mental pictures are (1) visual and mental, (2) verbal and mental, and (3) physical and mental.

The visual and mental approach is best illustrated by simply watching two brothers or a father and son move about in some type of activity. Their physical movements or mannerisms will likely be very similar. Perhaps their body makeup or structures are similar, but the mannerisms are similar, for the most part, because the younger person has seen the older person so many times that his mind has taught his body those movements. The mind has seen a physical movement, pictured it, and transferred it to the body. In the visual and mental approach to developing a mental picture, a coach may want to demonstrate or show films or pictures of the techniques he wishes to teach. Constantly seeing correct techniques can have a very positive result in learning a skill.

The verbal and mental approach to teaching mental pictures is also very important. This approach is likely the one that coaches use the most. Unfortunately, it is also the approach that produces the poorest results. A coach verbally feeds a mental picture to a hitter. To be successful at this approach, a coach needs to have a repertoire of different verbal statements that produce the same action. However, the statements that produce a proper mental picture for one player may do nothing for the next. For example, one hitter may not be able to form a picture based on the comment "Keep your back shoulder up in your approach to the ball." But this same player may tune in to "Aim your front shoulder at the ball." Or a coach may say, "Hit the ball hard," while another may say, "Drive through the ball." The point is that if the hitter is listening, you can make a verbal comment that will help him receive a good mental picture. The coach may need to use different phrases or verbal mental pictures to say the same thing, but it can be achieved. In connection with the verbal and mental approach, a caution should be made: Using negative verbal statements will, in most cases, result in negative mental pictures. The statement "Don't drop your back shoulder" will leave in the mind a picture of a hitter dropping his back shoulder. This statement does not leave a mental picture of what is desired. In teaching mental pictures verbally, you should be specific and positive to create a positive mental picture.

The final approach to teaching mental pictures is the physical and mental approach. This approach can be accomplished by the player himself. In this approach, a player may gain the desired mental picture simply by concentrating on that area until he feels the picture. A coach can help the player achieve this by devising isolated drills that give the player an opportunity to work on one particular area of his game. This may involve swinging in front of a mirror, hitting off a tee, throwing the ball into a fence, hitting a tire, or chopping down a tree. Whatever the drill, it can be an asset in helping the player feel the proper mental picture.

Confidence Development

Little needs to be said concerning the importance of confidence not only on the baseball field but in all walks of life. Building confidence in a player while identifying faults and working on corrections can be an awesome task. Certain avenues can be used that can help correct mistakes and also build confidence.

The first place that confidence needs to be built is within the player's own self-image. A coach can play a key role in this area. Helping the player to see himself as a good person is a beginning. This does not mean simply as a good hitter or ballplayer, but as a person. If the player has a good self-image, if he likes himself, he is more likely to be confident in specific areas. In breaking down this self-image to baseball, the coach might consider using the technique of one to one. This simply means that for every area in which the coach finds fault, the coach also tries to find one area of achievement. Too often coaches spend the entire practice finding and correcting faults. This is certainly an important part of coaching, but building confidence in a player is equally important. A good technique is for the coach to precede each fault-finding statement with a positive statement concerning the hitter's skill. Obviously, this cannot always be done, but coaches should consider the positives more often.

Practice sessions are the best time to help players build confidence. Coaches need to be sure that their practice sessions are designed to give every player a reasonable opportunity for success. This may mean shadow swinging with positive reinforcement from the coach. Hitting the ball off a tee or catching rolled ground balls can also provide this opportunity.

Practice sessions should include drill areas for isolating particular parts of the individual skill. A hitter will find it extremely difficult to concentrate on parts of his swing when a wild young pitcher is throwing batting practice. If faults are going to be corrected, the practice area must be constructed to give the player a good chance to concentrate on that correction.

Finally, the player must realize that improving his game is going to take time. The difference between a .200 hitter and a .300 hitter is simply one more hit in 10 trips to the plate. Noticeable differences do not always appear immediately. For a player, a good approach to practice would be as follows: "In some small way I can improve on yesterday today." Trying to become a great player in one day will leave the player discouraged or disillusioned. Letting each day and each practice have a positive influence on the next day and practice will help achieve team and individual goals. When a player improves one part of the individual skill at a time, the entire skill will eventually come together. The player and the coach must be patient.

As a coach, remember that the fundamental responsibility of your position is to develop not only the individual player but also the individual person. You, too, must bring all your talents, energies, and enthusiasm in a positive attitude to reach this goal. Winning is important for a lot of reasons. One reason is that striving to win develops the player and the person. Without the drive to win, players will not learn many of the lessons that the game offers.

As you plan your practice, make sure you are organized, and include some fun somewhere in the plan. Playing and practicing the game should be fun. The challenges that the game provides should be fun, exciting, intense, and pressure packed at times. Drill work is critical. It has been said that repetition is the father of learning. Break down the skill and work on each particular part of the drill. For example, in hitting, isolate the stance, the load, the stride, the hands, and the bat approach into individual parts—then put them back together. Working the process and not the result is a hallmark of outstanding players. Don't be overly concerned with results. The process is the key to learning and should always be the focus.

Practices should include activities that involve game-type pressure that duplicates—as closely as possible—the actual game. For example, a realistic activity could involve having a base runner steal second base (the pitcher tries to hold the runner) and having the catcher throw to second base. To add game-type pressure, you can add consequences for poor performance. If six players are in a group taking batting practice and your emphasis is on line drives and ground balls off the bat, a hitter who pops the ball up may have to run to the foul pole. Or, if the six players hit three fly balls, the entire group runs to the foul pole. Baseball is a game of failures. Have ample consequences in practice so players learn to handle failures. Players must learn to be comfortable in the uncomfortable.

And always remember the team. Be cognizant of the team's development in practice while working with individuals. Make everyone count. Insist that everyone puts an equal amount of sweat in the bucket.

Truths in the Power Areas of Baseball

As you make positive adjustments in the way your players throw and hit—the power areas of the game—be aware of one constant truth at the core of these areas: In the power areas of throwing and hitting, the weight transfer cannot occur before the initial start of the final summation of force. The back side (the side of the body farthest from the target) has to be loaded. It is the driving force in generating power and maintaining balance, control, and consistency.

When an athlete is trying to do too much, transfer occurs too early. Whenever the transfer occurs early, the front side receives the power and is forced to pull the back side through. The swing or the arm becomes longer and slower, reducing power and negatively affecting balance, control, and consistency. In pitching, pulling becomes a major culprit in arm injuries.

Poor adherence to this truth leads to lunging, rushing, drifting, leaking, dragging the back side, overstriding, and early transfer. Remember, balance and control create the power position. Keep the head over the rubber and keep the head quiet at the plate.

What It Takes to Win

Winning baseball games requires much more than just developing individual players who can run, throw, field, and hit. Much more. The end product of this endeavor is of no value if it does not mesh with winning the game.

How are games won? An abundance of answers could be given. One key is for a coach to help the team understand the game's inner game while developing the individual players. In addition, some very tangible goals should be set for each role that a player is given.

Everyone must fully understand that baseball is a game of percentages. You can do all the parts of the game correctly and still be unsuccessful on that particular day. Or you can do everything wrong yet be successful on a given day. Actuarial tables indicate that over the course of a season, the percentages for being successful will eventually place the team that plays the game correctly on top or near the top, depending on talent and whether the opposition is also playing percentage baseball. There will be games in which it does not seem as though these percentages will pan out, but they always do over the long haul. Remember, because of the nature of our game, the best team will lose 30 percent of the time, and the worst team will win 30 percent of the time. The remaining games will determine the champions—and in many cases, the results of the remaining games will be determined by a team's mental and emotional response to the 30 percent that went against the odds.

The following areas are major physical parts of the game that can be executed by a solid high school or college team. Execution in these areas can make the team champions if the players understand the percentages and stay true to their course (and if the team's talent is good). The team does not have to do extra as long as everyone makes these winning areas their priority. This requires a fearless trust by everyone. When a player gives in with two strikes and hits a soft 4-3 ground ball, or when a pitcher throws a 1-0 fastball down the middle and it gets ripped, the team must not buckle. They must stay with the percentages of winning baseball. Eventually, it will all work out.

Remember that the percentages get skewed if everyone is not committed to playing percentage baseball. The percentages do not work if only some of the players are involved. This fearless trust must be a committed team effort.

These are a few physical areas that can be executed if everyone is committed to the team and its goal. Obviously, for these to be executed, the mental and emotional areas must be strong, or the team will panic and buckle. The team will give in and play by the whirl of the wind, casting aside percentage baseball. This is why there are a lot of average teams; they simply do not execute percentage baseball.

Pitchers

- Should develop a minimum of two different pitches that they can throw for strikes, especially when behind in the count.
- Must be able to work both sides of the plate with a minimum of two different pitches.
- Must establish a low strike zone.
- Must get a strike in the first two pitches.
- Should not allow the leadoff hitter to get to first via a base on balls or to get on base more than twice in nine innings.
- Cannot allow more than three bases on balls or hit batters in nine innings.
- Should establish a minimum time of 1.4 seconds from the stretch to home plate (from the start of the delivery until the ball hits the catcher's mitt) and should be able to vary his hold in the stretch.
- Must be able to win with a man on base.
- Must consistently win the battles against the seven-, eight-, and nine-hole hitters.

Hitters

- Must be prepared and ready to hit the first fastball thrown for a strike that is not on the corners of the plate.
- Must hit 70 percent of the balls to the middle of the field.
- Should develop a line-drive or ground-ball approach, hitting no more than three fly balls in every 15 at-bats.
- Must put the ball in play, having no more than one strikeout for every 15 at-bats.
- Should get two bases on balls (or hit by pitch) in every 15 at-bats.
- Must understand that RBIs are bigger than hits and, therefore, must make every effort to not overswing and to use more of the middle and opposite side of the field in RBI situations.

- With no outs, should be able to move a runner at second base 8 out of every 10 times.*
- With fewer than two outs, should be able to score a runner from third base 9 out of 10 times with the infield back and 8 out of 10 times with the infield in (with no pop-ups or strikeouts).*

Outfielders

- Must make routine plays 99 percent of the time.
- Should consistently throw the ball to the proper base 100 percent of the time or to the cutoff man 98 percent of the time.
- Must keep the double play in order when there is less than a 40 percent chance of throwing the runner out at home plate.
- Must move to the correct spot 100 percent of the time when the ball is not hit to him.
- Should take no more than three steps between contact with the ball and the throw.
- Must understand that angles are critical so that all hits that move the outfielder directly toward the closest outfielder or in toward an infielder are singles. A normally hit ball to the left or right fielder toward the foul line at a 90-degree angle or less is kept to a single. Outfielders who understand angles will allow few triples.
- Must field at a .980 average.

Infielders

- Must learn to avoid in-between hops as much as possible, fielding the ball on either the big hop or the short hop.
- Must make routine plays 98 percent of the time.
- Must move to the correct spot 100 percent of the time when the ball is not hit to him.
- Should understand that accuracy of the throw is a priority over velocity and quickness. Regardless of the toughness of the play, bad throws place men in scoring position.
- Must realize that errors will happen, but multiple errors on one batter should not be allowed. Only one error per hit ball.
- Must consistently turn the double play.
- Must make a major effort to knock down the ball with a man on second base.
- Must field at a minimum .958 average.

---

* To be consistent in these game situations, the hitter must make every effort to achieve the goal before getting in a two-strike count.

Base Runners

- Must demonstrate 100 percent speed, 100 percent of the time.
- Must demonstrate 100 percent speed on all turns at all bases. Singles are always doubles until proven otherwise.
- Should freeze on all line drives.
- Must never make the first or third out at third base or the first out at home plate.
- Must never make an out at third base when on second base in a nonforce situation.
- Should always know where the outfielders are playing when at second base with fewer than two outs.
- Must tag on any deep, questionable catch if there are no outs.
- Should go a third of the way on any deep, questionable catch if there is one out.
- Must tag on all obvious foul balls hit in the air.
- Must tag at third base on all fly balls to the outfield even if they are questionable catches.
- Must always slide at second base, third base, or home plate if the base runner has any doubt about the fielder.

What Happens at the End of the Day

At the end of the day—after hours, days, months, and years of developing the individual player—what should that player expect? What results will be seen? What will he get? What will happen? Will he become a starter on the high school team, or perhaps an all-district player? Will his team win a championship? Will he receive a scholarship to play baseball at college? Or will he maybe even be drafted into professional baseball? Maybe, maybe not, but his efforts will not have been in vain. What a person gets for his work isn't really the question. What he learns will be considerably more than that.

The player should improve and move closer to his full potential as a baseball player. He should realize and enjoy the moments of total exhaustion that are required. He should develop mentally tough responses to adversity by not flinching or buckling at errors, bases on balls, strikeouts, losses, or bad calls. He should learn the importance of a healthy body. He should have more emotional balance and control. He should learn the importance of determination and perseverance. He should develop an acute awareness of the importance of the team and his teammates—and of his role in becoming accountable to each member of the team. He should develop social and leadership skills.

He should be keenly aware of the importance of his daily attitude in achieving his goal as well as the team's goal. He should realize and learn to enjoy the risk of stepping out on the field between the lines with no guarantee of success. He should develop a discipline within his person. That's just some of what he should get.

But at the end of the day, the most important measure is what he will become. John Ruskin said, "The highest reward for your toil is not what you get for it, but what you become by it." Developing individual players is a tremendously worthy endeavor. It empowers our young people to claim their inheritance and boldly affect their environment in ways that lead to a brighter day. To a coach, that result is priceless.

chapter 5

Building a Pitching Staff

DAVE SERRANO

A few years back, during the offensive explosion in Major League Baseball, there was a TV advertisement that depicted a popular perception of the status and importance of pitching in today's game. The spot showed a group of Cy Young-caliber pitchers taking batting practice and working on their home-run swings. It ended with one of the talented pitchers saying, "Chicks dig the long ball." This commercial was meant to be funny, but buried in the jovial tone was a truth about the state of the game: Offense puts people in the seats. If you turn on any nightly highlight program, the majority of the coverage is focused on offensive exploits rather than scrappy pitching and solid defense. The pitcher who induces two ground balls and a pop-out with only 10 pitches in an inning is overlooked by all but the keenest observers and most intimate students of the game. But how important is that stuff? In the age of the three-run home run, home-run derby, and fantasy baseball, how important is pitching? Any student of the game of baseball understands the importance of pitching. Great teams always have been and always will be built around pitching and defense. As a head coach who is also in charge of the pitching staff, I might be biased, but I firmly believe the old adage that pitching wins championships. Offense may get the fans excited, but to have a consistent chance of winning, a team must develop a good pitching staff. This chapter focuses on pitching philosophies and ways to build and prepare a pitching staff for success.

Building the Foundation

Every fall a new team steps on campus, and it is my job to give them the foundation for success. The first official gathering of the pitching staff has nothing to do with catch-play routines, arm exercises, or bullpens. Instead, our first official meeting covers philosophy and the characteristics I look for in a good pitcher and competitor. I believe this information is just as important as the Xs and Os of pitching mechanics or throwing the curveball. In my program, the foundation for pitching success is built around the intangibles that can be realized only by a staff with the ability and the aptitude for success. In my years of coaching, I have seen plenty of talented arms, but talent never wins if it isn't complemented by the right attitude and mentality. The following are some of the intangible aspects of pitching success.

Want the Ball

It is impossible to hide on the mound because everyone's attention is focused on the pitcher. A player who wants to be a pitcher had better love this aspect of the game and must thrive in the spotlight. Some of the best pitchers I have been around were good because when the spotlight was on them, they elevated their game to another level—most of the time a level they couldn't reach in practice. Give the ball to the players who want it the most because they tend to be the players with the confidence and competitiveness to succeed in games.

Pitch to Contact

From the first day we meet, I stress to pitchers that we are not going to be a staff that is scared to pitch to contact. As one of my assistant coaches likes to say, "If you are scared, buy a dog." When a pitcher delivers a pitch with the intention of missing the barrel of the bat, he usually ends up overthinking and being too fine with the delivery. Instill the "here it comes, hit it" mentality with your pitching staff. If you instill this mentality, your staff will challenge hitters with their best stuff, rather than worry about nibbling around the strike zone or trying to get hitters out by relying too much on trick pitches.

One thing I tell my staff to give them confidence in attacking the strike zone is to watch hitters take batting practice. Even in batting practice—when the hitter knows what is coming and the coach is throwing a batting practice fastball—hitters still make outs more times than they are successful. The mind-set of believing and trusting in pitching to contact is what we like to call the "nine-on-one mentality." This means we have a team of nine defenders against one batter. I ask my staff the following question: "If we were in a street fight and we had nine of us against one of them, would you like our chances of succeeding?" The answer is always an overwhelming yes. Take this analogy to the pitching mound. Make your staff concentrate on throwing effective strikes by pitching to contact. Just like in the street fight, the chances for success are very good.

The last area I address when dealing with pitching to contact is not changing based on the hitter. I have witnessed countless pitchers cruise through hitters they perceive to have limited ability. However, when the big cleanup hitter or All-American comes to the plate, the pitcher changes to try to miss his bat. Why? As noted earlier, pitching to miss barrels leads to a passive approach on the mound. I want my staff to be aggressive in everything they do. I can live with failure if we get beat while being aggressive, but I will not tolerate failure when the staff is being passive. Even when the best hitter in the world comes up or when King Kong steps to the on-deck circle, the pitcher should have the confidence to take the hitter out of the equation and focus on the glove. The result is a pitching staff that makes the same good pitches to the number four hitter that they make to the number nine hitter. This leads to better results. The idea is to maintain your approach no matter who is at the plate. Pitch to contact and trust your defense.

Learn to Pitch With the Fastball

Nothing frustrates me more than a pitcher trying to work on four or five different pitches without mastering the fastball. I see far too many young players come to campus thinking that having more pitches gives them a better chance of being successful. This is a myth that I believe is perpetuated by the video game era. Kids grow up playing video games featuring pitchers who are programmed to have unrealistic command of a vast array of pitches. In real baseball, this just isn't the case. I want my guys to focus on command of the fastball until they can put the ball wherever they want—inside, outside, up, or down. At least once a year, I give my staff the advice that Coach Wally Kincaid gave me when I was a young pitcher at Cerritos Junior College. When Coach Kincaid would talk about his simple theory, he would say, "If you want to be a good pitcher, learn to throw your fastball for a strike. If you want to be a great pitcher, learn to throw your fastball for a strike low in the strike zone. If you want to be an outstanding pitcher, learn to throw your fastball for a strike low in the strike zone to both sides of the plate." This is great advice to pass on to any young pitcher or pitching coach. Later in this chapter, I will explain how we go about developing pitchers who can execute this theory.

Establish Strike One

The last thing I say to a pitcher before he goes to the mound is simply "strike one." This tenet of pitching philosophy falls directly in line with the previous two of pitching to contact and learning to pitch with the fastball. I try to build a staff that rallies around simple and achievable goals such as commanding strike one to jump ahead of the hitter. Trying to get all my pitchers to throw

95 miles per hour or throw harder than their natural capabilities is unrealistic and unachievable. I would be wasting my time and their time. But focusing on commanding strike one is an achievable goal with enormous dividends for a pitching staff. Any hitter will agree that hitting with an 0-1 count is much more difficult than hitting with a 1-0 count. One of the ways I monitor the success rates of pitchers who throw strike one is by using a point chart to evaluate performance, which I will discuss as we move from philosophy to implementing a practice routine.

Be a Pitcher, Not a Thrower

I want a pitching staff that is schooled in pitching, not just a group of guys who throw hard or have good arms. In all honesty, the radar gun does very little for me when I evaluate my staff, and it has absolutely no influence on whom I decide to pitch. I want my pitchers to realize this and to take their focus off the radar gun readings and put it on the much more important art of being a pitcher. This involves knowing how to put a little on at times and take a little off at times. Any good hitting coach will preach that good hitters are able to maintain good rhythm and balance in the batter's box. As a pitching coach, I want my pitching staff to disrupt the rhythm and balance of a hitter by knowing how to throw strikes and change speeds. Again, batting practice can be used to demonstrate this point. If the coach unexpectedly takes just a little bit off the ball, it gives the hitter fits. The same is true of pitching in a game. If the pitcher follows the previous tenets and establishes strikes with the fastball, this makes it easier to change speeds and drop in a changeup or other off-speed offering to disrupt the hitter's timing. The reverse is true as well—a pitcher with a good changeup will make his fastball seem harder and tougher to hit because the hitter is dealing with a wide range of velocities. That is why I really don't get too concerned about radar gun readings. Instead, I focus my energy on instilling the importance of mixing it up by being able to add or subtract some velocity.

Sometimes, however, I do use radar gun readings to provide information about my pitcher. First, I see if the pitcher's gun readings change from bullpen sessions to game time. The pitcher who wants the ball often increases his velocity at game time because of the adrenaline rushing through his body. Sometimes, though, I see a player's velocity sharply decrease. If a guy who normally pumps it up there around 90 miles per hour goes into a game and is throwing 84 or 85 miles per hour, this tells me that he is holding back and not letting it fly; he is not trusting the work he has put in during bullpen sessions. This is a clear signal to me that we need to make his bullpen sessions more gamelike, or he may need more work on the mental side of the game to learn to control his body and mind during competition.

The second reading that is helpful for evaluating performance deals with a pitcher's velocity when he is throwing to the inner part of the plate. If a pitcher consistently throws 90 miles per hour and then dips to 85 miles per hour when trying to pitch inside, this tells me that he is not attacking the spot and is probably afraid of hitting the batter. For these instances, I believe gun readings can be valuable, but in all other cases, I stress to my pitching staff that success comes from mastering the art of pitching and not from trying to throw the ball hard.

If you do not have access to a radar gun, focus on the pitcher's arm speed. Does he guide the ball when trying to pitch to the inner part of the plate? It will be fairly easy to see without the luxury of a radar gun if a pitcher is losing his aggressiveness in certain situations. Identify these situations and find a strategy to attack them. In a case like this, we would use a stand-in hitter in all bullpen sessions.

Demonstrate Tempo and Mound Presence

Good pitchers work quickly and set the tone for the team. Baseball is a game of momentum, and momentum starts with a pitcher who is capable of setting a good tempo for the game. I teach my pitchers to get on the mound and attack. When a pitcher does this, he gets teams to play at the speed he wants. A well-coached team will be able to play at a fast tempo and overwhelm opponents who are not comfortable with playing quickly. When a pitcher takes the mound with tempo and attacks the strike zone, this keeps his defenders in the game and focused, which makes them more likely to make good plays in the field. Good tempo also keeps pitchers focused and in the moment because it doesn't give them a chance to overanalyze a previous pitch or to think about mechanical flaws. Instead, they must rely on their instincts.

Mound presence and tempo are natural partners. A pitcher who can pitch with good tempo is going to be an aggressive pitcher, and an aggressive pitcher has the competitive presence on the mound that makes him stand out against the timid or passive pitcher.

These are the simple philosophies that I use to build the foundation for pitching success. Remember that developing a good pitching staff involves keeping things simple for them. Trying to do too much or throwing too much information at players is counterproductive and inhibits focus on the few important skills that are most crucial to achieving and repeating desirable outcomes.

Now that we have laid the foundation, let's move on to implementing a practice routine that will lead to effective repetition and help build a successful pitching staff.

Implementing a Practice Routine

Skill acquisition comes from high-quality repetition. Pitching staffs develop the necessary skills to be successful by following a consistent program in practice. A pitching staff that completes all daily activity with a high level of discipline will be on the right track to becoming a successful staff.

The first area to focus on when developing a practice routine for a pitching staff is to establish a throwing schedule for bullpen and intrasquad work. A schedule keeps the throwing organized and allows the staff to get comfortable with a routine. Familiarizing the staff with a consistent routine is very valuable in preparing for competition because consistent hard work leads to improvement—and improvement and hard work together breed confidence. Figure 5.1 shows a simple sheet that I use to inform my staff of their weekly pitching responsibilities.

This simple plan is posted in the locker room and dugout at the beginning of each practice week. All pitchers are responsible for checking the plan and executing the routine established for them. Each area of the routine—catch play, bullpen, light bullpen (or loosen up, LU), and intrasquad innings—will now be explained.

Month _____

Player name	Monday	Wednesday	Friday
Pitcher A	Catch play Light bullpen (LU)	Bullpen	Game, two innings
Pitcher B	Bullpen	Game, two innings	Catch play Light bullpen (LU)
Pitcher C	Bullpen	Game, two innings	Catch play Light bullpen (LU)
Pitcher D	Catch play Light bullpen (LU)	Bullpen	Game, two innings
Pitcher E	Catch play Light bullpen (LU)	Bullpen	Game, two innings
Pitcher F	Bullpen	Game, two innings	Catch play Light bullpen (LU)
Pitcher G	Bullpen	Game, two innings	Catch play Light bullpen (LU)
Pitcher H	Bullpen	Game, two innings	Catch play Light bullpen (LU)
Pitcher I	Catch play Light bullpen (LU)	Bullpen	Game, two innings
Pitcher J	Catch play Light bullpen (LU)	Bullpen	Game, two innings
Pitcher K	Bullpen	Game, two innings	Catch play Light bullpen (LU)
Pitcher L	Bullpen	Game, two innings	Catch play Light bullpen (LU)
Pitcher M	Catch play Light bullpen (LU)	Bullpen	Game, two innings
Pitcher N	Catch play Light bullpen (LU)	Bullpen	Game, two innings
Pitcher O	Bullpen	Game, two innings	Catch play Light bullpen (LU)

Figure 5.1 Sample weekly throwing schedule for pitchers.

Catch Play

Like everything else we do during a practice, I want the pitching staff to make catch play as gamelike as possible. I constantly remind the staff that baseball is a game of catch and that the team that executes the game of catch better is usually the team that wins the game.

Players start catch-play time by working on underhand tosses and quick throws. For the first 5 minutes, pitchers simulate catching a comebacker followed by a hard pivot and underhanded toss to their partners. After working on their underhand toss, the pitchers move on to the type of snap throw they might use on a bunt down the third-base line when they have to execute a quick throw to first or third base. They also simulate fielding a squeeze bunt and throwing to home plate. This 5-minute routine gives them extra repetitions of throws they might practice only a few times during the course of regular practice. These throws are consistently a problem for pitchers because pitchers are used to taking their time with the delivery and being able to let the ball fly from the hand. When they have to make a quicker throw, this can lead to problems if they haven't been getting enough repetitions during practice.

Next, the pitchers move back at their own pace until they reach a distance of between 160 and 180 feet (48.8 and 54.9 m), depending on the individual. Playing catch at this distance helps pitchers build their arm strength. Once they reach their maximum distance, they throw long toss with a changeup grip. This has proved to be an extremely effective tool for developing the changeup because the key to a changeup is maintaining good arm speed. When pitchers try to develop their changeup from short distances, they tend to slow down their arm and push the pitch. However, by throwing long-distance catch with a changeup grip, they are forced to maintain arm speed to get the ball to their partner. By doing this in catch play, they begin to develop trust in their grip and extension on the changeup. They also develop confidence that they can repeat the same motion from the mound. After a few long-catch sessions, a pitcher should be capable of throwing a changeup using the arm speed of a fastball.

When the pitchers have completed their catch-play routine, which should last about 15 minutes from the time they start throwing, they move back in to about 60 feet (18.3 m) and start working on different pitches. This is the time when I like them to experiment with different grips and arm angles. I frequently get asked the question, "How do I develop better movement on my pitches?" My answer is always to take 5 minutes to experiment after playing catch. Pitchers should see what they can get the ball to do by using different grips or trying to cut the ball a little this way or that way. They should think of catch-play time as time for cultivating their craft. All good craftsmen continually look for ways to improve and try to find new techniques that work. It is the same with pitchers. Pitchers need to experiment to see what they can do with the ball.

Bullpens and Light Bullpens

In a typical week during the practice season, a pitcher will complete three sessions of throwing from the mound: one bullpen session, one light bullpen session (or a "loosen up" session), and one game or intrasquad game. Let's first address bullpen sessions (also called bullpens).

From my experience, I have found that a lot of bullpens are done more as aerobic exercises than focused pitching. Demand that your pitchers approach bullpens with a goal and purpose at all times. As with catch play, I demand that bullpens be thrown with gamelike intensity. Depending on the structure of your bullpen, this may involve kicking out pitchers who are not involved in the bullpen so the pitcher can do focused work. Pitchers who are waiting to throw often sit on a bench behind the bullpen mound. This is a distraction for the pitcher on the mound. Do not let this happen. Pitching, unlike most anything else in the game, can be done only for a limited amount of time and requires significant recovery time before a player can go back out there again. With this in mind, every pitch in the bullpen must have focus and purpose behind it. String together three days per week of focused prep work, and by the end of the month, you will have a disciplined pitching staff ready to execute in games.

The actual routine starts once a pitcher is done warming up and toes the rubber to begin throwing to the catcher. At this time, the pitcher must never throw a pitch to a catcher who is not down in his catching stance. If the pitcher needs more warm-ups, it is okay for the pitcher and catcher to step in front of or behind the mound to play catch. Remember, though, when a pitcher toes the rubber, the catcher should be down. You never want your pitcher to get used to throwing on a flat plane from the rubber. Pitchers need to develop a downward tilt to pitches because tilt and downward angle make it tough for a hitter to square up to the ball. The pitcher should envision standing on top of a two-story building and throwing down to a hitter at ground level. Think about how difficult it would be for the hitter to handle a pitch with that type of angle. Although it seems like a small pet peeve, I believe that allowing a pitcher to throw to a catcher who is standing up encourages bad habits that could lead to inconsistency.

Figure 5.2 illustrates a routine I developed that tries to simulate every situation a pitcher might encounter in a game. The far left column itemizes each pitch, from pitch 1 to pitch 40. There is no perfect number of pitches to throw during a bullpen session, but 40 is a good number for a bullpen if those pitches are thrown right. You want to avoid having pitchers who think they need to throw a ton of pitches in the pen or pitchers who are struggling and think they can throw their way out of the funk. Neither are good strategies. I settled on a structured routine of 40 because I believe it gets in everything we want to work on but keeps the routine short enough so pitchers have to focus on executing every pitch. They can't miss their spot five times in a row and then ask for a sixth chance. For a long time, I allowed pitchers to do this, but then I realized that come game time, they only get one chance to execute the pitch, not two or three.

Pitcher _____

Charted by _____

Number of pitch	Type of pitch	Score	Number of pitch	Type of pitch	Score
	Intentional base-on balls			*Stretch*	
1	Right-handed hitter		21	Pitchout to right-handed hitter	
2	Right-handed hitter		22	Pitchout to left-handed hitter	
3	Left-handed hitter		23	Fastball down the middle	
4	Left-handed hitter		24	Fastball down the middle	
	Windup		25	Fastball inside	
5	Fastball down the middle		26	Fastball inside	
6	Fastball down the middle		27	Fastball under the hands	
7	Fastball inside		28	Fastball outside	
8	Fastball inside		29	Fastball outside	
9	Fastball under the hands		30	Fastball elevated	
10	Fastball outside		31	Glove-strike changeup	
11	Fastball outside		32	Glove-strike changeup	
12	Fastball elevated		33	Changeup with count leverage	
13	Glove-strike changeup		34	Changeup with count leverage	
14	Glove-strike changeup		35	Glove-strike breaking ball	
15	Changeup with count leverage		36	Glove-strike breaking ball	
16	Changeup with count leverage		37	Breaking ball with count leverage	
17	Glove-strike breaking ball		38	Breaking ball with count leverage	
18	Glove-strike breaking ball			*Pitcher's choice*	
19	Breaking ball with count leverage		39		
20	Breaking ball with count leverage		40		

Figure 5.2 Bullpen routine of 40 pitches.

The bullpen routine starts with four intentional balls (the type of pitches thrown when a pitcher is executing an intentional base on balls). It confuses me that coaches expect pitchers to be able to execute an intentional walk without working on it. Usually, this action comes in a high-pressure situation with runners in scoring position. I want my guys to be prepared for this so they are not nervous when they have to do it in a game. That is why we start the bullpen session with intentional balls—pitches 1 and 2 to a right-handed hitter and pitches 3 and 4 to a left-handed hitter. Obviously, you hope your team doesn't need to intentionally walk batters very often, but when they do, it is going to be important to get it right.

Pitches 5 and 6 are the first regular pitches of the routine. Here the pitcher works on pounding the fastball right down the middle from the windup. Next, the pitcher throws two inside fastballs, followed by a fastball underneath the hitter's hands, two outside fastballs, and an elevated fastball. This all relates to being able to move the ball in, out, up, and down. We would rarely call for a fastball beneath the hitter's hands or an elevated fastball unless we had count leverage on the hitter and wanted to get him to chase the pitch. In that situation, these pitches could also be used to change the hitter's eye level in order to set him up for an off-speed pitch.

Once the pitcher finishes the fastball routine from the windup, he moves to off-speed pitches. He starts by trying to throw the changeup for a strike (glove-strike changeup). Typically, this pitch would be used either for a first-pitch offering or when the hitter is ahead in the count. Then the pitcher moves on to throwing the changeup in situations where the pitcher has count leverage. The final four pitches from the windup are breaking balls.

After pitch 20, the pitcher moves from the windup to the stretch position. A wise coach and ex-pitcher once said to me, "I'm only in trouble when I'm pitching out of the stretch." This is true, but a lot of pitchers forget to incorporate the stretch into their routine. The stretch routine starts with two pitchouts, one to a right-handed hitter and one to a left-handed hitter. After the pitchouts, the routine is the same as from the windup.

For the last two pitches, the pitcher chooses what he wants to throw. After completing this 40-pitch routine, the pitcher might finish with the catcher calling signs to simulate an at-bat.

While the pitcher is throwing his bullpen, another pitcher charts the progress and execution of the session, noting either a plus (+), minus (–), or X (strike) after each pitch. The pitcher receives a plus if he executes the pitch, a minus if he does not execute the pitch, and an X if the pitch is a strike. This gets a little confusing because it is possible to throw a strike but not get a plus. For example, if the goal is to throw an outside fastball but the pitcher throws an inside fastball for a strike, he receives a minus and an X. Likewise, if we want the pitcher to elevate the fastball and he succeeds in hitting the spot, the pitcher would receive a plus but not an X. After each session, the pitcher is given his chart, and he is encouraged to review what is working for him and what areas he needs to improve.

Another feature that can make the bullpen routine more gamelike is to add a stand-in hitter. The stand-in should be an offensive player because this will give the pitcher a game feel and will also help the hitter track pitches and work on his timing. Ideally, I try to get a right-handed hitter to stand in for half the time; then I change the look by bringing in a left-handed hitter for the second half. Over the years, I have found that using a stand-in is one of the best multitask drills (offense and defense, in this case) to do during bullpen time.

The final area of the bullpen routine to discuss is the light bullpen, or LU, which stands for "loosen up." This is a short 15-pitch bullpen session. It is meant to keep the pitcher fresh and to reinforce the feel of throwing off the mound—without blowing out the pitcher's arm by overextending him with multiple bullpens and game innings per week. Review the throwing schedule shown in figure 5.1 to get a good idea of how I use the LU, bullpen, and game innings during a practice week.

Scrimmage Games

In the fall practice season, scrimmage games are very important for the development of a successful pitching staff. To get my pitchers to buy into the system I implement, I have them pitch most scrimmage games using only their fastball and changeup. This teaches them to trust in these pitches and keeps them from falling in love with the breaking ball. Overuse of breaking balls puts unnecessary stress on the arm, and, as I stated earlier, the key to being a good pitcher is to be able to command the fastball and keep hitters off balance. Mastering the fastball and changeup before moving on to other pitches has helped my staffs simplify the game and learn to throw a high percentage of effective strikes.

Similar to bullpen routines, we chart and evaluate every pitch a pitcher makes in the scrimmage games. After each scrimmage, I write up a report and post two charts for each pitcher in the pitchers' dugout: the point chart (figure 5.3) and the pitcher's daily evaluation chart (figure 5.4, page 65).

Positive and negative points are allocated based on actions during the scrimmage game. Every positive point reflects something I believe is important to creating momentum and showing the aptitude necessary to compete during games. Every negative point reflects an area that can be a backbreaker for teams. I want my staff to realize that the little details of the game are very important.

Positive points are awarded for the following:

- First-pitch strike (+1): Strike one is the most important pitch in baseball. A staff that consistently jumps ahead will be a tough staff to beat.

- Shutout inning (+1): We like to think of the game as nine one-inning battles. Our goal as a pitching staff is to win every inning. Focusing on the game one inning at a time fosters a competitive edge that will give you an advantage over teams that aren't as focused.

- Inning of 12 pitches or less (+2): Pitch efficiency is vital to winning a game, and it also goes a long way toward setting up the pitching staff to win a series.

Pitcher _____

Date _____ Innings pitched _____

Positive points	+	–	Negative points
First-pitch strike			Base on balls or error
Shutout inning			Hit by pitch
Inning of 12 pitches or less			Runs allowed
Double play			Hit off two-strike count
1-2-3 inning			Missed sign
Pickoff			Failure to back up base
Pitch out of jam			20 or more pitches per inning
Totals			
Score			

Figure 5.3   Pitcher's point chart.

Quick innings are an enormous momentum swing and often put a positive feeling in your dugout. This positive feeling usually leads to offensive success.

- Double play (+1): This is another big momentum changer. Double plays deflate the other team and are another way to take the momentum.
- 1-2-3 inning (+1): As mentioned for an inning of 12 pitches or less, quick innings are great.
- Pickoff (+1): A pickoff is another big play that deflates the opponent and gets your team out of a jam.
- Pitch out of jam (+1): It is a lot easier to pitch when the bases are empty as opposed to when runners are on base, especially if those runners are in scoring position. This point allows me to see who steps up in big situations. These tend to be the guys whom I want to have the ball when the game is on the line.

Negative points are given for the following:

- Base on balls, error, or hit by pitch (–1): Free bases are a killer. Limit the amount of free passes, and your staff will be successful. The error is a deduction only if it was committed by the pitcher. The hit by pitch is deducted unless we were trying to throw in. If we were trying to throw inside, the hit by pitch is not counted as a deduction.
- Runs allowed (–1): We don't want to give up runs.

- Hits off a two-strike count (–2): Many pitchers lose focus when they get to a two-strike count, and they don't finish off the hitter. Minimizing hits off a two-strike count is a priority.
- Missed sign or failure to back up a base (–1): These are little things with big consequences. If the hitter is set up for a breaking ball but the pitcher misses the sign and throws a fastball, this could cost the team a win. Likewise, not getting to the proper backup position after a hit can lead to extra 90-foot advances for the opponent. Every 90-foot gain is important and can be the difference between a win and a loss.
- 20 or more pitches per inning (–1): Long innings give the opponent life and wear down the pitching staff.

The pitcher's daily evaluation chart (figure 5.4) focuses on simple but crucial aspects of pitching success. The chart is used to track innings pitched, number of pitches thrown, walks, strikeouts, first-pitch strikes, attitude, and mental focus. The chart includes columns for a letter grade (A to F) and comments on what the pitcher did well and what he needs to improve. I don't rely much on other statistics besides these simple measures. For my system, the ratio of innings pitched to pitch count provides a good indication of how my staff is throwing. I grade attitude based on how pitchers react to situations, and I grade mental focus based on how I think their mound presence was on the day they pitched.

Pitcher _____

Date _____

	Grade	Comments
Innings pitched		
Number of pitches		
Walks		
Strikeouts		
First-pitch strikes		
Attitude		
Mental focus		

Figure 5.4 Pitcher's daily evaluation chart.

Dry Mechanics

Pitchers get only two or three opportunities per week to throw from the mound. During the other days of practice, the pitchers should follow an established routine so they get the repetitions needed to build sound mechanics. I tend not to overcoach the mechanical side of pitching during bullpens or games, but I do believe that having repeatable mechanics leads to consistency. The most important thing to focus on while working on mechanical drills is for the pitcher to gain an understanding of how to control his body. A pitcher who doesn't control his body will have very little success repeating a consistent delivery and arm slot.

My pitchers develop body control and repeatable movements by going through a dry-mechanics routine every day in practice. Usually the routine is completed two or three times during the day. I want pitchers to focus on gaining control of a smooth delivery that stays on line to home plate.

The dry-mechanics routine is done without a ball. I emphasize to the pitchers that they should not simulate a pitch by whipping their arm as they would when throwing. Instead, I want them to focus on what their body is doing, and I have them try to repeat sound mechanics over and over until those mechanics become second nature. Here is the dry-mechanics routine that we use:

Windup Pitch Routine
- Four-pitch sequence
- Complete two times

Stretch Pitch Routine
- Four-pitch sequence
- Complete two times

Defensive Routine
Perform each scenario from the stretch a minimum of three times.

- Runner at first base; pitch fastball down the middle.
- Runner at first base; step off (competitive).
- Runner at first base; make pickoff attempt (competitive).
- Runners at first and third bases; perform third-to-first move.
- Runner at second base; perform look sequence and inside turn.
- Runners at first and second bases; pitch fastball down the middle and move into bunt defense.

The goal of this routine is to simulate every action that a pitcher might make during a game. If you want your staff to be good at something at game time, they have to properly prepare during practice.

Games and Game Management

As the fall practice season comes to an end, it is time to start distinguishing roles for your pitching staff. I break my staff into three roles: starting pitcher, long relief, and short relief. The back end of the short-relief designation will usually be my closer or stopper.

A good starting pitcher is a guy who can command the strike zone and throw multiple pitches for strikes. Ideally, starters should be able to throw three different pitches for strikes: fastball, changeup, and either a curveball or slider. Having the ability to be efficient with pitch count is also a major bonus. If the other team is able to get to your bullpen early in the series, they have a big advantage as the weekend plays out.

Long-relief guys will usually see action only if the starter gets chased early. Usually, they will come into the game in situations when you are behind by a lot and don't want to burn your short relievers until you get within striking distance. Long relievers may also come in when you are ahead by a lot and want to save your short relievers for a more crucial spot in the series.

Short relievers have the toughest job because they are almost always called on to protect narrow margins or to keep the game close enough for the offense to mount a comeback. These guys have to be tough mentally and can't be fazed by pressure-packed situations. Ideally, the closer is the player with the best stuff out of the bullpen, but it is also very important for a closer to come in the game and establish strikes.

Before the season starts, let your pitchers know what you envision their roles to be on the pitching staff. This helps them feel comfortable and gives the players who are unhappy with their position on the depth chart an opportunity to realize that they need to improve to get where they want to be.

Besides the game management aspect, theoretically, nothing should change between practice and games. Teach your players to practice at the speed they want to play at so they are not overwhelmed when the games get going. If your staff works hard during practice, they should have the confidence to be successful in games.

Conditioning Programs

Conditioning for pitchers is an important aspect of building a successful staff. Very few pitchers (or players in general) enjoy conditioning because it is hard work and can be monotonous. But conditioning is a key ingredient to the physical fitness that is needed in order to be a strong and durable pitcher. Plus, a good portion of the conditioning I have my pitching staff do in the fall is done with the goal of not only improving physical fitness, but also presenting them with a mental challenge. Mentally weak pitchers will give in when the conditioning gets tough. Either they won't complete the assigned tasks or they will complain about the need for running, believing it is in excess of what is required for physical strength. Mentally tough pitchers will see every conditioning period as a challenge and barrier they need to conquer. Conquering these challenges gives them confidence because they have completed a difficult task.

For a conditioning program, you should alter the schedule so it doesn't get boring for the group. Have distance days and short-sprint days, but always make it difficult and a mental challenge to complete.

Our running rules during the season are as follows: After a start, a pitcher runs at least 5 miles (8.0 km) in distance or 50 minutes in duration. A relief pitcher is required to run 1 mile (1.6 km) for every inning pitched.

Pitcher Recruitment and Development

To conclude this chapter on building a pitching staff, let's discuss what to look for when recruiting a young pitcher. Recruiting involves deciding which pitchers—if given the proper time and innings to develop—could turn into great assets for your team. Look for a pitcher with the aptitude and intangibles to be successful. To find out a little about a pitcher's character, I watch his presence and body language as well as his interaction with teammates. It is easy to treat the so-called best or cool players with respect, but how does the player treat the guy who is lower on the depth chart? At the high school level, I would take into account how the player interacts in the classroom with other students and the level of respect he shows for his teachers. Any pitcher who is on the mound showing up a teammate or showing negative body language will be crossed off my list—regardless of how talented he may be. I also like to watch a pitcher to see his level of competitiveness. A pitcher who lacks a little in the stuff category can make up for it with his presence and mental focus.

I also look for arm quickness, not velocity. A pitcher who throws hard but has a slow arm has probably reached his ceiling as far as development. On the other hand, a young pitcher who throws in the low to mid 80s with a quick, whippy arm is exciting and is a guy I want to follow in order to track his progress. Quick-armed pitchers will develop into hard throwers with electric stuff. Not only will their fastballs have life, but the arm speed on off-speed offerings will make it difficult for hitters to differentiate between pitches. Look for quick arms rather than hard throwers.

I look for a pitcher who can command one or two effective pitches. I try to find players who fit into the system I use. For example, I like my pitchers to use the changeup, so I look for pitchers who either have a feel for the pitch or have the arm speed necessary to throw an effective down-and-in changeup. I also try to find a pitcher who misses barrels. Sometimes you can't put your finger on exactly what you like about a pitcher, but you notice that he tends to miss barrels, or hitters tend not to hit balls square against him. It usually takes a few trips to identify the type of pitcher who might not wow you with his stuff but consistently misses barrels. In these instances, be persistent and try to watch him against the top teams in his league.

Developing a good pitching staff is a continuous grind. However, by focusing on the little details and implementing a consistent routine, you can help elevate your staff to a higher level.

chapter 6

Maximizing Batting Practice

GARY WARD

All coaches are products of their lifelong environmental programming and their life experiences. That programming and experience translate to an innate style of communication that includes body language, vocal tone, voice modulation, facial expressions, accent, sense of humor, story telling, and the choice of descriptive terminology. The verbal transcript is only a small part of teaching. Experts say that people communicate far more information about who they are and what they want through body language. The skill of teaching depends on an individual form of expression. If you expect players to be great students, you must be a great student yourself. Invest in yourself first and remain a student. Acquire all the knowledge available by seeking mentors who have gone where you wish to go. Study others who have achieved greatness in their respective fields of endeavor. Greatness leaves many valuable clues in its path. Become an avid reader, because readers become leaders. To teach, the instructor must allow himself to be taught. The coach can practice communication skills with the aid of a mirror, a tape recorder, or videotape. Accumulate and take ownership of the subject matter needed to become a master teacher. Present the information to the student with passion and a sense of urgency. Reflect joy and enthusiasm, and bring them from the depth of your soul. This assigns importance to the topic and encourages the player to follow, believe, and trust your leadership.

Practice time is a precious commodity. Place value on timely arrival and proper preparation for work. Foster an environment of interdependence among players. The culture of choice is one that embraces risk, change, and the desire to achieve greatness. Nothing about hitting is trivialized, and all comments between players are supportive of the efforts of team members. Interdependence provides no place for the independent or the dependent personality to exist. No alibis, no excuses. No one tunes his dial to WIIFM—what's in it for me. Interdependence allows for a synergistic rise of the collective group toward meeting the goal of winning championship-quality games. Knowledge shared is knowledge multiplied. Provide opportunities for your players to teach the hitting program to youth teams in your community. Teaching hitting means the player has ownership of the skill and can execute the fundamentals under game conditions.

The player controls the learning environment. Learning is a process of acquiring information through sight, hearing, and feel. Each player has his own method of processing new ideas. Players may rely on visual, auditory, or kinesthetic cues as their primary methods. Attempt to use video, a mirror, a lecture, and physical activity to teach each important idea. It takes 21 to 35 days to learn a new motor skill. It takes 6 weeks to replace and relearn a motor skill. The ultimate goal is to practice the action until it becomes an automatic response so that, under game conditions, the execution of the skill is an instinctive, productive reaction.

To teach motor skills, the coach must be relentless. The primary teaching technique is the power of spaced repetition. Expose the player to the idea 8 to 10 times over a period of 14 days. If you mention it only once, the player will lose about 95 percent of the idea. Practice patience, be resolved, and remain relentless. Bring the energy and effort to practice every day. Inspire your student rather than overwhelm or intimidate him. Failure is not final nor is it fatal. It is merely fertilizer for eventual success. Our society embraces the concept of being normal, socially acceptable, popular, and average. Dare to be different with a goal-setting program. Being mediocre is a self-imposed status and allows others to impose their limits on you. The teacher is not successful because of his knowledge of the subject. The teacher becomes successful when the player has learned the lesson. Once the player has learned, the coach should give the player the right to own the new skill and to be accountable for the results.

Expectations and Philosophy

Before teaching the offensive game of baseball, the coach must identify a personal set of core beliefs. Place a value on each phase of the offensive game. This includes many aspects of the game but also must address what is expected from each hitter. What does the coach expect in game performance as it relates to strike zone discipline, situational execution, baserunning, power production, bunting, and the number of pitches seen per plate appearance?

With a clear vision of the personal philosophy and expectations of the coach, each player can direct his energies efficiently. Do not give the player a map of Phoenix and expect him to find his way around Dallas. Answer these important questions:

- What message are you sending?
- What environment are you creating?
- What examples are you setting?
- What is the offensive identity of your team?
- Are you aware of the needs of each player concerning his mental, physical, visual, and emotional tools?

Specify your expectations of each player, taking into account his defensive position and spot in the lineup. Hitting can be defined as understanding the language of your hitting instructor.

Practice Environment

Every swing a player takes during practice—whether from a toss, off a tee, or off a live pitch—should have a precise, predetermined purpose. Each swing should require the player to compete at game-reaction speed. Drills should include several variables of decision making that are required under game conditions. For all drills, require the hitter to read whether the pitch is a ball or strike. The batter must decide to hit or take and must find the resulting body position at the conclusion of each pitch. This allows the coach to read the hitter's take position and to teach the initial movements of the proper swing. Pitches thrown at game-reaction speed allow the hitter to work on his response time. The coach can evaluate when the hitter is starting the stride, how much travel or information time he is getting with the ball in flight, and how good his reaction time is. Are the fundamentals the coach is attempting to impart to the player being practiced in each bat swing? Practice makes permanent, not perfect.

On many teams, a high percentage of batting practice is done with the hitter already knowing what type of pitch will be thrown. The speed of the pitch is replicated with predictability. The hitter is not required to read any change of speed or change of plane, which is rarely the case for a hitter in any competitive baseball game. In this type of batting practice, the hitter is allowed to work with the "dead red" mental set. He is expected to swing at every pitch without regard to whether the pitch is in the strike zone. In addition, the pitches are thrown as quickly as possible to get in a maximum number of swings in the shortest period of time. There is no time for the hitter to have a plan or to review his swing mechanics. Under these conditions, the hitter can make myriad mistakes in swing mechanics but still get in rhythm with the predictability of the pitch and perform like a successful hitter. Under these conditions, the player can put on a show of contact and power that gives the false impression that he is ready to play. The hitting drill has become a driving range and not a laboratory for preparing the hitter to be game ready.

The most important recommendation for every coach is to make the intervals between swings more than 13 seconds long. This is critical during more intense one-on-one instruction. The average visual memory of a hitter is 13 seconds. When pitches and swings are repeated every 5 seconds, the hitter is hitting with the visual memory residue of the last pitch. Double exposure on the visual film of any hitter creates confusion and failure. That process also overloads the sensory system and destroys the player's sense of kinesthetic awareness.

Slow down and put a premium on the quality of the exercise rather than the volume. Use a prepitch ritual for each hitter that allows the player to control the rhythm of hitting drills. Help the hitter develop a ritual similar to a free throw shooter in basketball. Encourage him to step away from the plate and reenter the box on each pitch. The prepitch ritual will allow him to learn from each repetition and make corrections. With responsibility for hitting or taking and the read of ball or strike, the player is gaining control of the learning environment.

On-field batting practice with full ball flight is the sanctuary. The hitter is easily motivated when he can see the result of his contact with the ball. It is possible to create two or more full-flight cages using the home plate area and on-deck areas of your field (figure 6.1). Batting tee drills and toss drills can be set up with full-flight capability. Each coach can practice with multiple batting

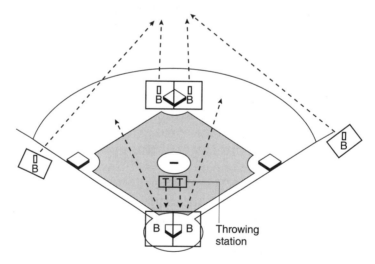

Figure 6.1 Setup for multiple batting stations. A split cage for two live-arm stations is set up at home plate. If you have small cages, make one side live arm and one side bunt. Protective screens are used in front of the dual throwing station in front of the pitcher's mound. Tee stations are set up at second base and along the right- and left-field lines on the warning track. All players are well protected at each station, and different balls (tennis, taped, marked) are used at each station to simplify ball pickup.

practice stations that allow for full flight. Be creative and multiply the options for work. With safety issues addressed and enough baseballs, the coach can organize a session of station drills that keeps the hitters highly motivated.

Being able to practice using multiple full-flight stations depends on the field area available, the size of the squad, the availability of protective barriers, practice time, and staff size. The creative coach can make a batting tee using a five-gallon bucket filled with sand and a radiator hose over a broomstick. Use the "beg and borrow" skill to find a radar gun, protective netting, restricted-flight balls (such as tennis, plastic, or cloth balls), available space, and extra staff (such as volunteers, parents, or students). Motivated coaches have conducted practice in city parks and parking lots.

Finally, for every practice, develop an atmosphere that allows for experimentation, change, risk taking, and role playing. As the coach, you are the primary person who dictates the instructional curriculum. The players may have been taught by many other coaches before being taught by you. Each player was already good enough to get to this point. You must help every player understand the meaning of each coaching term or command as it relates to his personal performance.

Change can be intimidating to players who have some insecurity about their talent or think that they have already mastered the game. It is easier for players to remain in their comfort zones. Players who are willing to take risks expose themselves to the possibility of suffering harm, loss, and ridicule. Experienced coaches understand that the students will likely regress before they begin to make progress. Change is often resisted and disliked; it is difficult to let go of the past. The coach must explain the why, when, and where of new ideas.

Invite the players to ask questions and engage in conversation. The coach should receive each question without making it personal. During the early stages of the coach–player relationship, conversation will be very guarded. Players cannot afford to look weak among their peers, so they learn to go along to get along. The coach must envision what the player can become, sell the athlete on the fact that it can be done, and provide work experiences that allow the player to see the potential benefits. A player who sees and believes that change is beneficial will embrace the change and implement it into his daily performance.

Create a relaxed practice that allows each player to role-play as his favorite professional player and to experiment with a new stance, swing, and personality. This alone sets an example of taking on new mental programming, new self-talk, new personality, and new results. By teaching with these concepts, you can set the player free to embrace the possibilities. The coach must remain nonjudgmental and ego free. Involve the player in conversation to learn what he thinks and what he feels. Do not overvalue the coaching role. Remain loyal to the teaching process and assure the player that failure is not final or fatal.

What Gets Measured Gets Managed: The Static Ball Test

The player hits a ball off a batting tee located in the middle of the strike zone. Place the tee slightly in front of a throw-down home plate. The player hits the ball into a net approximately 30 feet (9.1 m) from the batting tee. Record the ball flight with a radar gun. Evaluating with the radar gun can be done from directly behind the hitter or behind the net in front of the hitter. Repeat six to eight times to calculate an accurate average. The score measures bat speed, hand strength, and hitting mechanics.

Data on thousands of high school and college players have established a set of norms that can accurately predict the probability of hitting success. These norms also provide strong indicators regarding the power potential of each player. College coaches should use a range of 80 to 100-plus miles per hour to measure players and constantly monitor progress toward their personal goal. Scores in the high 80s indicate gap power with occasional line-drive home-run power. Routine fly-ball power is indicated as the hitter reaches the 95 score, and easy power is projected as the score reaches 100-plus. The uncontrolled variables in the test provide a margin of error of 1 or 2 miles per hour.

When the coach accumulates adequate data to establish norms for the level of competition, he can place values at increments of 2 miles per hour. The test can be expanded to include readings from additional angles that represent pull and opposite-field power.

Use a batting tee that has a grid directly in front of the plate to teach the proper impact area and ball flight pattern for hitting. Create a competitive game of tee accuracy by placing a scoring mat with point values on the receiving net. Players love to compete and measure their progress.

The numbers generated will help the coach determine each player's offensive skills and team offensive responsibilities. The coach's primary concerns are what position the player should play, where he will hit in the lineup, and what adjustments are needed to the bat's entry angle into the hitting plane in order to create ball flight angles that produce exit speed. These skills, or lack thereof, also indicate how much to emphasize the development of the player's bunting game and directional hitting.

Execution in this drill will involve a learning curve. Repeat the test every two weeks in the preseason and once a month during the regular season. The measurement is a motivator for all hitters. The initial test indicates the player's current status. Future changes in scores reflect the player's physical growth, the effect of training programs, and improvement in swing mechanics. It is not unusual to see an increase of 5 miles per hour in player performance in the first 60 days.

Commands for Maximizing Batting Practice

Develop your personal glossary of hitting commands. Here are some examples:

- Power base: This is the position of the body at the conclusion of the stride to hit.
- Heel to heel: This describes the timing of the lead heel touching down and the back heel elevating.
- Vertical stacking: The nose stays up to keep the head and eyes squared for the pitch; the nose stays over the navel throughout the swing.
- Stride takes you down, not out: Do not leak toward the pitcher, but load the body into the legs.
- Get back before you get down: Do not stride and separate the bat toward the catcher.
- Feel your energy flow: Gather energy from the ground through your feet.
- Do not hit on the rise: The stride lowers the body, and the swing is executed on that plane.

Use phrases to address the most important elements of your hitting system, and create a list of short, humorous, and colorful commands. Make a complete list, define each item, and test players until they understand the meaning of each. The coach now has a language that can be used in all batting practice situations.

Stride Takes You Down, Not Out

Teach hitters that the striding action of the front foot should be a reach that loads the energy into the back hip. At the conclusion of the stride, the hitter has established his power base. The distance between the feet at the power base should not be longer than the length of the bat that the player is swinging. The feet collect the energy flow from the ground and send it up to the knees and beyond. Use your primary team color to describe the feet plugged into the ground, collecting and distributing energy upward. Successful hitters describe the feeling of pressing their feet into the ground as they execute their swing. When the heel of the stride foot lands, the back heel immediately lifts. This is referred to as the *heel–heel dance*. This action allows the player to achieve an athletic position with the knees coordinated, ready to collect and direct the energy received from contact with the ground.

The coach can have the hitter preset the back heel at an angle with the toe pointed more toward the pitcher. The coach can also instruct the hitter to raise the back heel off the ground as part of the initial stance and setup. These techniques are referred to as *back heel cheats.*

If the back foot is not off the ground before the swing commitment is made, the hitter will not use the energy collected in the back hip (energy provided by a proper striding action). This common mistake is made even by performers at a high level, and it is easy to correct with the heel–heel technique. The coaching commands are "Down, not out," "Feel your feet," "Press your feet into the ground," and "Get some feet rhythm and deliver the energy to your knees." The heel–heel dance is not about being overly quick, and it certainly is not a commitment to the swing. Slow, controlled feet assist the flow of energy up to the front muscles. This energy is released sequentially and produces maximum bat speed.

Functional Knees and Elbows Lead to Flexible Feet and Hands

The knees are the functional joints of the legs, and the elbows are the functional joints of the arms. If a knee or elbow locks out early in the hitting action, energy flow is interrupted and misdirected. The back muscles activate and contract, taking over the delivery of the bat. Locking the knees or elbows reduces the control and quickness of the feet and hands. If the knees can function, the feet remain flexible and will maintain body balance and energy flow. If the elbows can function, the hands remain flexible and will control bat plane and speed. Hitting is done with the front muscles of the body. The back muscles provide a stable position, but if activated, they produce a long swing that cannot be adjusted to hit pitches that change plane or speed.

The coaching commands are "Make the knees work as a team; they are stars directed at the pitch," "Feel quick zone one," and "Feel the athletic position and do not lock out the energy flow."

Stay! Sit!

Using a balance board during live-arm hitting drills gives the coach an opportunity to emphasize a series of stay and sit commands. A basic 2-by-6-inch (5.1 by 15.2 cm) board is easy to acquire and works well on any concrete or turf surface. A dirt surface must be level and smooth. The coaching commands are "Stay on your legs to hit," "Stay tall and see the ball," and "Stay in the seat." These commands remind the player to keep the body stacked vertically. The board helps teach balance, so the player automatically stops bending from the waist and leading with the nose to the ball or to the strike zone. The player must be able to stay on the board at the conclusion of the swing. The coach may use a rotating adjustable bar chair with the board to create a kinesthetic feel for staying in the seat and using the legs to hit. Hitters who use the back muscles to swing the bat or lock out the functional and flexible joints of the legs and arms find it difficult to stay on the board.

The use of props during a live drill raises the concern of safety for the athlete. The apparatus added to the drill makes the hitting environment abnormal and reduces the normal avoidance response of the athlete. Monitor chair and board drills closely, and ask that pitches come at moderate speed. The primary purpose is to allow the player to experience the kinesthetic feel of the positions described by the coaching commands.

If You Can Feel It, You Can Fix It

Have players close their eyes and feel their swing mechanics as they swing the bat in slow motion. Players should identify where the body is and where the bat is throughout the total swing. Ask them what they feel. This is an excellent exercise to make the athlete more kinesthetically aware. Practice blind swings in an enclosed cage with the use of a tee. A teammate sets the ball on the tee, then commands the hitter to close his eyes and count to five. With his eyes still closed, the hitter attempts to hit the ball off the tee by using visual memory.

Extend the drill to involve a full-length mirror. A mirror is superior to video because it allows for instant feedback. The coach asks the player to take a slow swing with his eyes closed and to identify energy flow, quick zone one, or any part of the hitting system. The coach asks the player to stop at any given moment and open his eyes, using the mirror to see if his position is where he felt it was. If necessary, place the player in the proper position. Have him check it in the mirror and then close his eyes and feel what he just saw. This power technique activates the three learning senses simultaneously. Auditory, visual, and kinesthetic senses interpret the majority of information needed to practice the hitting skill.

Make the Move

The move is composed of five basic components:

1. The stride overcomes body inertia and establishes a loaded power base.
2. The heel–heel dance activates the functional joints of the knees and frees the flexibility of the feet.
3. The feet collect the energy flow from the ground and send it upward to the belly button to be collected and directed.
4. The knees work with the belly button to direct the energy.
5. The hands relax and move from the setup position into the launching area.

This is not a commitment to swing at the pitch but a preparatory action taken on every pitch. The move occurs while the pitch is in flight, based on each individual player's timing or rhythm adjustment technique. This is referred to as travel time and information-gathering time. The hitter uses this time to read the speed, arrival location, and type of the oncoming pitch.

The move can be practiced 30 inches (76.2 cm) away from a wall or a net with or without a bat. Caution players to be aware that the knees and belly button open to the pitch while the chest remains square to home plate, the wall, or the net. The hands and bat enter the launching area but are not committed to the swing. The move signifies the athlete's "hit or take" moment of decision. It is the preparatory move to function at the junction. The upper body remains coiled and loaded; the pressure is felt at the front of the back hip.

The front muscles of the chest—the pectorals—carry the energy and control the lever assembly of the arms and bat. The coach's command "TT harmony" reminds the hitter that the chest should remain level. The back and buttocks muscles remain tension free. "As the cat hunts" is a descriptive command that defines the buttocks as the tension release area of the hitter's body. Incorporate the move in all swing work in every drill at every practice.

Create Bat Speed With the Quick Zone System

Three quick zones create bat speed. The first quick zone is between the knees during the stride taken to establish the power base. Constantly monitor the distance between the knees because it is a strong indicator of the distance the bat must travel to make contact with the pitch. The shorter this distance and the more the knees work in harmony, the quicker the bat will arrive at contact and create the desired hitting pattern. A shorter distance between the knees allows the athlete to create greater rotational speed, resulting in more power and better access to the horizontal strike zone.

The second quick zone is the distance between the elbows as the bat moves into the launching area. This zone is not established within the hitter's setup or stance. The setup and stance merely reflect the individual style of hitting. When each hitter makes the move, his bat comes into the launching area. At that point, monitor the distance between the elbows (quick zone two). The more distance between the elbows, the longer the swing. A longer distance often locks out the elbows, creates undesired head movement, and transfers bat control to the back muscles. This causes a loss of centrifugal bat head control, creates a predetermined bat path, and results in a long, strong, but inaccurate swing path. This gives credibility to the coaching command "Get your elbows over your knees before the top hand is released." The coach who understands the proper technique for the second quick zone will be able to define bat speed for his players. Bat speed is how fast the bat head moves forward from the launching area to contact in relation to how far the hands move forward during that process. The instructor hopes to produce hitters whose hands move forward 4 to 6 inches (10.2 to 15.2 cm) as the bat moves from launch to contact. During launch to contact, the bat travels over one-third of the circumference of the swing circle and in as direct a line as possible.

The third quick zone is the distance of the bat head from the point of the back shoulder. The closer the distance, the greater the lag of the bat head. This results in more stored energy and enhances the speed and power of the swing. The greater the distance between the bat head and the point of the back shoulder, the greater the possibility that the hitter will cast or push the bat head away from the body. This results in the loss of centrifugal control and a more circular swing. This action makes it more difficult for the player to square the bat to the oncoming pitch. "Quick zone three" is the coaching command that reminds the hitter to drive the back hand and back elbow into the power slot past the belly button to release the stored energy and maximize the power potential of the hit.

Each player will discover his ideal distances for each quick zone. The coach should develop a series of drills and props that will assist the player in defining his most productive quick zone distances. The range of drills and gimmicks is limited only by the instructor's imagination. Build an adjustable stride box, have the hitter squeeze a tether ball between his knees, or use straps to control the elbows. The quick zone system simplifies coaching commands during batting practice.

Develop Control and Quickness With the Front Muscle System

Does the body swing the bat or does the bat swing the body? What does the coach want his hitters to feel when the bat is released to contact? This coaching decision will identify the central concept that directs the coach in organizing his instructional curriculum for teaching. Three front muscle areas of the body are emphasized to achieve the feeling of the body swinging the bat.

The first area includes the muscles inside and above the kneecap. You can find these muscles by placing a basketball or volleyball between the knees and squeezing inward. This pressure clearly identifies the muscles used to coordinate all knee action and assist the hitter in maintaining the functionality of quick zone one.

The second area of the front muscle system is the lower abdominal area surrounding the belly button. You can find these muscles by contracting the abdomen and grunting.

The pectoral muscles of the chest make up the third area of front muscles. The pectoral on the lead-arm side starts the bat on the correct plane to the hitting area. The pectoral on the back-arm side drives the top hand to the contact area. These pectorals work independently of each other or as a coordinated team, as do the knees. You can find the pectorals by cupping a hand and placing it over the functional breast while doing lead-arm and top-hand soft-toss drills.

The goal of the hitter is to emphasize, feel, and control the front muscles. This allows the hitter to create bat travel independent of the antagonistic action of the strong muscles of the shoulders, back, and buttocks. By doing this, the hitter helps ensure that the bat is delivered on a more linear and less circular path. The front muscles provide a greater kinesthetic feel for where the body is and where the bat is during the swing. These muscles are quicker and more responsive, and they allow the hitter to make more timely decisions regarding whether the pitch is a ball or strike and whether to swing or take. The hitter who gets more information from the pitch in flight can make a better decision on when to commit the bat. The coaching commands during efficient batting practice are "Let the bat travel," "Let your hands work," "Rake it, do not sweep it," and "Relax the three Bs: biceps, back, and buttocks."

Stay in Sequence and Unlock to Maximize Speed

Hitting is the sequential unlocking of body parts from the ground up to maximize bat speed at the point of contact. Energy is collected from the ground, drawn upward through the knees, and forwarded to the front muscles (the abdominal and pectoral muscles). In these muscles, the energy is collected and then directed and delivered in a powerful unleashing of bat head speed. If collection, direction, and delivery are executed with the front muscles, the hitter will maximize the bat speed at the point of contact with the incoming pitch. Sequential unlocking improves bat accuracy, minimizes centrifugal energy loss, decreases bat reaction time, and increases kinetic energy at contact. The coaching commands are "Stay in sequence," "Feel the gears work," and "Fix your transmission" or any reference to first, second, or third gear. Threaten to send a player to the mechanic to have his transmission linkage improved. The coach emphasizes the bat delivery package as the final portion of the hitting sequence.

Deliver the Package

When the player has mastered the move and can replicate it instinctively, the coach can introduce the refinements needed for bat delivery. This package defines the fundamental position that affects bat control, accuracy, and speed. Little is done with the upper body and the lever assembly of the arms and bat until the concepts previously discussed have been practiced to the point of becoming an automatic response—and the hitter trusts them. At this point, the coach must keep in mind the physical individuality of each player as it relates to hand size, arm length, and the player's static ball test scores.

The lever assembly of the upper body includes the grip, the lead-arm control of the starting action of the swing, the launching area, quick zone two, quick zone three, the power slot, power accumulation points, and the top-hand release. The control of all these functions remains the responsibility of the front muscles. Gripping the bat is done with the fingers and not the palms of the hands. A clenched fist decreases wrist action and finger function, resulting in the loss of hand speed, bat speed, and kinetic exit speed of the ball off the bat at contact. The fist action defers muscle control to the large muscles of the forearms and shoulders. This encourages the locking of the functional elbow and reduces the flexibility of the hands.

The launching area is the general zone from the top of the back pectoral reaching to the point of the back shoulder. Have the player point the bat at the pitcher with the arms fully extended. Then have him swing the bat back toward the catching position as fast as he can. This will identify for the coach and the player where his natural launching area is located.

The lead hand starts the bat on a direct plane to the pitch. The bottom three fingers of the lead hand provide the pressure point. It will feel as if the hitter is pulling the knob of the bat to the ball. The top hand passively follows the initial guidance of the lead hand until a swing decision is made. Coaching commands include "Start your hands," "Float load the bat when you start it," and "Melt the hands into the launching area." These actions allow the hitter's elbows to arrive in the launching area over the knees, prepared for the top hand to be released. This technique puts quick zones two and three in proper position. The master power accumulator of the lead arm is the distance that the lead armpit opens or flares upward and away from the rib cage. The master power accumulator of the back arm is the position of quick zone three and the subsequent drive of the back elbow directly to the oncoming pitch.

A player who can execute the move of the lower body and the delivery of the bat package in sequence is ready to perform at the championship level. He will be on his legs with the body stacked vertically, using the front muscles in sequence; the functional quick zones and the body stars will be aligned at the point of contact. The body stars are the knees, belly button, pectorals, and eyes. Aligning these body stars properly will let the hitter perform at his true talent level.

Execute the Game Without Changing Hitting Mechanics

One of the most overlooked and important keys to a hitter executing his responsibilities in game situations is called *rhythm adjustment*. When does the hitter initiate the striding action? When the hitter starts the stride, he is committed to the trained tempo of his swing mechanics. The hitter has trained his swing to be delivered from stride to contact at the same tempo for every pitch. Trying to make adjustments by changing the swing tempo increases the rate of failure. It is difficult to speed up or slow down swing tempo without stalling the bat or losing the sequential unlocking so critical to hitting success. The coach should design a majority of batting drills to define when the hitter is required to start the striding action.

This can be as simple as placing cones at intervals between home plate and the release point of the batting practice pitcher. For example, set cones at 10-foot (3.0 m) intervals with the batting practice pitcher throwing from 40 feet (12.2 m). Have each hitter experiment with starting his stride as the ball is released from the pitcher's hand. Next, have the hitter start the stride as the pitched ball passes the cone at 30 feet (9.1 m) away, 20 feet (6.1 m) away, and 10 feet away.

Rhythm adjustment drills can reveal some remarkable results. The hitter will discover the correct striding rhythm to hit the ball to the opposite field, to execute the hit-and-run, to perform the two-strike swing, and to hit the breaking ball. Hitters often discover that they can be more productive by staying in a breaking ball rhythm for every pitch and reacting to the fastball. Some excellent players at high levels have spent their careers sitting on breaking ball rhythm.

Zone hitting for power is about looking for a type of pitch inside a quadrant of the strike zone. The hitting plan is to cover the P-zone by preplanning the probable location, speed, and type of pitch. Any pitch that arrives without meeting the components is taken, regardless of whether it is a ball or a strike. In some game situations, the hitter will be asked to look for his power pitch early in the count—for example, with two outs and no runners on base.

The coaching commands are "Live in the power zone," "Tighten the rhythm," and "Invite them in and zone it in." The hitter understands that if he allows the pitcher to control his rhythm by throwing pitches of varying speeds, the hitter will often find himself between rhythms throughout the at-bat. Teach the hitter to execute rhythm adjustments. Then have the hitter arrive at the plate with a specific plan of execution for that particular at-bat and that specific pitcher. Rhythm adjustment should be the primary work of the hitter as he prepares in the on-deck position, awaiting the upcoming at-bat. When the coach asks the hitter to execute a situational hitting task through the team signal system, the player will immediately adjust his hitting plan and make a rhythm adjustment as needed.

Commitment to Mastery

Hitting a round ball with a round bat as the ball travels at 90-plus miles per hour is thought to be the most difficult athletic challenge in the world of sports. Teaching another person to meet that challenge is an even more difficult task. Do not be intimidated by difficulty or obstacles in your path toward becoming a great coach. Each obstacle will eliminate the weak coach who does not possess the resolve. The path upward is narrow, and do not expect a crowd when you arrive at the top.

When your critics attack you, do not argue. Continue the work. When your enemies mock you, smile and respond with "You could be correct." Value your enemies because they study what you do more than your friends and they help you identify where you may be weakest. Great work requires a single-minded focus and can result in a lonely journey. Learn to be alone without being lonely. Seek mentors who have traveled the path, and seek their knowledge.

Constantly evaluate your instructional program. Ask other baseball people to scout your practices and games. Ask them to provide you with a candid assessment. Have no fear of change. If you continue to do what you have always done, all you get is what you already got. If you want something different, you must do something different.

Hitting is a complex science that must be studied, dissected, and digested as required by any great intellectual discipline. Carry on and do the work. The regimen will challenge you to become the best you can be, and you will be proud of the effort. Parents and players who want a quick, simple solution to becoming a good hitter need to find a magician and not a teacher.

The end result of your labor and discipline will not always be reflected by the scoreboard. The teacher can hope to control the learning process, but the players play the game. Players win championships, and players can overcome coaching. Talent often prevails over teaching. Carry on, do what you need to do, do it for yourself, and do it now. The scoreboard will always be your judge, but it will not define you. Your products are not wins and losses. Your products are people who go on to be good parents and spouses and who go on to enjoy a successful life because of your mentorship.

chapter 7

Perfecting Positional Play

TIM JAMIESON

Developing the positional player is a long-term investment done daily that will benefit the individual and the team. Having players who have a solid foundation and a high level of confidence in games will help put the team in a better position to win.

We want to develop players who have the ability and background to help us win in a variety of ways. We need players who know how to move base runners with the bat and who are prepared and opportunistic when they are on the bases. We need these same players to have a similar level of contribution in preventing runs from being scored. As coaches, our job in developing these players involves organizing practices in a way that best prepares them for success at game time.

When organizing practices, a coach must consider several factors, including the constraints that are provided by time, weather, and facilities. At the University of Missouri, we have always begun organizing by creating a practice plan and setting goals for the week (figure 7.1).

The plan for the week begins with specifying scrimmage days, lifting days, and off days. After establishing those givens, we begin to fill in around them with what we want to work on in practice, and we prioritize the needs for each day. Having a practice schedule for the week helps keep us on task, making sure that we cover the areas of highest priority. At the end of each practice day, we evaluate the practice to determine if we need to make adjustments throughout the week.

Monday: Off day

Tuesday

    7:00 to 8:00 a.m.: Weights
    3:00 to 5:30 p.m.: Practice
- Baserunning: home to first, turns at second and third
- Outfielder throws
- Pickoffs and rundowns
- Team offense: sacrifice bunts and push bunts
- Bunting competition
- Defense for pitchers, catchers, and infielders
- Positional defense

Wednesday

    3:00 to 6:00 p.m.: Practice
- Baserunning: steal jumps with signs
- Catcher throws and steal defense
- First-and-third defense
- Team offense: hit-and-run, moving the runner
- Hit-and-run, moving the runner competition
- Positional defense

Thursday

    7:00 to 8:00 a.m.: Weights
    3:00 to 5:30 p.m.: Practice
- Baserunning: steal jumps, first-and-third steals
- Team offense: first-and-third offense
- Steals, early-break steals, hit-and-run, push bunts
- First-and-third competition, push bunts, hit-and-run
- Defense for pitchers, catchers, and infielders
- Positional defense

Friday

    2:30 to 6:00 p.m.: Practice
- Nine-inning scrimmage game
- Pregame batting practice, infield and outfield warmup

Saturday

    12:00 to 3:30 p.m.: Practice
- Seven-inning scrimmage game
- Pregame batting practice, relays throws for outfielders, fly-ball priority

Sunday

    12:00 to 4:00 p.m.: Practice
- Nine-inning scrimmage game
- Pregame batting practice, infield and outfield warmup

Figure 7.1 Sample weekly practice plan.

At Mizzou, we have tried to keep our approach as simple as possible in just about every area of the game. This includes designing practices that best develop positional players. We want players to walk away from practice with an increased awareness of how baseball is to be played. We also want them to walk away with more confidence and a sense of fun.

In baseball, as well as in life, many things are outside our control. On our team, we focus on the things that we have a degree of control over. Our players believe that confidence is an area that is within their control, and their belief begins with a simple formula:

Energy plus enthusiasm equals better focus.

Better focus leads to better performance.

Better performance leads to confidence.

The area of this formula that players believe they control is energy and enthusiasm. The players are responsible for coming to practice with energy and enthusiasm. The coaching staff is responsible for ensuring that those attributes stick around for the entire practice. Coaches need to do everything possible to organize practices that provide energy. We need to design practices that create enthusiasm.

Strength, conditioning, and nutrition are important parts of energy, enthusiasm, and performance. One of our goals each year is to be the best-conditioned team in the country. We combine this with education and practice in the area of how players need to fuel their bodies in order to sustain a high energy level. Eating the right foods and staying hydrated go hand in hand with being the best-conditioned team in the country. When to eat, how much to eat, and how often to eat are key components in the consistency and timing of energy. I am a big believer in strength, conditioning, and nutrition and their contributions to the quality and intensity levels of practices. This is another area we can control and is an important part of confidence and success.

The pages that follow detail some things we use in practice to help positional players develop confidence and improve their performance. We develop a foundation for each player through drill work in the areas of swing mechanics, situational hitting, bunting, baserunning, throwing, and positional defense. Some drill work is done daily in most if not all of these areas. We also include some work on one or two areas of team offense and defense. Most days we include some type of competition in conjunction with the specified areas of team offense and defense. The following sections start with an example of a practice schedule along with explanations of the organization and the thoughts behind the schedule. The chapter finishes with examples of ways we get players to compete in practice, which always helps increase energy, enthusiasm, and focus.

Daily Practice Schedule

Based on the weekly planner, we develop the day's practice schedule. The coaching staff meets to discuss what we want to work on and to devise the best way to get it done. When players arrive in the locker room, they find the practice schedule posted. This helps them begin to mentally prepare for what we want to accomplish in the upcoming practice. It helps them visualize the drill work, the necessary energy commitment, the length of practice, and the intended flow of practice. Players begin working on their confidence as they begin preparing for practice.

Figure 7.2 is an example of an early-season practice. The conditioning level of the positional players' arms will dictate how much we can do in each drill. Coaches must carefully manage the amount of throwing that players are required to do during the practice. For early-season practices, we try to do all of

---

Practice Schedule

1:30 p.m. Stretch and throwing

1:45 p.m. Baserunning
- Home to first
- Turns, first to second
- Steal jumps with signs
- Turns, first to third
- Turns, second to home

2:00 p.m. Outfielders live throwing with base runners
- Two throws with runners at home and first
- Two throws with runners at home and second

2:20 p.m. Defense
- Infielders, catchers, pitchers: fielding bunts and slow rollers, holding runners at second, executing pitchouts and intentional walks
- Outfielders

2:45 p.m. Hitting warm-up, sacrifice and push bunts

2:55 p.m. Team offense bunt competition
- Runner at first, sacrifice bunt; base runner earns points for moving 90 feet; payback is a half gasser
- Runners at first and third, push bunt; base runners and hitter earn points if base runners move 90 feet; payback is a half gasser

3:40 p.m. Hitting and defense rotation (five stations)
- Station 1: Nets, warm-up and drill work
- Station 2: Nets, situational rounds
- Station 3: On field, three rounds; round 1, time middle of the field; round 2, advantage count; round 3, situational round
- Station 4: Defense; infielders field fungo hits; catchers practice receiving; outfielders practice live reactions
- Station 5: Defense; infielders field fungo hits with double-play feeds; catcher practice blocking; outfielders practice live reactions

Figure 7.2 Sample early-season practice.

the positional throwing after the players' arms are loose. We want the players to have to get their arms loose only one time.

In this practice, players are also asked to do quite a bit of baserunning during drills. We need to be aware of the number of gamelike repetitions each player gets on the bases. Coaches must manage the amount of work for the players' legs in addition to their arms.

Stretch and Throw

We begin with dynamic stretching. Players run through several plyometric drills (these are drills that the players have been doing since the beginning of practice back in the fall). After the plyometric drills, the players do static stretching before moving on to baserunning drills. When stretching is complete, players loosen up their arms to get ready for drill work. This entire process takes about 15 minutes.

Baserunning

The baserunning portion of practice (figure 7.3) continues the warm-up process and provides some baserunning drills. One of the results that we are looking for is increased energy. Increased blood flow and heart rate are going to help increase focus.

For baserunning, the team divides into two groups. Group 1 runs from home to first. Their first technique is to run through the bag at first after a ball is hit in the infield. Their focus is to touch the front of the base without a lunge, break

Figure 7.3 Baserunning indoors during an early-season practice. The group in the foreground is running from home to first. The group at the back is running from second to third.

down quickly beyond the base, and look to the right for an overthrow. A coach stands 15 feet (4.5 m) beyond first base to indicate a stopping point for the base runner. Players begin 45 feet (13.7 m) from first base to maximize the number of reps touching first base; for more conditioning, we will sometimes have the players run the full 90 feet (27.4 m). Group 1 then works on turns at first base after a ball is hit to left field. A coach stands on the back corner of first base to make sure the base runner touches the inside part of the bag. Again, players start 45 feet from the base. Their focus is to run in a straight line between first and second after touching first. We also want players to accelerate through the base to put pressure on the outfielder. The base runner should run 30 feet (9.1 m) beyond first—toward second—before stopping quickly. We put a cone or a bucket at the 30-feet point as a guide. Group 1 will get two to five repetitions of both running through the base and turning.

Group 2 practices turns at second base when going from first to third on a base hit. They also practice turns at third base when going from second to home on a base hit. For both situations, a third-base coach communicates stop or go to the base runner. The base runner starts 30 feet from second base when going from first to third on a base hit placed behind the base runner. This allows repetitions during which the third-base coach decides whether or not the base runner should advance to third base. The base runner starts with his chest facing the pitcher so that he can also work on his first step in a manner similar to a steal attempt. The runner will be in line between first and second, so he will have to work harder to create the angle on his turn. While practicing his turn, he also works on his timing for picking up the third-base coach. We want the base runner to make eye contact with the third-base coach before touching second base, see his foot touch the inside corner of second base, and then make eye contact again with the third-base coach without slowing down or hesitating. The base runner then reacts to the third-base coach's instruction.

Going from second to home is done using the same focus and techniques as going from first to third. The base runner continues at full speed until he is stopped by the third-base coach. Group 2 gets two to five repetitions of both first to third and second to home. Groups 1 and 2 then switch stations.

After these two stations, we gather at first base as one group to work on offensive signs and steal jumps. Four players at a time practice getting the sign from the third-base coach. Another coach simulates the pitcher. The runners take their initial leads before reacting to the coach's delivery or pickoff attempt. Players are expected to dive back to first on any pickoff attempt. We use this as an opportunity to teach base runners what is expected in various situations using different variables. We also teach the signs during this activity.

The coach simulates both right- and left-handed pitchers. He can perform the pickoff or delivery with or without a slide step. Base runners must react properly whether there is no play, a straight steal, a delayed steal, a first-move steal, a hit-and-run, or something else. The main focus after the sign and initial lead is to get the proper reaction. We can also implement first-and-third situations on various days. The entire baserunning station lasts around 10 minutes or less.

Outfielders Throw With Live Base Runners

Instead of taking a regular pregame infield-outfield, we sometimes divide into two teams, one team of base runners and the other team on defense. This creates more pressure on the defense and forces decision making for both the defense and base runners. When necessary, base runners look to the base coaches. If involved in the drill, pitchers feign a delivery from the stretch. This initiates the base runner's secondary lead and the beginning of the drill repetition. After the ball is put in play, the pitcher backs up the proper base. If pitchers are not available, a coach can feign the delivery to start the base runner. Group 1 starts on defense, and group 2 starts as base runners. All base runners wear helmets.

One coach is at third base, and one coach is at home plate with a fungo bat and a baseball. With outfielders throwing to third base, we begin with two base runners. One base runner starts by sitting on or near home plate; this runner goes from home to first on a base hit. (He starts from a seated position so that he isn't too quick when going from home to first.) The other base runner starts at first base. He takes his secondary lead and then reacts to a fungoed base hit from the coach.

The coach at home plate hits the ball as the pitcher's arm comes forward. The base runners and defensive players react to the ball in play. Base runners are expected to react as if in a game, including sliding when necessary. After completion of the play, the two base runners switch starting points. Each outfielder makes two throws with a runner starting at first base, and then we reset with base runners at home and second base. We repeat the drill with the new situation. When the outfielders in group 1 finish their throws, group 2 moves to defense, and group 1 becomes the base runners.

Experiencing these situations in gamelike conditions helps prepare defensive players, base runners, and the third-base coach for the speed of the game. This entire drill should last 20 minutes or less, depending on how many outfielders you have.

Defense

The team is divided into two groups: The infielders, catchers, and pitchers make up one group; the outfielders make up the second group. This defensive drill lasts about 25 minutes. Outfielders work as a group on a couple of different defensive situations. The outfielders are done throwing for the day, so any drill work should involve little or no throwing.

Pitchers are divided into three groups. One group works with the corner infielders on bunts, slow rollers, comebackers, and third-to-first plays. A coach fungo hits or rolls balls, creating interaction between the pitcher and infielders. The focus is to make the play, but we also want to make sure players communicate properly on each play.

The second group of pitchers works with the middle infielders on holding runners at second base. This includes pickoffs at second and sign communication among the middle infielders and the pitcher.

The third group works with the catchers on pitchouts, intentional walks, and communication using all signs. The pitching groups rotate every eight minutes or so. During this drill, the catchers and infielders get repetitions with each member of the pitching staff. Familiarity will lead to greater confidence.

Hitting Warm-Up

This time is used to get ready for the competition coming up. Players get some swings from the tee, side toss, or front toss as well as some repetitions on sacrifice and push bunts. We want to do a little studying before the test. We want some practice repetitions before the game. Like all of our other warm-ups, we want these to help prepare players mentally and physically for competition.

Bunt Competition

The bunt competition is part of our regular practices. Players enjoy these competitions because kids love to compete. Competing in this format increases their energy and intensity, and as a result, their focus increases as well. The competition also makes the practice drill closer to game speed. In this competition, the pitchers and corner infielders have to quicken their reactions and decision making because the base runners are running full speed from home to first.

The competition must include a scoring system for each play in order to create point totals for each team. Each play is a scoring opportunity. A scoring system creates accountability. With this drill, players are not trying to score runs but to advance the base runner from first to second. The team on offense scores when they successfully advance the runner. The offense can also score by forcing the defense to hurry and make a mistake. The batter feels the pressure, similar to a game situation, because he is accountable for the outcome of his at-bat. The base runner also must make the correct read because he is the one who actually scores the point for the team.

Another key component is having some sort of payback for the losing team. The winning team may reap a reward, but the payback for the losing team is very quick. The payback immediately follows the completion of the competition, and it is more painful to the players' pride than their bodies. Kids love winning and hate losing, but the brief payback serves as an extra incentive for winning or an added reason to avoid losing.

We have two evenly divided teams made up of 10 players each. Team 1 starts on offense, and team 2 on defense. The hitter starts with a one-strike count so he has two strikes to execute the sacrifice bunt. For the team on offense, 5 players start as base runners at first base (wearing helmets), and the other 5 are near home plate to take their turn as bunters. Regardless of the result of the batter's attempt, he sprints from home to first. Even if the result is a strikeout or a pop-up to the catcher, the batter is expected to respond to failure positively with a full-speed 90. After the bunting attempt, the bunter becomes a base runner. After a baserunning attempt, the base runner becomes a bunter. This rotation continues until all 10 offensive players have had one repetition as a bunter and one as a base runner.

On defense, the infielders and catchers on team 2 play their positions, while the outfielders back up each base. One pitcher at a time is on the mound prepared to field his position. A coach or machine will pitch in order to speed up the repetitions. All competitions hold the players' focus and energy better if the activity moves quickly.

The base runner scores the points. He gets 1 point for each 90 feet he advances and is awarded an additional point if the defense overthrows a base. The batter is not the point scorer in the sacrifice bunt competition because his focus is to advance the runner, not try to bunt for a hit. Too many kids in a sacrifice situation focus more on reaching first base and not enough on executing a good enough bunt to move the runner. The offense has 1 point deducted for any double play. After all 10 players get their repetitions, the points scored by team 1 are totaled. Team 2 moves to offense, and team 1 moves to defense.

Team 2's objective on offense is to put up a bigger point total than team 1. The payback for losing this game is a one-half gasser (running the width of a football field over and back), which is executed immediately after the offensive repetitions for team 2. The team scoring the fewest points will do the running. This payback takes about 20 seconds; we try to keep paybacks at a minute or less. Immediately after the payback, we move on to the next situation.

The second situation for the competition is runners at first and third with less than two outs. The players on offense get a repetition as a bunter, as a base runner at third, and as a base runner at first. The batter starts with one strike, or we may choose to give the batter two strikes so he has only one strike to get his job done, creating more pressure on the hitter.

The batter is expected to push the ball to the right side to advance both base runners. The scoring is done by the base runners and the batter. Each base runner scores a point for each base he advances. The batter scores a point if he reaches first base safely. With the bunter's first strike, he tries to bunt for a hit while advancing the base runners. If the first strike goes foul, the focus on the second strike is to move the runners. Extra bases and points are awarded on overthrows. The teams trade sides after each player gets an at-bat and a turn as a base runner at both first and third.

Competitions in practice are as close to game repetitions as we can simulate for both offense and defense. The players want to win. They want to win their at-bat, they want to win on the bases, and they want their team to win. Pressure to win is present during every at-bat. The batter has pressure to win for himself as well as his teammates. He wants to succeed, and he does not want to let down his teammates. Keeping score creates a tangible accountability for each player. The more often each player has to deal with this pressure, the better he learns to handle it.

Hitting and Defense Rotation

Positional players are divided into five groups with one group at each station. Groups rotate from station to station until all five groups have completed all five stations. One group has its first rotation on the field for batting practice. The other four groups get some time in the nets to help prepare for on-field swings. The group starting on the field (station 3) is given some time to warm up before the rotation begins. We don't want any hitters using on-field swings as a warm-up. The warm-up also gives the hitters a better chance to take great swings. By the time all the groups reach the on-field station, hitters should be physically loose and focused for their confidence swings.

We put some thought into how the groups are divided. Early in the year, we make sure that returning players are included in groups with first-year players so the returning players can help prepare the younger guys. They can answer questions and help demonstrate the drills in the nets and on defense. One of the roles of the veterans is to help the younger guys build confidence by taking away some uncertainty and doubt. This also helps all the players get to know each other sooner, helping our chemistry and familiarity.

We try to have no more than three players of any one position in each group. This helps eliminate crowding in the outfield and infield during defensive stations. Catchers can work alone with a coach or two at a time doing defensive drill work. The groups rotate from station 1 to station 2, station 2 to station 3, and so on. Players at station 5 rotate to station 1. The hitting and defensive drill work is complete when all five groups get an opportunity at each station.

Station 1: Warm-Up in the Nets

The first net station is used to warm up for station 2 and station 3 (the on-field hitting station). Each player is encouraged to find his own method of warming up. Players may like to do certain drills, so each player is given the freedom to pick and choose what works best for him. By the time players finish this station, they should be ready to take live swings in a more structured setting. This station can also be used for a player to work on specific areas of his swing mechanics. The player may have been given drills to work on in order to focus on a specific area or two of his swing. These drills can be incorporated into the warm-up.

The four or five guys in this group can pair up and work together, or they can work individually off a tee. If they do pair up, we encourage pairing a returning player with a first-year player. The veteran can serve as an instructor to help the first-year player learn the process or learn a drill that he is working on.

Station 2: Situational Rounds in the Nets

In station 2, hitters are physically loose and ready for a little more structure. This station may include more drill work, machine pitch, coach pitch, or front toss, depending on the availability of a coach or pitching machine as well as the focus for this station on that particular day. Because the nature of this station is instructional, we include a coach. We want the players to know what is expected in the various game situations. Players spend time on their prepitch approach, focusing before each pitch or swing. They spend time making necessary swing adjustments for various situations. They also work on learning to make timing adjustments. This station is not about how many repetitions as much as it is about doing them right.

Although various game situations can be developed and used in station 2, here are some that we work on consistently because they are important to our team's offensive approach:

- **Two-strike approach.** We use timing adjustment drills, emphasizing the physical approach and the approach on the middle-in fastball, wearing a pitch inside off the plate. This usually includes coach-pitched or front-toss drills.

- **Advantage count.** In these timing adjustment drills, the emphasis is placed on the hitter sitting on a particular velocity in a specific location and taking pitches that are outside those parameters. In a hitter's count, good hitters swing at pitches they can hit, and they take the ones they can't hit. We define an advantage count as a count and a situation in which the hitter can take a strike if the pitch is something he is not prepared for. We will use coach-pitched, front-toss, and machine-pitched drills for this situation.

- **Hit-and-run.** The hitter must swing unless the pitch is in the dirt. The main emphasis is to hit the ball on the ground and to maintain the swing, placing greater focus on the top of the ball. Timing adjustments are important, but hitting the ball on the ground is the main focus. Coach-pitched and machine-pitched drills are the two types we use the most.

- **Advance runner from second base, no outs.** Bunting is an option in this situation, but we want to enable hitters to swing to move the runner to third base. We emphasize hitting a ground ball to the right side. Hitters work on timing adjustments, and they learn that they cannot wait for a perfect pitch. If the pitch is a strike, they need to get the ground ball to the right side. We generally use coach-pitched and machine-pitched drills to practice this situation.

- **RBI situation.** In drills, we usually work on RBI situations with less than two outs. The situations we use the most are runner at third with the infield in, runner at third with the infield back, and bases loaded. The prepitch focus is the most important thing, whether the hitter is trying to put the ball in play on every strike or trying to get a pitch that he can square up on the barrel and hit hard. These repetitions help improve and simplify the thought process of the hitter before the pitch is thrown. Like most of the previous situations, you can use a variety of ways to deliver the ball to the hitter.

With these situations as well as others, the primary goal is quality over quantity. The positional player gains confidence because he knows how to direct his focus in each situation. Confidence increases as the hitter has a higher success rate with his swings. Focus and mental preparation go further in determining the success of each repetition than simply having mass quantities of swings.

Ultimately, situational hitting comes down to seeing and reacting to the ball and being good enough to get the task done. We want to limit the amount of thinking the hitter does during the pitcher's delivery. However, the hitter must have a plan in place before he steps into the batter's box, and he must have a plan in place before each pitch. The confidence of our hitters increases because we give them a plan, an approach, and the repetitions in practice that help them gain experience before they have to get the job done in a game. By experiencing the thought process before the pitch and by executing the proper swings, the hitter becomes more relaxed and confident when he faces these situations in a game.

Station 3: On-Field Hitting

Stations 1 and 2 have prepared players to take good and aggressive swings on the field with a coach throwing batting practice. Players enjoy this station the most, and they see it as a reward for the work done in the previous stations. We try to keep rounds short (four or five swings) and stay away from the "one mores." If the hitter knows he has a mulligan on the last swing, his focus is not as sharp as it is when he knows this is really his last swing. The coach throwing batting practice may tell the hitter to take one more, but that is the coach's decision.

The focus of on-field work can be in a variety of areas, but we usually give players the freedom to swing aggressively at good pitches. For the first round, we ask hitters to focus on hitting up the middle and not being pull happy. After the first round, the hitters are in a better rhythm with the batting practice pitcher. After the first round, the focus usually becomes swinging at pitches that the hitter can drive, focusing on the top half of the baseball (staying away from fly balls), and taking an aggressive swing while staying behind the ball. We want hitters to take a loud batting practice, meaning that a large number of balls are squared up on the sweet spot. Like everything else we do in practice, we want players to learn and to move on to the next drill with a sense of accomplishment.

Stations 4 and 5: Defense

In this practice schedule, defensive work is done in back-to-back rotations. The infield and outfield are occupied with players who are working on defense, but because of the grouping, neither location will be overcrowded. Catchers have their own area and will work individually or with a partner. It's virtually impossible for the coaching staff to pay attention to all of these players, so the players must know what is expected and must understand any drill work that is to be done. Any drill work done during a practice like this one will have been done with the coaches at previous practices. Again, it is helpful to have veteran players to help guide the younger guys. We group the players to allow for this, but the experienced players must embrace this role on behalf of the team.

We have a minimum of two pitchers hitting fungoes to the infielders at their positions. During the first defensive station, the infielders field ground balls either live off the bat or from a fungo. During the second defensive station, they take ground balls and make double-play feeds. At least two infielders will be included during each rotation so they can take turns covering second base and receiving the throw from the other infielder.

During the defensive rotations for outfielders, the focus will be on reactions and reads from balls off the bat. This cannot be simulated with a fungo, and players do not get enough repetitions during a game to develop the instincts necessary to play the outfield at a high level. We do multiple drills every day in practice, but the benefit of practicing live reactions is immeasurable.

Be sure to keep anyone shagging balls (usually the pitchers) out of the way of the outfielder who is going after a ball that has been put in play. The outfielder should prepare before the ball is pitched and then react to a ball hit to his area, whether it is hit in the air, on a line, or on the ground. He may not be able to go after every ball hit in his area, but he should react when he has time to set up before the pitch. Outfielders need to communicate with other outfielders using the same rhetoric that will be used in games. We love to see outfielders laying out for balls, communicating, and getting behind routine fly balls. As coaches, we need to sell the value of this practice time for the outfielders, let them know we are watching, and let them have fun learning how to attack a ball hit in their direction.

With so much going on during this rotation, it may be difficult to have a coach available to work with the catchers during their defensive time. When we do not have a coach available, catchers work in groups of two or all together so they can drill each other. The catchers will have knowledge of the drills that are to be done, and they can be entrusted to do the drills together.

The two areas that catchers work on daily are receiving and blocking. For either skill, a pitching machine can be used, making it easier for the catchers to be without a coach. To work on receiving, we isolate an area of the strike zone, and catchers practice catching the baseball properly. The catcher sets up so that the ball is coming in at the proper angle. Instead of adjusting the machine to throw to different locations, it is much easier to reposition the catcher. One round may consist of 20 to 30 balls, depending on the number of catchers, the time allotted, and the number of different locations to work on. We may also put different spins on the pitches to give the catcher the opportunity to work on pitches with movement.

Blocking drills can be done the same way with the machine. We set the machine to throw fastballs or right- or left-handed breaking balls. We want some pitches right at the catcher, and we also want to make the catcher move to his left and to his right. Again, it is much easier to reposition the catcher when he begins to work on moving right and left.

For both blocking and receiving drills, a machine is not necessary. Plenty of other drills can be used to work on blocking and receiving fundamentals. Other areas of defensive work for the catchers can include plays at the plate, bunts, fly balls, pitchouts, intentional walks, and throwing drills that work on the footwork and exchange during a throw to second or third.

During the defensive rotations, each position has two 15- to 20-minute opportunities. We also refer back to our weekly planner and set up the drills that we want to do on that day based on what we will be doing the rest of the week. We may adjust the drills for individuals based on their needs in specific areas. We may put extra emphasis on things that happened in live play. We have planned for the entire week and have set goals for what we want to accomplish; however, we need to remain flexible and adjust if necessary to help the positional players.

Practice Competitions

Earlier in this chapter, I described a bunt competition that we use during practice. This section describes other types of competitions that can be used to increase the intensity of drills so they are closer to game intensity. We can turn just about any situation into some sort of competition. Some of the competitions require a foundation of drill work and explanation before the players jump in to the actual competition. Some of the competitions can be done the first day of practice. A learning curve and some growing pains may be involved with all the competitions, but once the players get the knack, you will see immediate results. Table 7.1 summarizes the practice competitions described in this section.

When setting up each competition, you need to come up with a scoring system that emphasizes the successful execution of the situation. For our competitions, we also select an appropriate payback for the losing side. We use a plethora of different paybacks, mixing them so we do not use the same payback all the time. Paybacks differ in terms of difficulty, but they will take about the same amount of time to perform. We created a list of potential paybacks that we use, from postpractice tarp duty to runs up a hill called "the summit" (which is located south of our baseball field). Usually, we use one- or two-minute exercises that don't tax the players' throwing arms—something that players will feel but will not affect their performance in the rest of practice. Losers of intrasquad games or practice competitions have to do the paybacks. Paybacks for losing intrasquad games are usually a little more intense, such as triangles or summits; the quantity is based on the score differential.

Hit-and-Run

The first competition is the hit-and-run with a base runner at first (figure 7.4). A successful execution of the hit-and-run is defined as advancing the base runner at least one base. The offense gets 1 point for each base the base runner advances. The base runner knows his responsibility—break to second base when he knows the ball will be delivered to the plate, track the ball after the third stride, and react to the ball when it is put in play. Ideally, we would love for the runner to go from first to third or even score, but we consider it successful if he moves at least to second base.

Table 7.1 Practice Competitions

Title	Description	Goals	Scoring
Hit-and-run	This is a coach-pitched or machine-pitched game. Defense vacates opposite side. Hitter swings until ball is put in play or until he swings and misses.	Live baserunning Live hitting Team defense	Base runner and batter earn 1 point for each base they advance. A point is subtracted if the hitter hits into a double play.
Bunt or hit-and-run: first-and-third offense	This is a coach-pitched game. Hitter starts with one strike. Hitter gets sign from third-base coach.	Push bunt, hit-and-run, squeeze play Live baserunning Live hitting Team defense	Base runners and batter earn 1 point for each base they advance. A point is subtracted if the hitter hits into a double play.
Live-pitch situations, part I	Pitcher and hitter are on same team. These situations are included: sacrifice bunt with runner at first; push bunt with runners at first and third; runner at second, zero outs.	Live pitching Pitcher's mound work between games (four or five batters or pitch count)	Base runners and batter earn 1 point for each base they advance. A point is subtracted if the hitter hits into a double play. Defensive team earns bonus points for a wild pitch or passed ball.
Live-pitch situations, part II	Pitcher and hitter are on opposite teams. These situations are included: bases loaded, less than two outs; runner at third with one out, infield in; runner at third with two outs; runners at second and third with less than two outs.	Pitchers learning to pitch in these situations Instilling philosophy and approach at the plate Pitcher's mound work between games (four or five batters or pitch count)	Runs scored. A point is subtracted if the hitter hits into a double play. Offensive team earns bonus points for a wild pitch or passed ball.
Batting practice	This is a coach-pitched or front-toss game. Players compete with other groups. Each hitter is responsible for the team's success. Each player gets four or five repetitions per round.	Sacrifice bunt Advancing a runner Hit-and-run RBI	Batter earns 1 point for each successful attempt as defined by the coach.
Cutoff and relay drills	Players are divided into two teams. Each team makes the same total number of throws.	Playing catch with the cutoff man Communication Gamelike pressure	The team with the fewest points wins. Points are given when the ball hits the ground or when there is an overthrow.
Rundowns	Players are divided into four or more teams to work on rundowns.	Defensive goal is to minimize the number of throws. Offensive goal is to force bad throws.	Base runner earns points for total time spent in pickle and total number of throws. Bonus points are given for reaching base safely.
Bunt defense	This is a machine-pitched game. Bases are set at 75 feet (22.8 m). Hitters start with one strike.	Speeding up the game on defense Defensive decision making	Defense earns 1 point for an out, 2 points for a lead out, and 3 points for a double play.
Four corners	Infielders and catchers are at the four bases.	Throwing quickness and accuracy Playing catch Conditioning of throwing arm	Throws continue for one minute. Players earn 1 point for each throw. Overthrows are returned to the base before the next throw. Players receiving throws must step on the base or home plate before throwing.

Figure 7.4 Hit-and-run indoors: *(a)* competition setup; *(b)* runner at first runs with the pitch on the way.

The batter also knows his responsibility—swing unless the ball is in the dirt, focus on the top half of the ball, and hit a ground ball. Ideally, the batter times the pitch correctly to hit it through the vacated hole on the opposite side of the field. The batter scores a point when he reaches base as a result of putting the ball in play or an error by the defense. He earns 1 point for each base he reaches.

A hole is created on the opposite side of the infield before the ball is pitched. For a right-handed batter, the second baseman starts on second base. For a left-handed batter, the shortstop starts on second base, opening the opposite side of the infield for the batter to use.

Double plays result in a 1-point deduction from the offense. A ground ball turned into a double play, a line drive or fly ball caught so the base runner is doubled up, or a swing and miss all count as a double play.

A coach pitches from behind an L-screen. A pitcher stands beside the coach, ready to react to the ball put in play. The team is split into two teams—nine players on offense and nine players on defense. Each offensive player gets one repetition hitting and one repetition as a base runner before we trade sides. The pitching staff is included on defense, divided between the teams. Here is an example of an inning of hit-and-run:

- **First batter, right handed.** The pitch is made. The batter hits a ground ball through the hole on the right side. The play stops with the base runner at third base and the batter at first. The offense earns 3 points—2 points for the base runner going from first to third and 1 point for the batter reaching first.

- **Second batter, left handed.** The pitch is made. The batter hits a line drive at the second baseman. The base runner is doubled up. A point is deducted for the double play.

- **Third batter, left handed.** The pitch is made. The batter hits a ground ball to the third baseman, who throws the ball away. The base runner ends up at third base. The batter, hustling all the way, winds up at second base. The base runner and batter each score 2 points for a total of 4 points.

- **Fourth batter, right handed.** The pitch is made. The batter hits a line drive down the right-field line. The play stops with the base runner scoring and the batter at second base with a double. The base runner gets 3 points for three bases, and the hitter gets 2 points for two bases (for a total of 5 points).

All nine batters hit before the teams trade sides. After the inning, the points are totaled to come up with a grand total. For the first four batters in this example, the point total is 11. Both teams know the score and make sure they know the running total as the second team is taking its turn on offense. After both teams complete their turns on offense, everyone gathers in the middle of the diamond. The losing team does the payback, and then we discuss coaching points for what may have occurred. After the payback, we move on to the next inning or game situation and begin a new competition. In the event of a tie, we carry over the points to the next inning, and the losing team has to double up on the payback. Or we may use some type of tiebreaker, such as a sign quiz, a baseball trivia question, or even rock-paper-scissors.

Bunt or Hit-and-Run: First-and-Third Offense

This is a continuation of the previous inning in the competition but with a different situation—runners at first and third with less than two outs. The main difference in this inning is that the defense doesn't know what the offense will do. A third-base coach gives signs for a push bunt (safety squeeze) or the hit-and-run. If we use the same set of signs for both teams, we ask the defense to turn their backs while the sign is given to the batter and the base runners. We may also use different signs for each team. The batter starts with one strike; therefore, in the case of a bunt, he has two strikes to get it done.

For the push bunt play, success is defined as advancing both base runners. The hitter wants to bunt the ball in a manner that takes the pitcher toward first base, allowing the runner at third to score. The runner at third is instructed to take an aggressive secondary lead and read the bunt. We want him to be aggressive with his secondary lead to ensure a better chance of scoring. The base runner at first treats the bunt like a sacrifice. Ideally, we would like the batter to bunt well enough to give himself a chance of reaching first base. The scoring system is the same as in the first inning (the hit-and-run competition)—both the batter and the base runners earn 1 point for each base. Here is an example of an inning:

- **First batter.** The pitch is made. The hitter pushes a bunt away from the pitcher, allowing each base runner to advance 90 feet. The batter is thrown out at first. The base runners earn a total of 2 points, 1 point for each base.

- **Second batter.** The pitch is made. The hit-and-run is on. The batter grounds into a 1-6-3 double play. The runner at third base scores. If we are playing with zero outs, the base runner who scored earns 1 point for advancing one base. If we are playing with one out, 1 point is deducted because a double play would have ended an inning.

- **Third batter.** The pitch is made. The hitter pushes the bunt past the pitcher. The first baseman fields the ball and throws it away with the pitcher covering first. The base runner at third scores, the base runner at first goes all the way to third, and the batter advances to second base on the error. The base runner at third earns 1 point, the base runner at first earns 2 points, and the batter earns 2 points, for a total of 5 points.

Each offensive player gets repetitions as the batter and as a base runner at both first and third. Then the points are totaled and the teams trade sides. At the conclusion of the inning, we meet in the middle, discuss any coaching points, and have the nonwinners complete their payback.

These innings move quickly. Sometimes we go through six or seven different situations in a little more than an hour. Sometimes we have time for only one inning, but we want to finish practice with a competition. At times we use the same situation for two or three straight innings to get more work on that one situation. The combinations, as well as the possible situations, can be endless, but we prioritize the areas of need and devote the majority of our time in that direction.

Live-Pitch Situations and Batting Practice

During live-pitch situations, the batter has a gamelike at-bat. When the ball is put in play, the defensive players, base runners, and batter react as they would in a live situation.

For batting practice, each batter gets a certain number of swings. To keep the focus on hitting, there are no gamelike reactions during batting practice, just swinging.

Cutoff and Relay Drills

Defensive competitions emphasize the fundamentals of playing catch, communicating, and making plays when time is a factor. Players also condition their arms. Unlike the offensive examples previously described, in the defensive competitions, points are scored by the defense. Two of the defensive examples use a clock, creating a greater urgency and putting the emphasis on quickness.

Outfielders and infielders intensify their focus during outfield throwing drills. We use this competition to practice situations in which the outfielder makes a throw to a single cutoff man on a base hit or sacrifice fly. We also use it to practice the relay after the batter hits a sure double and the outfielder makes a throw with two infielders used as the relay. We usually do not use base runners during this competition; the simple focus is playing catch and communicating. The team is split into two even teams. Each team gets a turn on defense, making throws to the designated bases. The defense is trying to avoid scoring points because the team with the fewest points wins. In a perfect cutoff situation, the outfielder makes a throw that is caught by the cutoff man, the cutoff man then throws to the appropriate base, and the defensive player at the base also catches the ball. The ball cannot touch the ground. If the ball lands short of the target, the team is given 1 point; if the ball is overthrown, the team is given 2 points. Each outfielder makes the same number of throws to the same bases.

For the cutoff drill, a coach hits a fungo to the outfielder. The outfielder throws to the cutoff man, who then throws to second. On the next hit, the outfielder throws to the cutoff man, who then throws to third. And on the next hit, the cutoff man throws to home. Each outfielder throws twice for plays to each base, for a total of six throws. All throws from the outfielder are handled by the cutoff man, who then throws to the intended base. Infielders and catchers play their positions and are involved just as they would be in an actual game. After the first team completes all their throws, they total their points (zero is the perfect score). The other team gets the same number of throws and then totals their score. The team with the most points has to do a payback in the center of the diamond after any instruction.

Next, we work on relays after sure doubles. Each outfielder will participate in three relays to third base and three relays home. A coach hits a fungo to the wall. The outfielder will need to make a longer throw to one of two infielders who are working together as a relay team. They must communicate regarding who will receive the throw. That player will catch the throw from the outfielder and then throw it to the appropriate base. The ball cannot touch the ground. If the outfielder throws the ball and it lands between the two infielders (showing a lack of communication between the infielders), the defense is given 1 point. If the ball is then picked up by the infielder and he throws a short hop to the third baseman, another point is given for a total of 2 points.

We limit the total number of throws in each practice, depending on where the players are in their conditioning. We may also combine the two drills so the outfielders make three cutoff throws and three throws from the wall. This drill is pretty stressful on the arms of both outfielders and infielders, so we rarely do it more than three times in a week.

Rundowns

This tough drill usually gets the players excited. As younger kids, we all enjoyed having a base runner in a pickle. This competition is used during practice, but we have also used it at camps with younger players. It is often the highlight of the day at practice or camp. This is the one drill that showed me that creating a competition can turn the simplest drill into a must-win situation. Kids love to compete, even in rundowns.

We include all players in this drill, even the outfielders. The players are divided into teams of six. Two teams compete against each other at a time. For example, if we have six teams total, three different competitions will go on at the same time, or we can do one at a time. One team is on defense. The other team is on offense, serving as base runners. On defense, three players are in a line at one base, and the other three are at the other base. One defensive player has the baseball. The base runner starts 5 yards (4.6 m) from the player with the baseball. The rundown begins when the player with the ball runs toward the base runner. The base runner continues to run until he is tagged out or reaches base. The defensive goal is to complete the rundown by getting an out as quickly as possible.

A coach begins a stopwatch as soon as the rundown begins. He stops the watch when the base runner is tagged out or reaches a base. If the base runner reaches base, he gets to run again, thus increasing the total time. An overthrow by a defensive player results in a five-second runoff, adding more time to the total. All six offensive players get a turn until each player is tagged out. The defensive team accumulates a total time, then the teams switch. The team with the lowest accumulated time wins.

To determine the overall winner, the two teams with the lowest total times compete against each other. The five teams that do not win do some sort of payback. This is the best way that I have found to get the base runners to run hard in a rundown drill. No one wants to lose.

Bunt Defense

The team on defense makes gamelike reactions to the bunted ball. Batters and base runners also make live reactions.

Four Corners

This competition is for infielders and catchers. These positional players are split into two teams. Each team competes against the clock. Players stand at all four bases. The goal is to throw the ball around the horn as quickly as possible, completing as many throws as possible in a designated amount of time (usually one minute). We run the drill twice, once clockwise and then once counterclockwise. The infielder or catcher receiving the throw must make contact with his base before he throws to the next base. If there is an overthrow, the ball must come back to the overthrown base before it goes to the next base. The stopwatch begins with the first throw. The team that makes the most throws in the designated time is the winner and gets to enjoy watching the other team do a payback.

Developing a positional player is a daily process. During the season and off-season, coaches will have to adjust to the ups and downs. We try to create a foundation for the team as well as for each individual, and we go back to that foundation during difficult times. We keep the players' thoughts as simple and direct as possible while giving them a large menu to work from. The most important ingredient in the development of the individual player is the player's passion for becoming his best. We need guys who love to compete and want to get better. Along the way, we all want to enjoy the game. At the end of the day, we want our players to be excited about tomorrow's practice.

chapter 8

Fine-Tuning Team Fielding

STEVE JAKSA

Every coach talks about the importance of pitching and defense to the success of his team over the course of a season. We all realize that good pitching can keep a good hitting team in check and that we need to focus on trying to keep other teams from scoring.

To fine-tune defensive fielding, your team also needs to spend a considerable amount of time on the individual aspects of fielding. I believe in developing individual players progressively. First, a player needs to be able to field a ground ball and throw it to another player, usually to get an out (for example, a 5-3, 6-3, or 4-3 ground ball). This is a basic skill of all defense, but it still requires sound execution for defensive success. Remember, nothing is routine until you get an out; do not take any play for granted.

Next, players advance to finishing a standard double play with three people involved (4-6-3, 6-4-3, 5-4-3, or 3-6-1). These examples demonstrate the need to develop the individual fielder and then add additional fielders to the sequence.

The drills in this chapter allow each player to improve his individual defensive skills while recognizing the need to progress to working with other fielders—which ultimately allows you, the coach, to fine-tune your team's fielding. Fielding is a daily fundamental. As this chapter shows, many drills help build team defense. However, daily individual work needs to be done to refine individual fielding skills.

107

Establish fielding expectations for your players and your program. These expectations are the heart and soul of your team. Your players have to believe in you and in each other.

Infield Fielding

The following guidelines enhance individual fielding skills; however, you should keep searching for new ideas to keep your program top-notch.

Guidelines for Infielders

- Take read steps with each pitch. This enables you to get a good jump on a ground ball by creating some momentum.
- Extend your hands out to get a ground ball. Try to put your glove at a 45-degree angle and cover the ball with your throwing hand. It is better to flick your fingers up. Do not flip your glove up.
- Remember that those watching you field should be able to see the ball disappear into your glove. Emphasize keeping your head down and your hands out.
- After fielding a ball, work to get your feet in throwing position and get through the ball as you field it. Point the shoulder of your glove side to the target.
- When warming up, catch the ball with two hands (except for first basemen). Catch each ball in front of your chest. This forces you to move your body if the throw is off line. Work to catch the ball with two hands.
- When throwing the ball, always throw to a spot. Work on being accurate with every ball you throw.

We practice infield play during pregame warm-ups. In addition to taking ground balls and making throws to bases, we emphasize catching and tagging during pregame infield. During a game, if a ball tips off an infielder's mitt, this could cost a run, an out, or a chance to keep the opponent out of scoring position. Practicing this situation during pregame infield forces players to recognize the importance of securing the ball; after a while, securing the ball becomes a good habit.

Between innings, infielders throw to each other. This is an opportunity to work on accuracy when throwing the ball to first base, and it keeps arms loose every inning. When we are on defense, players throw to first base before every inning. The more players do it, the more accurate they become.

We have specific rules for where players line up between innings. The third baseman is on the foul line, 15 to 20 feet (4.5 to 6.1 m) behind third base. The shortstop is deep in the hole, near the outfield grass. The second baseman is near the grass on the shortstop side of the infield on a straight line through first and second base.

Keep your rules for fielding easy to understand. Some rules are constant for all infielders:

- Middle infielders fake turning two on fly balls and pop-ups in order to mislead the runner on the location of the ball.
- Infielders arm fake when there is no play and multiple runners are on base. A runner often rounds a base, and an alert infielder might be able to back pick him.
- Infielders turn and run on all pop-ups over their heads. They do not backpedal.
- On slow rollers, infielders are quick and sprint to the ball, swinging their arms. Then they quiet down on the last two steps and scoop up the ball with the glove.

One of the most exciting plays for infielders, especially middle infielders, is turning a double play. When turning a double play, infielders have many options in terms of footwork. An infielder should have a standard way to turn two. Early on, the coach should determine the best pivot and should make that a priority.

When the ball is hit to the shortstop, the second baseman should arc to the base, keeping his shoulders square to the shortstop. He comes across the base, touches the base with his left foot, and steps forward with his right foot toward third base. He then plants on his right foot, turns, and throws to first base. The second baseman will end up on the third-base side of second base. This is the best pivot. Another pivoting option is to straddle the base, receive the ball, and rock to create momentum for the throw to first. The second baseman will touch second base with the inside part of his foot and will be ready to throw to first.

The shortstop has a couple of pivot options. The option he uses will depend on whether the ball comes from the second baseman or the first baseman. If the feed is from the second baseman, the shortstop goes to the middle of the base on the right center-field side. When the throw comes from the first baseman, the shortstop gets inside and puts his left foot on the base. He must keep his left shoulder closed so he can make a quick and accurate throw to first base.

When catching the ball, both the shortstop and second baseman must catch the ball with their fingers up, keeping their palms in. This makes it easier to handle a low throw. Catching the ball closer to the chest while staying compact allows for a quicker exchange.

When making the feed, the infielder's chest is open to the base and comes up a little as he pivots. He must not feed the ball with a straight overhand throw because this makes the ball go down.

For the third baseman, turning a 5-4-3 double play is important, but his ability to field slow rollers and bunts may be even more important. Many games can be changed through the use of the small-ball concept. On slow rollers, the third baseman takes one step toward the third-base line; this helps line up the throw to first. He fields the ball off his left foot, then switches to his right foot and throws off his right foot. The throw will be similar to an underhand throw. The third baseman should practice this technique while using a glove and also with a bare hand.

The only time we discourage the backhand play (at the expense of fighting to get in front of the ball) is when a base runner at second base would score if the ball goes into the outfield. For the backhand play, the fielder carries his glove low as he approaches the ball. His knees are bent as he extends his glove so that the upper part of the body does not hinder the full extension of the arms. It's better to field the ball with the left foot out, well bent at the knee. This enables the infielder making the backhand play to field the ball with the left foot forward and take a bracing step with the right foot in order to throw the ball to the proper base. This is not mandatory in all situations for all fielders. The glove must be extended well out in front of the left foot; the elbow is slightly bent and also in front of the body. This enables the infielder to see the ball into the glove. The good backhander times his approach to the ball so that his glove hand is out and away from the forward foot. Once he fields the ball with the left foot forward, he takes a small step with the right foot to brace for the throw to first or second base. As the right foot hits the ground and the weight transfers to that leg, the infielder bends his knees. The right leg should be under the right shoulder.

Team Defense

Now that we have covered some basics of individual defense, I want to focus on team defense. Coaches must recognize the importance of individual defensive skills, but they also need to develop the concept of team defense. During practice, the work on team defense needs to be as gamelike as possible. A number of situations may develop during a game, and fielding may also be affected by the score or the inning.

Team Drills

We have six series of team drills that focus on total team defense and communication for all players. A total of 17 drills make up the six series. When we practice team defense, we use one series each practice (we do the six series in sequence).

The team series are done at the beginning of practice after stretching and warm-up. The quick-paced team drills set the tone for practice and involve everyone, including coaches, players, and managers. Someone is in charge of keeping time because each drill is run for 4 1/2 minutes with 30 seconds between drills for explaining the next drill in the series. Any players who play multiple positions will move at the 2-minute, 15-second mark so they can benefit from each segment of the drill. Communication is emphasized. Players must talk, be loud, and take charge.

As mentioned, we do one series per day. Therefore, each week we go through all six series of team defense drills. Once we start playing games, the amount of practice time is reduced. As the coach, I determine which series to do during practices based on the results seen during actual games. We perform these drills throughout the entire season.

FUNDAMENTAL 1

Setup
5-minute stations; catchers at home plate, infielders at the four positions in the infield, pitchers in left field, outfielders and a coach in right field (figure 8.1).

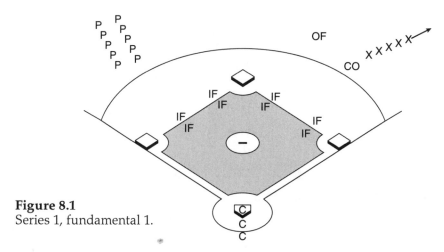

Figure 8.1
Series 1, fundamental 1.

Infielders and Catchers
Infielders and catchers work on force plays at home plate. With the infield in, the infielders field ground balls (coach fungos) and throw home to the catchers for a force play. Catchers then throw the ball to first base for a double play. For the last 2 minutes, the infielders move to halfway, and the catcher performs a tag at the plate.

Pitchers
Pitchers field ground balls in left field. Pitchers throw balls to partners from 60 feet (18.3 m). For the first 2 minutes, the pitcher fielding the ground ball steps and fakes a throw to an imaginary first baseman. For the last 2 minutes, the pitcher fields, steps, and fakes a throw to an imaginary second or third baseman.

Outfielders
Outfielders work on fence communication in right field. One outfielder stands in right center field, yelling distance and fence at the proper time. Other outfielders line up as right fielders and break for the fence to field fly balls.

Setup

5-minute stations; catchers at home plate, infielders at positions in the infield, pitchers with a coach in left field, outfielders with a coach in right field (figure 8.2).

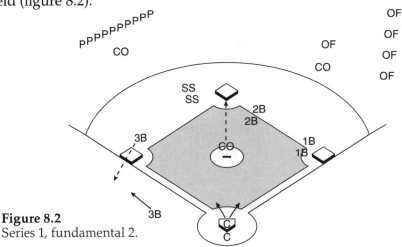

Figure 8.2
Series 1, fundamental 2.

Catchers and First Basemen

Catchers field bunted balls and throw to the first basemen. A catcher throws out the bunted ball and yells inside. First basemen come from different depths to cover the base, yelling inside. For the last 2 minutes, the first basemen make a return throw to the catcher for a tag play.

Shortstops and Second Basemen

Shortstops and second basemen work on communicating on ground balls over the base. A coach hits from in front of the pitcher's mound. The shortstops and second basemen cheat slightly. No throwing to first base is done.

Third Basemen

Third basemen field fly balls at the dugout and the fence. The third basemen throw to each other.

Pitchers

Pitchers form a straight line in left field. The pitcher reacts to a quick steal by stepping back, looking the runner back to third base, and then turning and throwing to middle infielders who call the ball right away. The coach calls out what the runner at third base is doing. The pitcher reacts to the situation and backs up home on the first-base side.

Outfielders

Outfielders work on going back on fly balls in right center field. They can throw to each other, or a coach can throw. The outfielder must get in proper position to catch the ball with his throwing-arm side to the base.

FUNDAMENTAL 3

Setup

5-minute stations; catchers at home plate, infielders at positions in the infield, outfielders in positions in the outfield, pitchers with a coach at the pitcher's mound (figure 8.3).

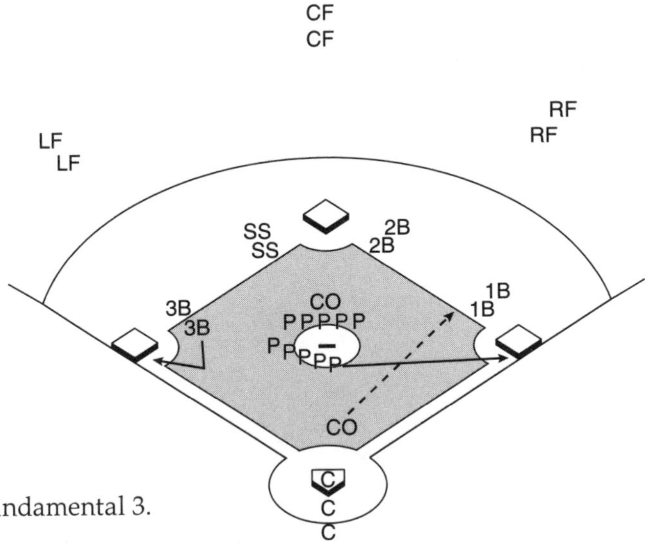

Figure 8.3
Series 1, fundamental 3.

Pitchers and First Basemen

Pitchers and first basemen work on 3-to-1 ground balls. A coach fungo hits from in front of home plate. The pitcher delivers to home plate and then takes a straight line to first base to cover. For the last 2 minutes, the players work on drag bunts with the first basemen holding a runner on.

Catchers and Third Basemen

Catchers field bunted balls on the third-base side and throw to third base. Third basemen charge and then go back to third base. A catcher or coach throws the bunted ball. For 2 minutes, players work on bunt defense with a runner on second base; then they work on tags. Players should focus on being more aggressive.

Shortstops, Second Basemen, and Outfielders

Shortstops, second basemen, and outfielders practice communication on fly balls. A coach throws fly balls from behind the pitcher's mound.

FUNDAMENTAL 4

Setup

5-minute stations; catchers at home plate, pitchers on the pitcher's mound, infielders in the infield positions, outfielders with a coach in center field (figure 8.4).

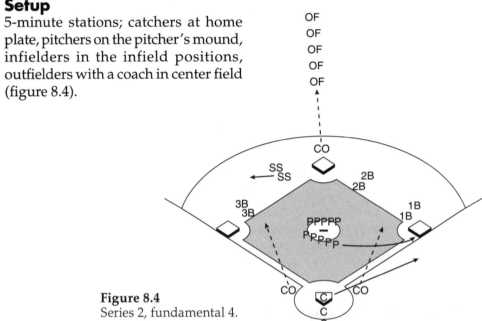

Figure 8.4
Series 2, fundamental 4.

Pitchers, First Basemen, Second Basemen, and Catchers

These players practice communication on ground balls hit to the right side of the infield. The catcher backs up the play at first base, yelling to the pitcher to get over. A coach fungo hits to the first-base side. The pitcher throws to home plate and then takes a straight line to first base to cover. First and second basemen play deep.

Shortstops and Third Basemen

Shortstops and third basemen practice communication on ground balls when a runner is forced from second base and the shortstop fields a ball to the right (6-5). If the third baseman fields the ball, he fakes a 5-4-3 double play. For the last 2 minutes, there is an imaginary runner on second. The fielders then work on tags at third base and 5-3 plays. A coach fungo hits from the third-base side of home plate.

Outfielders

Outfielders charge ground balls from deep center field and make a play in the infield. A manager is in a cutoff position behind second base. A coach fungo hits from second base.

Setup

5-minute stations; catchers at home plate, infielders in position in the infield, outfielders divided between left field and center field (with a coach), pitchers near the pitcher's mound in two groups (figure 8.5).

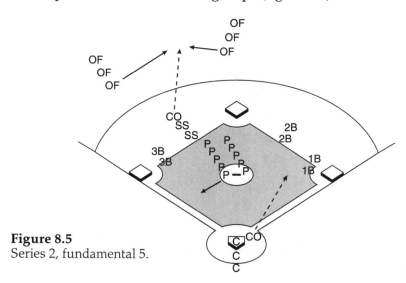

Figure 8.5
Series 2, fundamental 5.

Pitchers

Pitchers are split into two groups. The groups switch locations at 2 minutes.

Third Basemen, Catchers, and One Group of Pitchers

These players practice 2 minutes of force plays and 2 minutes of tag plays. They work on communication on bunts to the third-base side with runners at first and second or a runner at second with less than two outs. If the catcher yells "one," the pitcher fakes the throw to first base. A coach rolls the bunted balls. The pitcher fakes pitches to the plate.

Second Basemen, Shortstops, First Basemen, and One Group of Pitchers

These players practice communication on ground balls hit to the right side of the infield (3-6-1 ground balls). A coach fungo hits to the first-base side of home plate. The first baseman plays deep and also holds a runner on. Switch every other play.

Outfielders

Outfielders practice communication on line drives. Outfielders line up in center field and left field; they are positioned closer together than normal. A coach throws line drives from behind the shortstop position.

Setup

5-minute stations; catchers at home plate, pitchers in the infield, infielders at positions in the infield, outfielders with a coach in right field (figure 8.6).

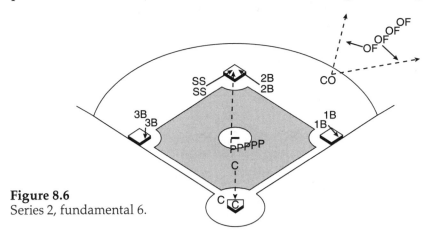

Figure 8.6
Series 2, fundamental 6.

Pitchers, Shortstops, and Second Basemen

These players practice pickoffs in and out, .001 second delay, no daylight. A manager acts as a base runner at second base. Use pickoff signs.

Catchers, Third Basemen, and First Basemen

These players practice pickoffs at third and first. Use signs. One catcher throws to the plate from the front of the pitcher's mound, one catcher swings a bat, and one catcher throws. The catcher alternates picks, throwing to third and first base.

Outfielders

Outfielders field ground balls in right field. Balls go left and right. The outfielder sets up to throw. A coach throws from deep second base. A manager is in a cutoff position.

FUNDAMENTAL 7

Setup

5-minute stations; catchers at home plate with a coach, infielders in the infield positions, pitchers near the pitcher's mound with a coach, outfielders in the outfield positions (figure 8.7).

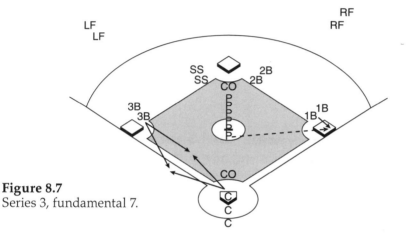

Figure 8.7
Series 3, fundamental 7.

Pitchers and First Basemen

Pitchers and first basemen practice pickoffs and bunt defense with runners at first and second base. A manager acts as the base runner at first base. Switch picks after 2 minutes.

Catchers and Third Basemen

Catchers and third basemen practice communication on fly balls between third and home. A coach throws from home plate.

Outfielders, Second Basemen, and Shortstops

Outfielders practice throwing behind a runner who is rounding second base. A coach hits or throws balls to outfielders from in front of second base. An infielder puts his arms up if he wants the ball.

Setup

5-minute stations; catchers at home plate, infielders in positions in the infield, pitchers in left field, outfielders in right field with a manager (figure 8.8).

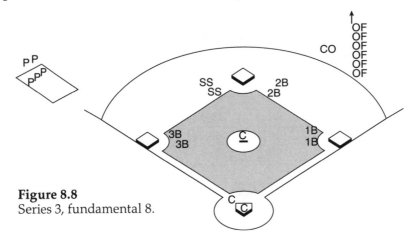

Figure 8.8
Series 3, fundamental 8.

Catchers, Second Basemen, and Shortstops

These players practice pickoffs (regular pick behind and first-and-third play). One catcher throws to the plate from in front of the pitcher's mound. A manager acts as a base runner at second. Switch picks after 2 minutes. The middle infielder must get to the base.

First and Third Basemen

First basemen field bunted balls down the first-base line and throw to the retreating third baseman. At third base, half of the plays will be force plays and half will be tag plays. Once in a while, the bunt should be thrown down the third-base line to keep the third basemen honest.

Pitchers

In left field, pitchers work on inside pickoff moves. They throw to each other.

Outfielders

Outfielders work on picking up a ball at the fence and throwing it to a relay man. A manager in a cutoff position acts as the relay man.

Setup

5-minute stations; catchers at home plate, pitchers at the pitcher's mound, infielders in positions in the infield, right fielders in right field (figure 8.9).

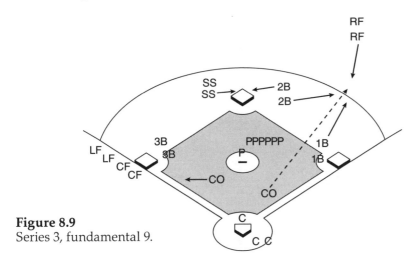

Figure 8.9
Series 3, fundamental 9.

First Basemen, Second Basemen, and Right Fielders

These players practice communication on fly balls to right field. A coach throws from in front of home plate. In order, priority moves from right fielder to second baseman to first baseman.

Pitchers, Shortstops, and Second Basemen (as available)

These players practice above and inside pickoff moves at second base. A manager acts as the base runner.

Catchers and Third Basemen

Catchers and third basemen practice rundowns between third base and home. No pitchouts are allowed. Include the shortstop for the second 2 minutes.

Left Fielders and Center Fielders

Left fielders and center fielders act as base runners at third base.

FUNDAMENTAL 10

Setup
5-minute stations; catchers at home plate, pitchers on the pitcher's mound, infielders in the infield positions (figure 8.10).

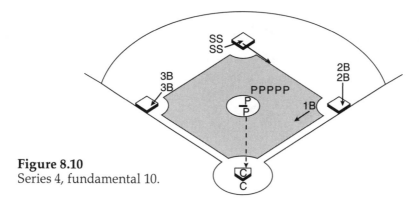

Figure 8.10
Series 4, fundamental 10.

Half Pitchers and Third Basemen
Pitchers and third basemen practice pickoff plays at third base. The coach gives proper signs. No rundowns are allowed. Pitchers alternate groups.

Catchers, First Basemen, Second Basemen, Shortstops, and Half Pitchers
These players practice defending against a runner who gets an early break on a pitchout off a bunt defense. The runner may get in a rundown. Pitchers throw pitchouts from side of pitcher's mound to practice timing. Pitchers alternate groups.

Outfielders
Outfielders act as base runners at first and third base.

Setup

5-minute stations; catchers at home plate, pitchers on the pitcher's mound, infielders in positions in the infield (figure 8.11).

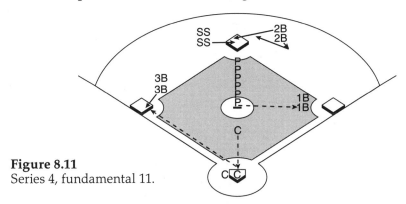

Figure 8.11
Series 4, fundamental 11.

Pitchers, First Basemen, Second Basemen, and Shortstops

These players practice pickoff bunt defense with a runner at first. Rundowns are only allowed during the first 2 minutes.

Catchers and Third Basemen

Catchers and third basemen practice pickoffs (first-and-third play). For the second 2 minutes, they practice play number 3 with the shortstop. They also practice rundowns during the second 2 minutes; the rundowns will include the shortstop. One catcher throws to the plate from in front of the pitcher's mound. Another catcher swings and misses the pitched ball. Switch picks after 2 minutes.

Outfielders

Outfielders act as base runners at first and third base.

Setup

5-minute stations; catchers at home plate, pitchers at the pitcher's mound, infielders in the infield positions, outfielders in the outfield positions (figure 8.12).

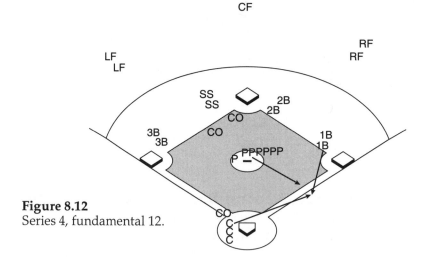

Figure 8.12
Series 4, fundamental 12.

Pitchers, First Basemen, and Catchers

These players practice communication on fly balls. They must know who has priority. A coach throws the ball from home plate.

Outfielders, Third Basemen, Shortstops, and Second Basemen

These players practice communication on fly balls. Coaches throw the ball from behind the pitcher's mound.

FUNDAMENTAL 13

Setup

10-minute stations; catchers at home plate, pitchers at the pitcher's mound, infielders in the infield positions (figure 8.13).

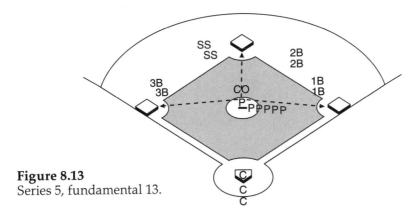

Figure 8.13
Series 5, fundamental 13.

Infielders, Catchers, and Pitchers

These players practice rundowns between bases. The pitcher throws a pick to a designated base. The coach calls which pick play is live. Picks at first base: either runner at first and second or bases loaded. Bunt defense: runner at first only. Picks at second: choice. Picks at third: use sign, left-handed pitcher use sign.

Outfielders

Outfielders act as base runners at first, second, and third base. They get in a rundown when picked off a base.

Setup

5-minute stations; catchers at home plate, pitchers on the pitcher's mound, infielders in the infield positions, outfielders in the outfield positions (figure 8.14).

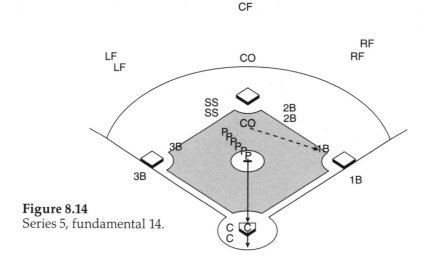

Figure 8.14
Series 5, fundamental 14.

Pitchers and Catchers

Pitchers cover home on a wild pitch or passed ball. The catcher goes back to the backstop and makes the throw to the pitcher.

First Basemen

First basemen take bad throws at first base from a coach who throws from behind the pitcher's mound. The coach moves in a semicircle.

Outfielders, Second Basemen, Shortstops, and Third Basemen

These players practice tandem relays with a play at third base. A coach hits or throws the ball from behind second base.

FUNDAMENTAL 15

Setup
5-minute stations; catchers at home plate, pitchers at the pitcher's mound, infielders in the infield positions, outfielders in left field (figure 8.15).

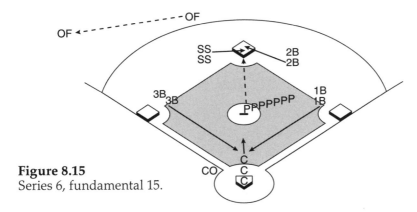

Figure 8.15
Series 6, fundamental 15.

Pitchers, Shortstops, and Second Basemen
These players practice daylight pickoff plays at second base with the second baseman or shortstop backing up. A manager acts as the base runner at second base.

First Basemen, Catchers, and Third Basemen
These players practice communication on fly balls in front of home plate. A coach throws the ball up at home plate. Move home plate back. The first and third basemen cheat up. Priority order for the catch is first baseman, third baseman, and then catcher.

Outfielders
Outfielders execute a cone drill.

Setup
5-minute stations; catchers at home plate, pitchers at the pitcher's mound, infielders in the infield positions, outfielders in left field (figure 8.16).

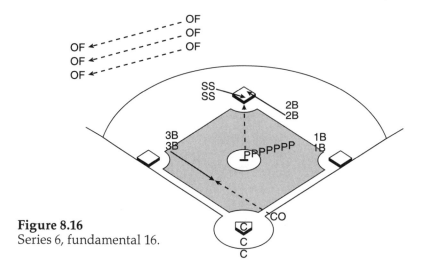

Figure 8.16
Series 6, fundamental 16.

Pitchers, Catchers, Shortstops, and Second Basemen
These players practice a pick at second base. Pitchers throw from the stretch and pick when the catcher gives the signal. A manager acts as the base runner at second base.

First and Third Basemen
Third basemen field slow rollers and go to first base. A coach hits balls from the first-base side of home plate.

Outfielders
Outfielders throw ground balls to each other. Players throw to the side, not always directly in front of each other. Make these ground balls do or die.

FUNDAMENTAL 17

Setup

5-minute stations; catchers at home plate, pitchers on the pitcher's mound in two groups, infielders in the infield positions, outfielders in right center field with a coach and manager (figure 8.17).

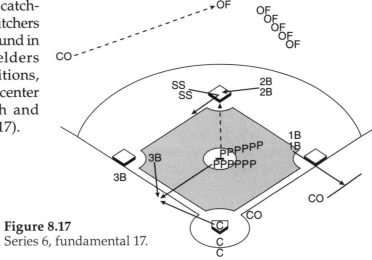

Figure 8.17
Series 6, fundamental 17.

Pitchers

Pitchers are divided into two groups. The groups switch locations at 2 minutes.

Shortstops, Second Basemen, and One Group of Pitchers

These players practice pickoff plays at second base off bunt defenses with runners at first and second base. Managers act as base runners.

First Basemen

First basemen field fly balls at the fence. A coach throws the fly balls from in front of the first-base dugout.

Outfielders

Outfielders practice the line drill using a head swivel from the left-field line. As the outfielder runs back along a straight line at full speed, he looks over his shoulder. When the coach throws the ball, the outfielder quickly swivels his head to look over the other shoulder. This is an excellent practice drill for outfield play because it forces the outfielder to lose track of the ball for a split second just like in a game.

Catchers, Third Basemen, and One Group of Pitchers

These players practice communication on pop flies. They must know the priority order for the catch: third baseman, catcher, then pitcher. A coach throws the pop flies from the home plate area.

Script Series

The script series are composed of two types of drills for different defensive coverages: total defensive practice situations and first-and-third situations. The first script series covers all defensive coverages. In this series, we practice all defenses, including bunt coverage, first-and-third situations, and so on. Essentially, we script all offensive plays versus every defensive play for any combination. Sometimes the offensive sign may be better than the defense called, but the whole idea is to force players to read the play as best they can and communicate what is happening. Generally, we run three groups of defenses for 6 minutes per group and get in as many plays as possible for this 20-minute drill. We keep track of where we leave off on the script sheet (figure 8.18) and pick up at that point the next time we run the series. So that the series can do double duty, we also use our offensive system, making it a true offense versus defense situation.

Play	Situation	Defense	Offense	Outs	Notes
1	Runners on first and second	Play 3	Double steal	1	
2	Runner on first	Play 4	Sacrifice	0	
3	Bases loaded	Verbal	No sign	0	Only with right-handed hitter
4	Runners on first and third	Play 2	Safety squeeze	0	
5	Runners on first and second	Play 4	Sacrifice	1	
6	Runner on first	Play 3	Sacrifice bunt	0	
7	Runner on first	Play 1	Sacrifice	1	
8	Runners on first and second	Play 2	Slash	0	
9	Runners on second and third	Belt	Squeeze	1	
10	Runners on first and second	Play 5	Slash, hit-and-run	0	
11	Runners on first and third	Play 2	Verbal versus left-handed pitcher	2	Only with left-handed hitter
12	Runner on second	Play 2	Sacrifice	0	
13	Runners on first and third	Play 1	Safety squeeze	1	
14	Runners on first and second	Bud	Sacrifice bunt	0	
15	Runners on first and third	Sign	Straight steal	1	Only with right-handed hitter
16	Runner on first	Play 2	Slash, hit-and-run	0	
17	Runners on first and second	Play 3	Double steal	1	

Figure 8.18 Sample script series.

Play	Situation	Defense	Offense	Outs	Notes
18	Runners on first and third	Play 2	Suicide squeeze	1	
19	Runner on first	Play 1	Sacrifice	1	
20	Runners on first and third	Verbal	Double steal	2	Only with left-handed hitter
21	Runners on second and third	Sign	Safety squeeze	0	
22	Runners on first and third	Play 5	Squeeze	1	
23	Runners on first and second	Play 5	Sacrifice	0	
24	Runners on first and second	Play 1	Sacrifice	1	
25	Runners on first and third	Sign	Run-and-hit	1	Only with right-handed hitter
26	Runner on first	Bud	Delayed steal	1	
27	Runner on first	Play 2	Slash, hit-and-run	0	
28	Runner on first	Play 1	Delayed steal	0	
29	Runner on first	Play 3	Hit-and-run	0	
30	Runners on first and third	Sign	Quick steal	2	Only with right-handed hitter
31	Runner on first	Play 1	Hit-and-run	1	
32	Runners on first and second	Play 3	Double steal	1	
33	Runner on first	Play 4	Sacrifice	0	
34	Runners on first and second	Verbal	Sacrifice	0	
35	Runners on first and third	Verbal	Double steal	1	
36	Runners on first and second	Play 5	Sacrifice	0	
37	Runners on first and third	Play 3	Suicide squeeze	1	
38	Runner on second	Play 4	Sacrifice	0	
39	Runners on second and third	Sign	Suicide squeeze	1	
40	Runners on first and second	Play 2	Slash, hit-and-run	1	
41	Runners on first and third	Play 4	Double steal	2	
42	Runners on first and second	Verbal	Sacrifice	0	
43	Runners on first and third	Belt	Steal	2	Only with left-handed hitter
44	Runner on first	Play 2	Slash, hit-and-run	0	
45	Runners on first and third	Play 2	Fake squeeze, steal	0	

(continued)

(Sample script series, *continued*)

Play	Situation	Defense	Offense	Outs	Notes
46	Bases loaded	Verbal	No sign	0	Only with right-handed hitter
47	Runner on first	Play 2	Slash, hit-and-run	0	
48	Runners on first and second	Play 5	Sacrifice	0	
49	Runners on second and third	Sign	Safety squeeze	0	
50	Runner on first	Play 3	Hit-and-run	0	
51	Runners on first and third	Play 3	Double steal	2	
52	Runners on first and third	Play 4	Suicide squeeze	1	
53	Runners on first and second	Play 3	Double steal	2	
54	Runners on first and second	Play 4	Sacrifice	1	
55	Runners on first and third	Verbal	Double steal	2	Only with left-handed hitter
56	Runner on first	Play 1	Hit-and-run	1	
57	Runners on first and third	Sign	Run-and-hit	1	Only with right-handed hitter
58	Runners on first and second	Play 2	Sacrifice	0	
59	Runners on first and third	Play 5	Steal	0	
60	Runner on first	Play 3	Hit-and-run	0	
61	Runner on first	Play 1	Bunt for hit	1	
62	Runners on first and third	Play 2	Double steal	2	
63	Runner on first	Play 1	Slash, hit-and-run	1	
64	Runners on first and third	Play 1	Safety squeeze	1	
65	Runners on first and second	Play 4	Sacrifice	0	
66	Runners on first and third	Play 2	Verbal versus left-handed pitcher	2	Only with left-handed hitter
67	Runner on second	Play 2	Sacrifice	0	
68	Runners on first and third	Play 4	Fake squeeze, steal	0	
69	Bases loaded	Verbal	No sign	0	Only with right-handed hitter
70	Runner on second	Play 5	Slash, hit-and-run	0	

Figure 8.18 *(continued)*

This script series is very effective, especially during preseason practice before we begin playing games. Generally, we use the script series twice a week, including it either in the middle of practice or at the end. We always try to keep a high-paced, focused practice. In essence, the script series puts our offense against our defense; therefore, it allows us to see vividly how players react to real-time, real-game situations.

As often as possible, we record these sessions and break down the video with the players afterward. The importance of video cannot be overstated. Video reveals exactly what happened, so there is no misunderstanding.

Defensively, we ask these questions:

- Did we execute the correct coverage?
- Did we throw the ball to the proper base?
- Was our spacing good for pickoffs?

Offensively, we ask these questions:

- Did we get the proper sign for the batter and runners?
- How was the execution?
- How did base runners react to the batted ball?

We rotate players from defense to offense to baserunning, usually every six outs. At three outs, we clear the bases. This gives us a gamelike atmosphere. The team coming off the field must get ready to hit, and the team that was hitting rotates to the field. The need for communication is similar to an actual game.

The second script series is more specific and is designed for first-and-third situations only. Again, it is offense versus defense, and the drills are scripted accordingly.

Rope Series

The third area of emphasis takes place during a live batting practice with the focus on successfully defending any offensive situation. Rewards are given for great diving plays. We call this our *rope series*. We set up a field for batting practice and assign each player to a group; four or five players are in each group. Each group takes turns hitting, baserunning, and fielding. This intense 40- to 45-minute segment focuses on total defense. Figure 8.19 on page 132 shows the defensive statistics we record during the rope series. We use a chart similar to figure 8.20 on page 133 to record offensive statistics.

Name	Putouts	Assists	Fielding errors	Throwing errors	Total errors	Web gems	Double plays	Touches	Total chances	Range factor	Fielding percentage
Team totals											

Total errors = fielding errors + throwing errors

Total chances = putouts + assists + total errors + web gems + double plays + touches

Range factor = [total chances + touches + (web gems × 3) + (double plays × 2) – fielding errors] ÷ total chances

Fielding percentage = [putouts + assists] ÷ [putouts + assists + errors]

Figure 8.19 Rope series defensive statistics.

Name	Round 1	Round 2	Round 3	Round 4	Total rounds	Total swings	Swings per round
Team totals							

Total swings = round 1 + round 2 + round 3 + round 4
Swings per round = total swings ÷ total rounds

Figure 8.20 Rope series offensive statistics.

Specific instructions are given to the hitter, base runners, and fielders. The outfielders play shallow to make diving plays. The hitters are told what they need to accomplish in the at-bat (figure 8.21). If a hitter is unsuccessful, the next hitter in the group must complete the assignment. Baserunning is outlined to specify which base the runner is on and what the defense is attempting to do (figure 8.22). Players are evaluated, and this information is recorded and posted so that all players can see their progress. The rope series encourages outstanding team defense while rewarding the great plays. It helps players learn how to play good hard-nosed defense.

Hitting Assignments

Round 1: Hit power ground balls. The goal is to drive in the runner from third base with the infield halfway. If the batter is unsuccessful, the next batter jumps in. The batter gets five swings.

Round 2: Move the runner from second to third. The goal is to move the runner by hitting fly balls to right field or ground balls to the right side. If the batter is unsuccessful, the next batter jumps in. The batter gets five swings.

Round 3: Hit low line drives as hard as possible. If the batter is unsuccessful, the next batter jumps in. The batter gets five swings.

Round 4: Perform a hit-and-run or a slash as hard as possible. The batter gets five swings. If the hit-and-run or slash is not on the ground, the next batter jumps in.

Figure 8.21 Sample hitting assignments for the rope series.

Baserunning Assignments

Round 1: The runner is on third base, and the infield is halfway. The batter is attempting to hit a power ground ball. The runner must read the ball through the infield or recognize the high chopper. The runner tags up on a fly ball only if it is deep enough to score on.

Round 2: The runner on second base reacts to power ground balls and line drives—three times with zero outs and three times with one out. The runner must read the ball to advance. If the ball is not deep enough for the runner to tag up, the runner must get as far as he can before returning to second base.

Round 3: The runner on first base reacts to low line drives and power ground balls. He tries to break up double plays and freezes on line drives.

Round 4: The runner is on first base in a hit-and-run situation. The runner reacts to low line drives and power ground balls. He reacts to the hit-and-run. If the ball is in the air, the runner finds the ball and retreats, if necessary. The runner tries to make it to third base on a single.

Figure 8.22 Sample baserunning assignments for the rope series.

Although it is impossible to cover every aspect of individual and team defense in one chapter, I would be remiss not to point out the importance of each individual in the success of the team. Team defense is very important, and the series of drills in this chapter are the building blocks to making it work on the field. We emphasize individual improvement by giving each player a specific set of drills to work on during individual of group defense time. In general, we take approximately 15 mintues a day for the team defense series and 20 minutes two to four times per week for the script series, depending on the needs of the team. the script series is very intense for team development, forcing players to think on their feet and be aware of every situation. This practice prepares fielders in every defensive position.

chapter 9

Preparing for Every Game Situation

DAVE PERNO

Victories and championships don't come by accident. Although winning starts with talent, the next step is championship practice, which includes preparing for every game situation. At Georgia, I've found that frequent scrimmaging is the best way to prepare.

Evaluating a team to learn its strengths and weaknesses allows a coach to create a clearer, more vivid practice structure to best prepare for games. Scrimmaging is a more economic method of honestly evaluating your own personnel. You've got to know how much horsepower you have. Strong preseason scrimmaging can also teach lessons that players would otherwise have to learn in games. When players have to learn those lessons in games, this can cost wins.

Scrimmaging will inherently lead to the same situations seen in games. The game teaches players by itself—the more games they play, the more they learn. At Georgia, we treat scrimmages like real games. The thing that players love to do the most is play. In all areas of the game, I preach tempo. When using a scrimmage, we never have a problem with tempo, and we find it much easier to get players up for a practice. For a second baseman, playing a game is a lot more fun than fielding 200 ground balls and taking three rounds of batting practice.

Scrimmaging has been a large part of my playing and coaching careers. In college, when I was playing for Coach Robert Sapp at Middle Georgia College and my brother Donn was an All-Southeastern Conference second baseman at Georgia (during the Bulldogs run to the College World Series), our teams often scrimmaged. This kept me much sharper in practice and better prepared me for game situations. Later, I became a graduate assistant under Howie McCann at Marshall University. We scrimmaged frequently, and it proved beneficial. I returned to Middle Georgia to be an assistant to Coach Sapp. He had an amazing record there, winning three national JUCO championships and frequently contending for the title. We had tremendous talent, especially compared to the opposition, and we again found that the best way to maximize our potential was through scrimmaging.

I followed Coach Sapp to Georgia after the 1996 season. Our record was not very good, and Coach Sapp was replaced by the legendary Ron Polk. Through a lot of campaigning and arm twisting, Coach Polk agreed to keep me on as an on-field, active recruiting coach. I'd brought in a great deal of talent as an assistant, and Coach Polk inherited a talented roster. What struck me most about Coach Polk was his organization. I was aware of his success at Mississippi State. Not only had he won big there, but he made college baseball a big deal in Starkville, Mississippi, and the rest of the Southeastern Conference followed suit. Coach Polk was in Athens for only two years, but in his second season, he guided us to the school's first SEC championship in 47 years. Behind a superhero performance from our All-American shortstop Jeff Keppinger, we made it to the College World Series.

Coach Polk's handpicked successor, Pat McMahon, decided to take the coaching job at Florida instead of Georgia. Florida had fired another one of my mentors and favorite coaches, Andy Lopez, who wound up at Arizona. After about six weeks and six or seven big-name coaches declining to sign with Georgia, I sold myself to athletic director Vince Dooley and was named the head coach of the University of Georgia baseball program in 2001. Three years later, Georgia and Arizona met in the College World Series. Coach Lopez had been the first domino, and I had been the last, but we made it to the mecca of collegiate baseball before Florida or Mississippi State returned there.

To get there, we had to start fast. Keppinger and most of the firepower from the 2001 College World Series team were gone. Straight to work we went. I incorporated all that I had known and learned about the game, going back to my dad's Little League guidance and the insights of all the coaches I'd played and worked for. Fate had given me this opportunity, and I was going to do everything in my power to take advantage of this chance of a lifetime.

It's been said that baseball is unique because it is the only American sport in which the defense has the ball. In this chapter, I'll break down our practice routines and go into depth about how we work on every aspect of the game, from hitting to pitching to defense to baserunning. We'll start where the game starts—on the mound.

Pitching

Developing pitching is a key to success at any level. You must prepare your pitchers for games. Before fall or spring practice starts, we begin with bullpen sessions. Pitchers get four bullpen sessions and one batting practice session in which they actually throw to a hitter.

The focus of the first bullpen session is helping the pitcher establish a clean delivery and making sure the pitcher's mechanics are strong. All we're concerned with at this stage is what's going on at the mound. At this point, we are not even concerned about where the ball winds up. We are trying to establish the pitcher's tempo and find matches for each individual. As an example, let's consider Alex McCree, a six-foot-six left-handed pitcher. Our first step with this 48th-round draft choice out of high school was to make him more compact in his delivery. He went through some growing pains as a freshman, but we could see the potential. As a sophomore, he was one of our most valuable players, going 7-1 and earning three NCAA tournament wins, including one in the 2008 College World Series. With a pitcher like McCree, sometimes you have to take a step backward to go two steps forward. Initially, taking steps backward—changing deliveries, rhythm, and tempo—can be uncomfortable. We tend to increase tempo and delivery. Momentum is key and a huge part of pitching. Most kids are programmed to be much more deliberate; however, working too slowly causes inconsistent and inaccurate release points, leading to a lot of disadvantageous counts and too many walks.

The second bullpen session is intended to help the pitcher establish command of the strike zone and location. Throwing strikes with good tempo provides two enormous benefits. First, the pitcher does not give up many walks, and he finds himself in advantageous counts. Second, the team will naturally play better defense. The players will be more alert and alive. People want to play defense behind guys who throw strikes. From a pitcher's perspective, we've gone from making the pitcher feel good about his delivery and creating the proper tempo to helping the pitcher throw strikes and locate pitches.

The third bullpen is about the pitcher's stuff. Our philosophy calls for proper tempo and command, which should have been established by this point. Now the pitchers focus on their stuff, adding that extra 10 percent to every pitch. This could be movement on the fastball, bite on the curveball, or sink on the changeup. In the first two bullpens, the pitching coach begins to refine a pitcher's talent. The third bullpen is based on recruiting and luck in the draft. This is about having talent. This is where a pitcher shows his goods.

For the fourth bullpen, we incorporate game situations, which means that the entire bullpen is thrown from the stretch. We do this because all of the tough outs—all of the big outs—are worked from the stretch when base runners are on base. This is when the pitcher has to get outs to win. This is when tempo is the most important (ahead of command, location, and stuff). In the end, the guy on the mound makes all the difference. We only hope we have prepared him for the situation. Good tempo will give the catcher a chance if the opposing team wants to run. A pitcher who doesn't throw strikes is never going to get the tough outs. With runners in scoring position, the pitcher has to get pitcher's counts to have success. Scoring position in the big leagues is second or third base. With the aluminum bat in college ball, our philosophy is that first base is scoring position. Solo homers rarely beat you. Not only is the fourth bullpen thrown from the stretch, but every pitch is thrown with different timing. This bullpen is thrown on the game field in the stadium. We simulate pickoffs and bunts. We roll bunts, and the pitcher has to make plays. In this bullpen on the field, the pitching coach is positioned right off the mound behind the pitcher. The pitching coach counts aloud, switching from "one thousand one" to "one thousand five" counts. For example, he says, "one thousand one—pitch" or "one thousand one—pick" all the way through one thousand five.

Defense

I've never found it wise to be overly concerned with flaws during drills. Drills are just that—they are performed with the purpose of preparing players to perform at their peak and to be able to handle any game situation that arises. I never want to turn players into robots. I don't want to take away their instincts. Every player has different nuances, which is fine as long as the end result is what the team needs.

Baseball is a sport of repetition and confidence. Confident players who get the proper repetitions will be prepared for any game situation. For a pitcher, the most important aspect is to be able to handle the elements that he can't control—such as the umpire, weather, poor defensive play, or hostile fans. Therefore, many aspects of the pitcher's game can be experienced only during actual games or intrasquad scrimmages. Pitchers must keep a positive demeanor and must control their emotions at all times. Although a pitcher can control much of the game, he must have a symbiotic relationship with his defense, from the catcher to the infield to the outfield.

We move from pitching to the often overlooked aspect of baseball—defense. Defense includes many areas that must be addressed. Let's start with team defense, specifically outfield play.

We do a fly-ball communication drill in which we use our Fungoman machine. The device shoots fly balls to different outfielders in various spots with greater consistency than an outfield coach can. However, the fungo works just fine if you don't have a machine. The drill is done to build excellent communication, and it works. The center fielder is the captain. The execution and communication need to be very solid. However, sometimes we change the drill, telling the players that they can't say anything. The outfielders must know where they are on the field. This teaches instinct. At schools with big stadiums, the outfielders can rarely hear. We use the same philosophy of silent communication for cutoffs, tandems, and relays. Every coach knows that one play can determine the outcome of a game, which can determine your success in a season. This comes from experience. College players are 18 to 21 years old. They haven't been through the number of conference championship races and postseason games that successful coaches have. They might not fully appreciate and understand how something as simple as hitting the cutoff man can determine whether you win a game that determines whether you have the chance to be a champion.

I have a painful memory related to this. In 2004, we went to the College World Series, won the SEC championship, and finished number three nationally. The following year, we were in a dogfight to make our conference tournament (the top 8 in the 12-team SEC go to the tournament), which virtually ensures an NCAA regional bid. In the second of a three-game set with Vanderbilt, we led 5-1 going into the ninth inning. During that inning, we threw away a bunt play, our fly-ball communication broke down on another play, and we gambled at the wrong time in the outfield and lost. A potential diving catch turned into a loose ball rolling to the warning track, which by cruel coincidence happened to have been hit by the fastest player in the SEC. The play resulted in an inside-the-park home run. We lost 6-5. It was inconceivable. Because we were also rained out of a game earlier that year against the worst team in the league, we wound up half a game out of our conference tournament. Had we not blown that game against Vandy with defensive breakdowns, that win would have earned us the number seven seed in our conference tourney, which most likely would have guaranteed us an NCAA regional bid. I am living proof that one ill-fated and ill-timed dive, one miscommunication, and one bunt-play breakdown can demolish an entire season's dreams. Mississippi State got the number seven seed that year—our number seven seed—and went on to win the SEC tournament, getting the automatic bid. We finished a half game behind them, despite having beaten them two out of three games.

In practices, I often borrow from a quote: "You don't have to do extraordinary things. You just have to do ordinary things, the things that show up the most, extraordinarily well." In baseball, this means executing the basics such as bunt defense. If we had done that properly, we would have been back in the postseason that year.

In the Georgia defensive drill series, we try to cover as many game situations as we think may come up. The following drills are designed to fine-tune double-play defense. A manager keeps time on a stopwatch. Because the average time for a base runner out of the box is 4.3 seconds from home to first, this is our standard.

28-OUT DRILL

Players have to turn 14 double plays, and each double play must be completed in 4.3 to 4.4 seconds, although the time may fluctuate depending on the situation. We tell defenders what type of runner is at the plate. A coach does the hitting, and there are no actual base runners. Using the clock instead of actual base runners allows us to get more repetitions, providing a cleaner, crisper routine. Yet players still understand the speed of the game because of the clock. A sample situation we use is the runner at first plus the runner at the plate. This means defenders have to turn the double play in 4.2 seconds or better.

GOTTA DO 10 DRILL

In this drill, runners are at first and second, and the defenders have to turn 10 double plays. The only way it doesn't go 6-4-3 or 4-6-3 is if the ball is hit right to the third baseman or if the ball takes the third baseman to his backhand side toward the bag. We hit some balls to the pitchers and go 1-6-3 instead of 1-5-3. A lot of young pitchers are tempted in that situation. Communication is essential. Communication is one of the fundamentals we instill during all of these double plays. The second baseman has to be the first one to recognize the play and make the call. He has the best view of the runner at first, and he sees the contact of the ball. His eyes are working in the direction where the runner is going to go. Everybody recognizes a "two ball." The communication, beginning with the second baseman, becomes ingrained.

FIRST-AND-THIRD DRILL

With runners at first and third, the corners have to recognize a softly hit ball. If the ball is softly hit, the corners must look to throw home. A softly hit ball that an infielder has to come in on is rarely a double-play ball.

All teams are offensive in first-and-third situations with the double play in order. The runner is going from third on a ground ball, so we get the out at home. We are not willing to trade one out on the bases for a run, although the game situation might dictate otherwise.

BASES LOADED WITH ONE OUT

We finish with the bases loaded and one out when the double play is in order. If the ball is hit to the pitcher, he goes home first. For the corner defenders, the bases-loaded scenario is similar to first and third with one out. The only time they are sending the ball home first is if the ball is hit softly. The drill work with the bases loaded and less than two outs is mainly for the pitcher to work on the 1-2-3 play. The 1-2-3 has to be practiced.

When the bases are loaded with no outs, the correct play for the defender depends on the score. I don't think a lot of these situations should be simulated in practice. If you script everything, players lose their instincts. This is where scrimmaging comes into play. Players just don't feel the same pressure if they are not in a game situation.

We have a segment just for pitchers on double-play balls, and it covers 1-6-3, 1-2-3, and 3-6-1. The infielders have the script. The segment with the pitchers is separate.

Players know the variables and that the ball can be hit anywhere. We have a script just for infielders and a script for infielders and pitchers.

PITCHERS ON DOUBLE PLAYS

On the 1-6-3, we preach to middle defenders that they must get to the bag and try to be as much of a stationary target as possible. They should always square up to the baseball—regardless of the angle—so the thrower has the biggest target. We call this fronting the baseball, and we tell players to make sure of one.

However, in some situations, you do what you do. Timing is the key factor here, and we trust that the fielding receiver is going to be there. The thrower has to recognize that the target may differ because of the timing and the position in which the middle infielder may have been playing. This goes for 1-6-3, 5-4-3, and 3-6-1.

We have a saying: "We don't turn double plays; people hit into them. All we try to do is execute one out at a time and realize that one good feed leads to another."

In 2004, we turned 73 double plays, the second most in school history. It wasn't just the standards in the middle. We turned that many because we could turn them on both corners. Our third baseman was a shortstop in high school. Our first baseman was a third baseman in high school. Both middle infielders had great pivots. They both had the ability to feed, to secure a feed, and to follow with a quick and accurate release. This made them a lethal combo. That was the first year that we started using the stopwatch, and we enjoyed a tremendous increase in production. We also had an All-American closer who had an incredible knack for inducing the twin killing. It got to where I would tell him during mound visits that we needed a double play. Being a bullpen guy, he would see the hitters and know where to pitch in order to induce the ground ball (low and away, down and in). He was our guy because of his pitching, his defense, and his incredible ability to get the double play.

Offense

I'm a true believer that great pitching and great defense can ignite an offense. It's uncanny how the emotion can carry over to the plate. And the other team feels it, too.

You have to score to win. If you don't score, the best you can do is tie—and that doesn't happen in baseball.

Hitting

In 2004, we came up with a unique strategy to prepare our hitters. This strategy involved using early hitting groups instead of the proverbial method of setting up for batting practice and trying to do three things (with pitchers shagging, guys on bases, and so on). We do early hitting groups on game days or Thursday practices before a Friday to Sunday series. Early hitting groups are a bear for the coaches, but they do a great job in preparing hitters and giving them more individual time for instruction.

Early hitting groups take place two hours before practice. Four different players rotate every 30 minutes. That gives you four different blocks of 16 hitters. All players have a cage routine to warm up 15 minutes before their field time. Nothing else is going on except hitting. We emphasize that we don't want fungoes being hit, guys running the bases, or anything else. We want players to concentrate on the different rounds we assign them to, and we want them to focus on seeing success on the field. Every round involves a game situation—everything from hitting with a 0-0 count, to leading off an inning, to hitting with a 3-1 count with runners moving, to moving over a runner on second with no one out.

We pair hitters accordingly, and the situations vary from group to group. For example, we try to keep our potential one and two hitters together and our eight and nine hitters together. We call these hitters *action guys*—they see more hit-and-run calls, perform more slashes and bunts, and take more pitches. These hitters must be able to identify the strike zone. Then we group the players who will hit in the three, four, five, and six spots. These are the RBI guys and the potential power threats. Number seven hitters float among the one-two, eight-nine, or three-six groups.

Not only do we have game situations, but we also have approach rounds in which hitters are asked to be aggressive, to be selective, or to identify pitch locations. Hitters have to know what they are looking for. They are not fastball hitting; they are zone hitting. In our philosophy, the best way to drive in runs is early in the count. For example, more than half of the homers hit by our All-American shortstop Gordon Beckham, who led the country with 28 home runs in 2008 (the season of our run to the College World Series), were hit on the first pitch of the at-bat.

On certain days, we bring all left-handed hitters into a group of four or go with all right-handed hitters. We work on the mechanics of the swing on the field. We try to prepare the hitters for every game situation. We work hitters against pitchers.

When nothing else is going on but swinging the bat, hitters can feed off each other and better learn our philosophy, both in mechanical terms and with situational hitting. Players are able to concentrate on the flight of the ball and contact, and they feel the rush in the cage during batting practice. Players are out there for only 30 minutes; then they go back to the locker room or the lounge in order to relax and get ready for batting practice.

In the end, early hitting groups allow our practice times together and team situations to be crisper. We don't have to take all the time for the whole team to do batting practice. Batting practice leads to a lot of standing around. From a teaching standpoint, it's better to break it up.

This is a long day for the coaches, but we believe that it's important to work on the individual aspects in a teaching mode. Hitting is such a high priority for us. When our players are hitting, we want that to be their sole focus. Sometimes we'll go from four hitters for 30 minutes to eight players, or we'll have four hitters and four base runners (our situational hitting and baserunning segment).

We specify where the runners are at first (all four runners and a new runner every pitch). There are no defenders, just a batting practice pitcher. Early pitchers work in the bullpen, and early offensive work is done at the same time. The offensive players use the field, and early pitchers use the bullpen. We then come together and work on our drill series.

Baserunning

To a lot of folks, there's hitting and pitching and then there's defense. But baserunning is one of the most overlooked aspects of the game. We put a priority on baserunning by incorporating it as part of our warm-up before practice starts.

After the hitting groups, we sometimes use baserunning as a warm-up. Players seem to engage and be more interested if you put something at the front end of practice instead of at the back end. Putting baserunning at the front of practice helps to emphasize its importance. When we add baserunning at the front, it becomes a segment, whether the segment involves a simple run from home to first or any of the various run-throughs that players will encounter in a game. Before some games, we'll do a baserunning segment at first base and use all the different strategies from varying situations.

For some players, we'll teach more of a 90-feet-at-a-time approach. For other players, we'll be much more aggressive.

Early baserunning work is incorporated into the aforementioned situational hitting. There are no defenders here. Imagination is needed.

During scrimmages, we sometimes remove our base coaches in order to help players learn baserunning instinct. Instead of merely relying on the base coach, the base runners must use those instincts, know where people are playing, and know the situation. If runners can see the ball, they can make their own decisions. However, runners sometimes need to rely on the coach, especially when the ball is behind them. We work on those situations through our Dawg drill, which is done in warm-ups at a 75 percent clip. This is a controlled drill. We want players to be precise in their leans and where they touch the bag, and we want them to be accurate in their decisions.

Just being fast doesn't make a player a great base runner. We use the term *technique strong*. We tell players, "Make the defense stop you." Base runners should never assume on the bases. When the runner knows where the ball is, he gets to his spot, and he waits to see what the ball and the defender do. A base runner at first base is responsible for knowing where the right fielder is. The base runner at second base is responsible for knowing where all fielders are. (A base runner at third base can depend on the base coach.) We call this evaluating the situation. The first thing to do after reaching a base is to check the scoreboard. The runner should note the inning, the score, and, of course, the number of outs. He should define the importance of his run. Then he is responsible for picking up the base coach. Next, the base runner is responsible for picking up the outfielders that he needs to account for.

DAWG DRILL

The Dawg drill uses three base runners: one at the plate, one at first or second, and one at second or third. The runner at each base has a specific technique to work on, such as hitting a corner of the bag or reacting to the ball off the bat. A coach fungo hits the ball. We emphasize what kind of turn to make. On a ground ball, a runner goes straight through. On a line drive to the outfield, a runner makes a more aggressive turn.

During the drill, the runner at first or second is told the number of outs and the situation. The runner on second or third is told the situation, including the variables of the score, the number of outs, and the inning. The runner must react accordingly.

POST PRACTICE

Our post practice is what we call baserunning specific. We divide players into base stealers, hit-and-run guys, delayed-steal guys, and guys who go 90 feet at a time. We work on the techniques that each type of base runner will use the most.

The base stealers work with various pitchers. The pitchers vary their deliveries to give base runners different reads and to create more opportunities for them to steal bases. The runners also get the opportunity to do this in our team steal offense and defense, which is listed in our team drill series. A strong-armed catcher is a plus in intrasquad scrimmaging.

Stolen bases may be the most glamorous aspect of baserunning, but I've found that moving from second to home and from first to third is more important. Stealing bases does not necessarily lead to run-scoring success. Getting good jumps and being able to advance from first to third and from second to home are directly related to run production. Another reason I'm not a huge fan of the stolen base is that I don't like to take the bat out of the hitter's hands.

Hit-and-runs, run-and-hits, and starting the runner on a full count are called in order to get the runner going early. The majority of the responsibility for moving the runner falls in the hitter's lap. You have your stealers, and you have guys who are getting head starts. Your players just need to realize the difference.

In our system and philosophy of baserunning, we want to be aggressive but extremely smart. We want to make the opposing team earn their 27 outs—we don't want to give them any on the bases.

Fall, Preseason, and In-Season Practice

Our preparation throughout the calendar year is broken into three phases. During the fall, we primarily evaluate strengths and weaknesses of the team and individuals. This is done primarily through scrimmages, our drill series, and work on team fundamentals.

January is an extension of the evaluation period from an individual standpoint. This is a key time for getting everyone sharp, up to speed, and ready for the speed of the game. January is mainly used for individual teaching, focusing on what's good for each player.

Once February starts, we focus on identifying the roles for developing the kind of execution we're looking for in the spring. February and March are specifically for identifying roles. April, May, and June are used to put it all together, reaping the benefits of understanding the process.

Most scrimmages are done in September and October and over the first three weekends in February. We don't hold intrasquad scrimmages during the season.

In our most successful years, the professionalism and leadership present during practice sessions carried over into the season. The players' level of focus stood out. All of our College World Series teams had different strengths and weaknesses. However, their preparation habits were consistent and fundamentally sound.

Player Mix

Most coaches would agree that to have success, a team needs to have a combination of veterans and impact newcomers. The key to preparation and actual success during the season is having a productive senior class. It's always easier to set up championship practice with a solid senior class that understands the importance of preparation and the discipline that is needed daily.

We have a structured system and blueprint in place. However, the length of time we deal with team situations and individual situations depends on the strengths and weaknesses of the team for that particular season. For example, our 2004 Omaha team was a very businesslike and overachieving baseball team with very few stars. Practice and good execution were important. More time was spent on defense, in part because our pitching staff didn't get a lot of strikeouts. All four infielders developed into All-SEC players. More emphasis was placed on team defense and our drill series. All four infielders were already good players, but they got much better through practice and drills.

By contrast, the 2008 team that made it to the College World Series finals was a much looser team. The fresher they were, the better they executed at game time. We practiced very little once the season started. This team was filled with veterans. It was a team that was at its best when players were mentally fresh. The 2008 team didn't do a lot of the repetition drills that helped the 2004 club thrive.

You have to play the game. You have to play the scoreboard. You can drill until the cows come home, but you have to understand how to perform at the real speed of a competitive scrimmage game. That has been the best and most effective way for a young man and team to develop. The mold has come from Major League Baseball. They drill and do their fundamentals, which we also do. But at the end of the day, game time is when you see the substance of the players. At the college level, we don't have spring training; all games count.

I don't use the same structure every year. We change how we spend our time based on personnel. We use comparisons, but that does not mean we'll do it the same way the next year. In one season, you may have a veteran outfield and a young infield, then vice versa the next season. When we have veterans, a majority of our practice time is spent on our team series. With freshmen, we focus on our drill series, when our players break into smaller groups.

chapter 10

Focusing on the Forthcoming Opponent

DAN HARTLEB

As a coach, you have many options available to help you prepare for your next opponent. You can use historical experience, current statistics, recent box scores, or information gathered by the opposition's recent opponents. Each method of obtaining information can provide important knowledge that may give your team the edge needed for a victory.

The most important question a coach must answer is "What is your coaching philosophy?" The philosophy of our coaching staff over recent years has been to prepare our team with a solid fundamental base that allows us to be successful against all types of opponents. As information on future opponents is gathered, coaches often spend too much time worrying about what the opponent can and cannot accomplish instead of concentrating on their own team's strengths and abilities. Coaches must understand the importance of coaching their own team first rather than coaching against an opponent. Many coaches are not confident or do not commit to a specific philosophy. These coaches may confuse their players and create mental and physical discord within their team.

The best coaches in the country are the ones who pay attention to detail in all aspects of the game, stick with their coaching philosophies, and are concerned with their own team regardless of the opponent, game, or time of year. Once a coach has evaluated his team's strengths in a given year, he must decide what the team's style will be for that season. Players must be coached to use their strengths. This teaching method will help create mental stability and toughness in individual players, which in turn will facilitate growth and solid team chemistry. Players who understand their strengths and possess a strong self-image create opportunities to win.

As we delve into the use of scouting materials, keep in mind that the material presented to the team is meant to educate players on what to expect from the opponent. The information should not be presented in a manner that will divert players' focus from the team's philosophies and strengths. Consider how the information obtained about an opponent may be used by your players while your players still focus on their strengths.

Dissecting Statistics, Box Scores, Clippings, and Broadcasts

In the Internet age, it has become very easy for coaches to find multiple sources of information on upcoming opponents. Whether it be season statistics, box scores, newspaper clippings, or audio broadcasts available on the Web, advance scouting of opponents has become much easier. Over the years, the most common way to gather information has been to use stat sheets and box scores. Statistics can reveal many things about a given opponent. A team's offensive statistics will tell you the team's best hitters; the players who consistently get on base through hits and walks (on-base percentage); the hitters who are free swingers (strikeout-to-walk ratio) with high strikeout totals; the power hitters; the base runners who can create havoc and apply pressure; and whether the team uses the short game to manufacture runs. These statistical categories provide insight into the opposition's players and team tendencies.

Players and coaches may evaluate a team's defensive abilities by looking at fielding percentage and paying specific attention to individual players' assists and errors. When evaluating a team's defensive ability, you must be sure to evaluate the statistical information for all of the pitchers and catchers. With this information, you will be able to make more educated decisions on your running, hitting, and bunting approach against each specific pitcher and catcher.

For example, while evaluating the pitching stats of an upcoming opponent, you may identify a pitcher who has a low ERA and gives up fewer hits than innings pitched. These individual stats indicate that short-game strategies may be your best option against this pitcher. However, you should also consider the abilities and past performances of your own pitchers—you must determine how many runs you think your team needs to score to offset the runs your pitcher may allow. Calculate how many runs per game the opposing team averages. Also pay special attention to the number of walks and strikeouts, as well as the number of innings per outing, by each pitcher.

Remember that many pitchers are strong for a given number of innings but begin to falter in the middle to late innings. This tendency may dictate whether you play for a single run or a big inning at different points during a game. A high number of walks, hit batters, and wild pitches often indicates a pitcher's lack of control, but hit batters may also indicate a pitcher who throws on the inner part of the plate regularly. When looking at box scores from a team's recent games, you can often identify the hitters who appear to be hot and productive in RBI situations. Box scores can also give you a feel for the positioning of the hitters in a lineup. The positioning of the lineup helps coaches better understand the overall statistical information of their upcoming opponents. In addition, recent successes or failures, possible positive or negative control issues, and the recent workload of specific pitchers can be obtained through box scores. In many situations, overall statistics and box scores give players and coaches information that helps them to make educated decisions throughout a game.

Other useful information can be obtained on the Internet in the form of press releases, articles in local newspapers, or radio broadcasts that are archived on the Web. Reporters and broadcasters will often note the players who have been consistent, hot, or cold over a given period.

Using Scouting Reports From an Opponent's Opponent

One of the most common methods of gathering information on a future opponent is to obtain information from a previous foe of that opponent. This may be in the form of verbal communication or written reports and charts. Generally, this information consists of the opponent's tendencies, both offensively and defensively. For example, the information may identify the counts in which the opponent steals bases, sacrifices, calls the hit-and-run, or hits behind the runner. The report may also describe the team's hitting philosophy and the team's philosophy on taking pitches early in the count. Defensive tendencies include the handling of specific situations such as bunts, pickoff plays, and first-and-third situations. Spray charts on individual hitters will assist in the positioning of defenders for the opponent's hitters. Charts and reports generally provide information on the specific abilities of each player in the lineup. Charts should have specific information on players who have the ability to beat teams with their speed, players with power potential, or players who can handle the bat well in short-game situations.

Information on a specific pitcher will show the types of pitches he throws (along with velocities), the pitcher's out pitch, and the pitches that the pitcher will go to in advantage and disadvantage counts. Good reports will identify those pitchers who struggle to field their position in short-game situations.

Involving the Catchers

When looking at the responsibilities given to catchers, go back to the first question posed in this chapter: What is your coaching philosophy? In today's college game, many coaches dictate and control the entire game—offensively, defensively, and on the mound. Many coaches think that they must call each pitch throughout the entire game. In rare cases, catchers are given complete control of and responsibility for the pitching staff and calling the game. As a former catcher who was given the opportunity to call my own games, I believe that catchers should be developed so they are able to call the game themselves.

My reason for this stance is that some information can be recognized solely from behind the plate. A catcher is in a better position to evaluate any adjustments or movements the opposing hitter makes in the batter's box. The catcher can also better evaluate the movement, velocity, and location of pitches, as well as the overall sharpness of the pitcher. A catcher may find it difficult to evaluate inside and outside locations if he has been coached to make subtle body adjustments behind the plate. If a coach allows the catcher to call pitches, the coach must be sure to teach the catcher to recognize the three basic types of hitters. The catcher must understand the strategies for attacking each of these hitters with regard to the pitcher's strengths and abilities.

The first type of hitter is the spin hitter. This hitter rotates through his motion, causing the bat to enter and leave the strike zone without consistent plate coverage throughout the zone. To attack this type of hitter, a pitcher would pitch hard and soft down and away. The pitcher would also use the fastball up and in to create swings and misses or hard-hit foul balls.

The second type of hitter is the dive hitter. This hitter strides hard toward the plate and strike zone. To pitch against this hitter, the pitcher should pound the inner part of the plate regularly.

The third type of hitter is the balanced hitter. This hitter presents the most problems for a pitcher because the pitcher must be able to attack by working the inner and outer parts of the strike zone with multiple types of pitches.

The catcher needs to be able to recognize these types of hitters, but so do defenders. If defenders can evaluate and recognize the different types of hitters, the defenders will be able to make subtle positioning adjustments based on the tendencies of each hitter and the pitcher's strategy for attacking him.

The college catcher can gain valuable information on opponents from game film, statistics, box scores, and scouting reports. However, catchers must be able to recognize a hitter's strengths and flaws during individual at-bats in a game. To learn this skill, catchers should work on helping pitchers attack the hitters on their own team during practice and scrimmage sessions. A cookie-cutter approach may not work because of ever changing adjustments by various hitters. Great catchers learn to recognize the adjustments that hitters make from pitch to pitch.

Defending Against Various Opponents and Hitters

Individual defenders and the defensive team as a whole must understand each hitter's tendencies. Many hitters pull pitches on the ground in the infield but hit fly balls straightaway to the slightly opposite field. Some hitters mechanically dictate pull side on the ground and in the air. For other hitters, their mechanical approach and bat speed may dictate opposite-field hitting on the ground and in the air. The most difficult hitter to defend against is the mechanically balanced hitter who is able to use the entire field on the ground and in the air, depending on the location of the pitch.

The coach must decide if he is willing to make exaggerated defensive shifts that may leave large gaps or weak areas in the defensive alignment. Are you willing to play the percentages and live with the consequences of giving up a cheap hit or gap hit throughout the game? Will exaggerated shifts create a negative mental thought process for the opposing hitter? Will these shifts force the opponent to try to do something that he isn't comfortable with and has not done throughout the season?

These are questions that you must answer to determine a portion of your coaching philosophy. You need to develop a defensive placement strategy that is dictated by pitching counts. Early in counts or on 0-0 counts, the defensive alignment is usually determined by the overall tendencies of the hitter (figure 10.1). Hitter-advantage counts often lead the defense to play straightaway or slightly toward the pull side (figure 10.2, page 154). Pitcher-advantage counts

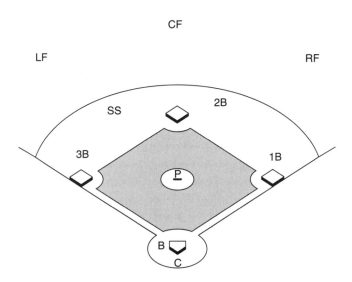

Figure 10.1 Early in the count versus a right-handed hitter.

and put-away counts often call for opposite-side positioning (figure 10.3); the opposite-side outfielder will move in and toward the foul line because many hitters become defensive in these breaking-ball counts.

One factor you must consider is the ability of your pitcher to throw inside regularly, as well as your philosophy about throwing inside late in games. A team that throws inside late in games often opens itself to the possibility of hit batters, risking putting a runner on base without the hitter having to earn the base through making contact.

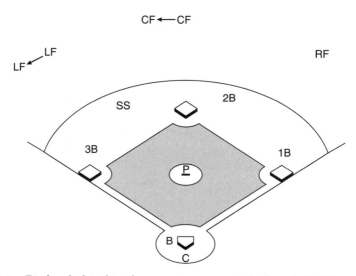

Figure 10.2 Pitcher behind in the count versus a right-handed hitter.

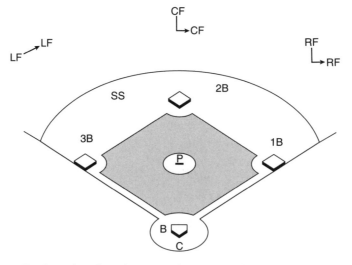

Figure 10.3 Pitcher ahead in the count (two strikes) versus a right-handed hitter.

Other tendencies that the defensive team must evaluate include hitters who are aggressive and look dead red for a fastball early in the count and hitters who regularly chase pitches out of the strike zone. Hitters who are very aggressive and look for fastballs early in the count can be attacked in several ways. If a pitcher chooses to use a fastball, the pitch must be located in an area that will produce an early strike or early contact in the pitcher's favor—for example, a fastball down and away or a fastball in on the hands.

Hitters who chase pitches out of the strike zone often fit into one of two categories: (1) hitters who swing at fastballs at the letters or above the hands or (2) hitters who consistently chase off-speed pitches below the knees and in the dirt. In all situations against all hitters, the pitcher needs to get ahead and stay ahead so the pitcher is in an advantage count. More often than not, balls are not hit as hard when pitchers are attacking the zone and are ahead in the count.

The coaching staff needs to use scouting reports or game evaluations to determine if a team is apt to move runners through sacrifice bunts, hit-and-run calls, stolen bases, or by hitting behind runners. Although coaches often lean toward one method, many teams will use all methods of moving runners throughout a season. In sacrifice situations, defensive players need to understand that they must get one out while keeping in mind that cutting down the lead base runner is a bonus. However, in certain situations, such as late in a game with the winning run on base, defenders need to gamble on getting the lead runner out. Against teams that steal, the defense must control the running game. Teams that use the hit-and-run can be deterred with occasional pitchouts, along with pitchers staying in advantage counts. Teams that consistently hit behind runners to the right side of the field can be countered by pitching hard to the third-base side of home plate.

A coach must have a plan for defending first-and-third situations. For example, on a steal attempt, the plan could be for the catcher to throw through to second base with options for the infielders to cut off the ball and throw out the runner breaking for home. Other options could include the catcher throwing behind the lead runner at third base or holding the ball if the pitcher can dominate the hitter. Your defensive philosophy should also include options for defending the suicide squeeze, such as pitchouts, pitch-ups, or pitches thrown up and in. Whichever scenario fits your philosophy, you must be sure to practice these situations throughout the season.

One of the most important areas of team defense is controlling the running game. Doing this effectively will enable a defense to deter aggressive teams throughout the year. You must have a pitching staff that is quick to the plate (the time from the pitcher's first movement to the ball's contact with the catcher's mitt should be 1.3 seconds or less). The pitchers should vary the counts from the time the pitcher comes to the set position to the time of initial movement toward home plate; longer holds should be used when base runners who are aggressive base stealers are on base. The longer hold will force the base runner into making antsy movements or settling his legs into uncomfortable positions that will break up the rhythm of his jump.

Another way to control the running game is to vary the point at which a pitcher picks to a given base. For throws to first base, a pitcher should develop pickoff moves when moving his hands up to set position, when moving his hands down to set position, and from the set position. The most difficult pitcher to steal against is one who takes the sign from the catcher with the baseball in his throwing hand, which gives the pitcher the option to pick at any time. Pitchers must also develop quick feet and a short arm swing to make the base runner uncomfortable. The last deterrent is the ability of the coaching staff to call pitchouts at opportune times to prevent the opposing coach from creating movement on the basepaths. (Coaches may have differing opinions on pitchout situations. In most cases, a pitchout is called by a member of the coaching staff. However, certain catchers who have a great feel for the game of baseball, game situations, and the pitchers' abilities may have the green light to call pitchouts on their own.)

As you consider your game plan for a given team, pick out a few players whom you will not let beat you in a game or series. These are hitters who thrive in RBI situations and at crucial points in the game. In strategic situations, you can pitch around or intentionally walk these hitters in order to get to a hitter in the lineup who hasn't shown the same ability to drive in runs.

From a coaching philosophy standpoint, you should decide if you are willing to play the infield in to cut down runs early in the game. With this concept in mind, do you pull your infield in against a hitter who bats at the top or lower part of the batting order? Do you pull the infield in against middle-of-the-order hitters or only in pitcher-advantage counts? My philosophy is to cut down runs throughout the game, but certain game situations will dictate my decisions. I'm not comfortable pulling the infield in with a multiple-run lead or against strong hitters early in the count. I often pull the infield in late in the count against strong hitters when the pitcher has the advantage; however, I rarely pull the infield in with runners at second and third unless the winning run is on third base in the last inning.

From a defensive standpoint, a general rule for any team is to avoid big innings. Many games are lost when the opponent scores more runs in one inning than they score in the entire rest of the game. The teams that consistently allow the fewest runs per game normally do two things. First, the team consistently gets at least one out in bunt situations. Second, the team's outfielders consistently throw to the correct base to keep the double play in order.

Another key is to make base stealers and aggressive base runners earn their way on base. Generally, these types of players will not hit extra-base hits. Therefore, pitchers need to throw strikes and make these hitters hit their way on base. The sole goal of base stealers is to find a way to get to first base so they can work their way into scoring position with their legs.

Developing an Offensive Approach Against Opponents and Pitchers

As you develop an offensive approach for the season, you must evaluate the skills and talents of your players. Some offensive teams are built on speed, some on manufacturing runs, and some on power hitting. Teams with speed can create havoc for pitchers and defenses while lowering the number of sacrifice bunt situations throughout the year.

Teams with little or no speed must rely on manufacturing runs with the short game. Teams with multiple power sources can play for the big inning. If your team relies on speed and you can move runners by stealing bases, you need to gain information on the opposing pitcher's ability to control the running game and the catcher's ability to throw out runners consistently. When evaluating the opposing catcher, first look at the catcher's ability to receive and catch the ball consistently. Also look at his ability to move his feet with quickness and agility in order to position himself to throw quickly (you should determine if he can throw with a pop time of 2.0 seconds or less). You also need to evaluate the catcher's ability to throw with accuracy. Against teams that have speed and are aggressive on the basepaths, pitchers commonly elevate pitches in the strike zone, which often leads to better offensive numbers. Speed on the basepaths disrupts the pitcher's concentration and command more quickly than anything else you can do offensively. As you evaluate the pitcher's and catcher's ability to control the running game, develop an alternate plan for moving runners in the event that your running game is shut down in a given inning or game.

Sacrifice bunting, using the hit-and-run, and hitting behind runners are important tools for any solid game plan. The most important overall aspect of your offensive attack is your hitters' approach, mind-set, and ability to recognize and execute at the plate in any situation. Our teams take a middle-of-the-field hitting approach while concentrating on using the gaps and hitting hard line drives. With this hitting approach in mind, we look at the opposing pitcher and his statistics, and we work to make minor adjustments.

A team's pitching staff will have similar tendencies throughout the staff. These tendencies may include pitching away, pitching in, mixing in and out, using the fastball, and throwing many off-speed pitches or a combination of hard and soft. Many right-handed pitchers attack right-handed hitters with combinations of fastballs and breaking balls, but they attack left-handed hitters using fastball–changeup combinations with occasional breaking balls (either backdoor or wrapped around the back knee). Conversely, left-handed pitchers employ fastball–changeup combinations with occasional breaking balls (backdoor or wrapped around the back knee) against right-handed hitters, and they use combinations of fastballs and breaking balls against left-handed hitters.

Coaching staffs and players should gather information from scouting reports and should watch in-game tendencies of pitchers and the types of pitches they use in specific counts. For instance, many pitchers fall into patterns of throwing a specific pitch in a given count, such as always throwing a fastball when behind in a count.

Pay particular attention to the change in velocity, the sharpness of pitches, and the elevation of pitches when runners reach base. With runners in scoring position, many pitchers tend to rush to the plate and lose command, velocity, and life on their pitches. It is sometimes difficult for hitters to adjust their positioning in the batter's box based on the velocity, style, and pitch repertoire of an individual pitcher. For example, against a soft-throwing pitcher who consistently throws pitches down and away, a hitter should move closer to home plate and farther up in the box. In this scenario, the hitter is adjusting so that he has more plate coverage to the outer third of the plate. In addition, this adjustment cuts down on the amount of time the hitter must wait for a pitch. The hitter should also have a middle-to-opposite-field approach in this situation. To make this adjustment successfully, hitters must be confident enough in their abilities that they will be able to handle any pitch thrown on the inner part of the plate.

In our practices, we spend many hours working on situational hitting and bunting. Each practice begins with a bunting program, which includes sacrifice bunts, bunts for hits, and suicide and safety squeezes. We also work daily on driving the ball on the ground between the first and second basemen. This can be accomplished by placing cones in the desired area to set up a hitting lane. We also work on moving runners, scoring runners with the infield in and back, and game-winning hits.

Another aspect of your coaching philosophy will be to decide when you should slow down the game and make offensive changes (pinch hitters or runners), defensive changes, or pitching changes. You will also need to decide when to use pitching mound conferences or offensive conferences. The thought behind using a pinch hitter is to bring a fresh bat off the bench to create a positive offensive matchup. In many cases, the opposition hasn't seen this hitter and likely doesn't have extensive scouting information on his abilities and tendencies. A pinch hitter is often used to try to neutralize the pitcher's out pitch in multiple situations. Many times, coaches play percentages by pinch hitting a right-handed hitter against a left-handed pitcher or vice versa. This often neutralizes the effect of a good, hard breaking ball. These changes are dictated by percentages as well as gut feelings, and they are made when a starter is not seeing the ball well or is not having good at-bats on a particular day. Through scouting reports and in-game evaluation, you may find that a given pitcher doesn't command a particular part of the plate consistently, which will set up your pinch hitter to get a good pitch to hit.

Pinch runners, on the other hand, are used mainly to upgrade speed on the basepaths. You may do this in an effort to manufacture runs through stolen bases or to increase the probability of a runner scoring from second on a single or from first on an extra-base hit.

Mound visits are a vital part of keeping the game under control from a defensive and pitching perspective. They are used to slow down the game, refocus the pitcher and defense, and discuss a strategy against an upcoming hitter or in a particular situation. My philosophy is that on a mound visit, all players need to understand the task at hand while also being given reinforcement that will help calm the situation. If you are confident that the group on the mound understands the situation at hand, then making a joke, smiling, or saying something to take their minds off the pressure situation is time well spent in your short mound visit.

Deciding on the correct time to bring in a relief pitcher may be the most important but most difficult job of a coaching staff. When managing a pitching staff, you have to understand that you are managing to win the day while also looking at giving your team the opportunity to win an entire series or week. If at all possible, you should give your pitchers specific roles out of the bullpen. Throughout my coaching career, my best teams have had starters who consistently went deep into games and relievers who had a feel for specific and tangible roles. However, each game brings specific challenges, and great athletes and competitors will adapt to subtle changes when needed. You must be aware of how a pitcher's legs feel, because tired legs will lead to poor performances and short outings. Tired legs may indicate when a pitching change needs to be made. When you are considering pitching changes, you must also be aware of the game situation. If you are contemplating a pitching change in a bunt situation, you should decide whether the current pitcher or the possible reliever is a better fielder. Also keep in mind that the pitcher chosen to throw the pitches in the bunt situation must throw strikes. If the situation dictates an intentional walk and you are contemplating a pitching change, you will likely want to bring in the reliever to administer the intentional walk. This will allow you to make another pitching change if the offense counters with a pinch hitter after the intentional walk. Remember that a reliever must face one hitter before you can make another pitching change.

With a lead late in games, I prefer to insert my best defensive lineup. This forces the opposing team to beat our best defense, and it also gives us an opportunity to keep multiple players involved by playing substitutes in crucial situations. This helps team morale and gives some little-used players a great sense of worth, helping to create good team chemistry.

Scouting Pregame Infield and Outfield Practice

Coaches and players often learn a great deal by watching the opposition's pregame infield and outfield practice. As you evaluate a team's outfielders, look at arm strength, accuracy, trajectory of throws, footwork, and release time. Arm strength and accuracy will dictate your team's ability to take extra bases. Trajectory will be an indicator of the batter–runner's ability to get into scoring position on throws where an outfielder is attempting to cut down the lead runner (when the outfielder overthrows the cutoff man). Footwork and release time are major factors that are often overlooked. Many young players look merely at arm strength while ignoring all other factors. All of these criteria are important to your ability to advance base runners during game situations.

When evaluating infielders, watch for fielding ability, exchange and throwing ability, footwork, and, most important, agility. The evaluation of these factors will indicate the players who may have difficulty on routine balls, first-and-third steal attempts, or slow rollers such as bunts. Coaches and players can use this information to decide if using the short game is a viable option for getting hits in the game.

When evaluating catchers, look at receiving ability, exchange, arm swing, arm strength, accuracy, and foot agility behind the plate. As with outfielders, many players and coaches are fooled by arm strength alone. Take into account the quickness with which the catcher releases the ball and the accuracy of the throw.

Evaluating and Scouting Unfamiliar Ballparks

Players must understand unfamiliar ballparks when playing on the road or at a neutral site. All ballparks have different dimensions, fence angles, foul territory, mound slopes, baseline tilts, and backstop materials, all of which can greatly affect on-field play and the outcome of a game. Players must understand their surroundings and the way the ball will react in those surroundings. In your evaluation, include weather and field conditions such as soft fields, hard fields, wind direction, sun position, and artificial lighting. You should inspect and test various areas of an unfamiliar ballpark when you arrive at the park, during pregame batting practice, and during infield and outfield practice. Have players throw balls off surfaces and angled areas to test the ball's reaction. The players should also roll balls down the baselines to test how bunts or softly hit balls will react. Hit ground balls down the left- and right-field lines to test reactions off the side fences.

A team must be well prepared for the season and for upcoming opponents. Coaches have different philosophies, and there are many ways to prepare a team. In the off-season, you need to prepare your club to handle all types of teams and situations. During the season, make your team aware of the opposition's strengths, but more important, make sure your team believes that the principles and fundamentals they have practiced will lead to success against any opposition. Be aware of your opponents and surroundings. Believe in the abilities of yourself and your team, and that will make you champions.

chapter 11

Taking Practice Indoors

BOB WARN

Overall I have never thought that coming inside for practice was a bad thing. It allows for small-group instruction and gives coaches more quality one-on-one time with athletes. Small-station instruction leads to large success in skills. We consider it the part-to-a-whole approach. I believe that learning the game should always precede playing the game.

Practicing inside has two additional positive carryovers. The small-ball idea is much easier to plant in a team's mind during indoor practice. Also, after an indoor practice, the ball seems to look bigger to hitters when they return outdoors for practice.

Every coach must bring his team indoors for practice at one time or another. In climates where weather is a factor, coaches must be extremely creative if they are to prepare for any early-season success, which will often need to take place on the road.

A coach designing an indoor practice must first understand and then learn to optimize certain variables that are essential to successful indoor practices. He must consider the variables of space, time, number of athletes involved, number of instructors, setup time, and practice objectives. In addition, to construct his practice plan, each coach must be aware of the basic minimum needs.

Ideally, a space the size of two basketball floors is needed, although one floor can work.

Figure 11.1 shows a possible floor plan for an indoor practice using the following equipment:

- One or two batting tunnels
- Mobile sock nets (approximately 5 feet [152 cm] square) for tee work
- Two pitching L-screens
- Two or three indoor mounds
- Four tumbling mats (4 feet by 8 feet [122 by 244 cm])
- Three sets of indoor, nonsliding bases
- One pitching machine
- Six to nine orange cones (field markers)

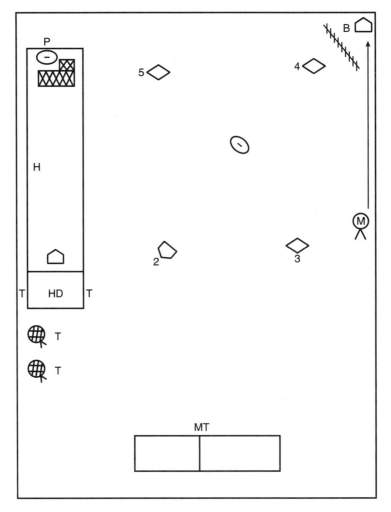

Figure 11.1   Floor plan for an indoor practice. 2, 3, 4, 5 = indoor bases; B = bunting station; T = batting tee or hitting sock screen; H = hitting cage; P = indoor pitching mound; HD = area of cage for hitting drills; MT = tumbling mats for diving.

- A bucket of soft cloth balls and rubber balls
- Four batting tees, minimum
- Usual practice equipment, such as balls, bats, catching gear, batting helmets, and fungo bats

Practice Planning

When conducting an indoor practice, the coach should have basic ideas that determine how the valuable minutes of practice will be used. For example, hitting and pitching should take place during the entire workout because these two areas are the most time consuming. For pitching, I recommend having a veteran and rookie work together because of the example of pitching mechanics shown by the older player to the younger. Also, the rookie sees that he is learning the same fundamentals and making the same mistakes as the returning player.

A circuit approach can be used for skills that are needed by a large number of players. For example, the hitting circuit illustrated in figure 11.2 allows 15 hitters to perform several different drills:

- Cage. Two players throw to each other. One player practices a hitting drill at the other end of the cage.
- Pepper. One hitter hits to two players as they throw to him. Each player takes a turn hitting.

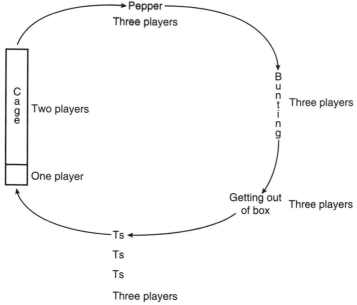

Figure 11.2 Hitting circuit.

- Bunting. Players bunt off a pitching machine using fungo bats. Each player takes a turn hitting.
- Getting out of the box. A hitter hits a soft rubber or cloth ball that is tossed to him from behind a screen. He then runs to a designated spot on a baseline. This is a timed drill.
- Ts. Players hit from tees (into sock nets) and practice hitting to all fields.

Consider using a schematic approach to drill work. This simply means practicing two or more skills at once. For example, use baserunning for conditioning as well. A pitcher or coach mock throws from the mound, and the first player in line performs the task that is asked of him. (For some examples, see figure 11.3.) Any of these efforts can be timed.

Pitchers can develop control by throwing to targets, such as a target made with strings. Create a target by extending three strings over the plate, horizontal to the ground. Strings may be fastened to the cage poles and another object, or you may use a pair of volleyball or badminton standards. Hang two vertical strings on each side of home plate, tying them to the top horizontal string (figure 11.4). Add a weight such as a small ball of tape to the bottom of each vertical string to maintain the size of the strike zone. Pitchers begin by throwing to the target created by the strings. Then, at a certain point, the pitchers start throwing one half of their pitches to targets and one half to hitters in a cage.

Another way to develop a pitcher's arm is to use a progressive pitch count. The coach must decide how many pitches are to be thrown per day by each pitcher based on the pitcher's individual development plan. This plan will also determine the number of different kinds of pitches to be thrown, as well as the number and frequency of days off. The coach must also decide on the percentage of maximum effort at which the athlete will throw. Does he throw at 50 or 75 percent of his maximum, or does he throw at his maximum effort?

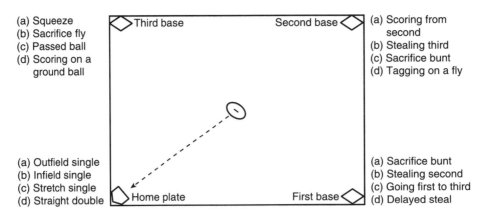

Figure 11.3 Baserunning conditioning drills.

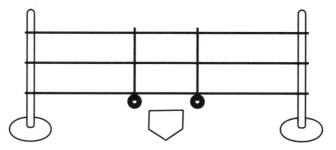

Figure 11.4   Use strings to create a target for pitching practice.

When a coach is planning indoor practices, long toss and bunting are also considerations. Long toss will be done outside regardless of the weather. Pitchers who are scheduled for long toss can go outside for 15 to 20 minutes even if it's snowing. The only other skill (other than long toss) that cannot be covered indoors is fielding balls in the air at all positions. Our solution to this problem is to take everyone outside regardless of the weather at least three days each week to practice fielding balls in the air. All types are worked on— fly balls, pop-ups, pop fouls, and balls over a player's head. We allow 15 to 30 minutes for these drills, depending on weather conditions. Selling this idea to our athletes is not difficult; we remind them that they may have to play in rough conditions. Our motto must be "Weather will not prevent us from preparing our team for the upcoming season."

For bunting, I recommend using a machine filled with soft rubber balls. Use orange activity cones or other target objects to set up bunting lanes for bunts for hits, sacrifices, and suicide squeezes (figure 11.5). Add a scoring system to create better concentration. Using fungo bats to bunt will challenge hitters to truly learn the skill.

Plan practices so that each practice begins with group instruction, branches off to individual instruction, and ends with more group activities. Remember, this is a team, and the players should do as much together as possible.

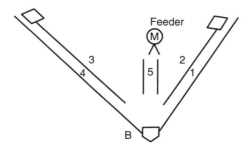

Figure 11.5   Bunting lanes. M = machine; B = batter; 1, 4 = bunt for hit lanes; 2, 3 = sacrifice bunt lanes; 5 = not used for any bunt, except suicide squeeze. Any lane can be used for the suicide squeeze.

Indoor Practice Segments

The following indoor practice segments can be inserted into your plan when you have access to one basketball court. The entire team is working at all times.

Every indoor practice must begin with a brief explanation period during which the coach identifies the areas of the facility that players must stay in for safety reasons. The coach also explains the execution of each drill. The use of screens and nets (as shown in the illustrations) will help address all safety concerns. At first, the coach should explain the next segment during every time change. As the indoor sessions progress, the coach can usually yell out the name of the segment, and the players will go directly to their allotted space. This will save valuable time.

Each practice segment has a central activity for which it is named (three-line drill, multiple-work drill, and so on), but small satellite drills will take place at the same time. The small satellite drills ensure that everyone is kept busy at all times.

SEGMENT 1: MULTIPLE-PICKS DRILL

Pitchers
From the center of the floor, pitchers practice picking off runners at first base. On one side of the floor, two pitching alleys are set up. In one alley, a pitcher pitches live to a hitter. In the other alley, the pitcher pitches to a target.

Base Runners
Base runners work with the pitchers in the center of the floor, taking leads and returning to first base as the pitchers try to pick them off.

First Basemen
First basemen work with pitchers and base runners, making tags on the pickoffs at first base.

Catchers
One catcher is in one of the pitching alleys, catching live pitching. The other catcher is in a corner of the floor working on blocking.

Hitters
Two hitting stations are set up on one side of the floor. At these stations, hitters hit into sock nets off batting tees.

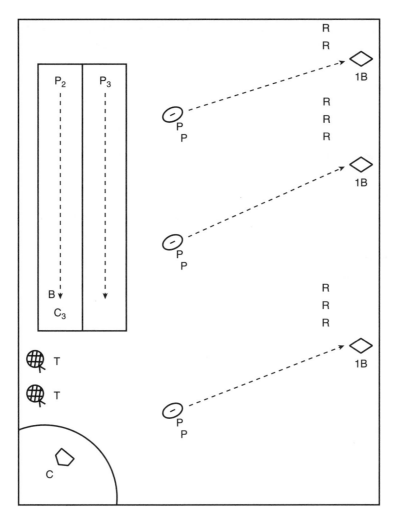

Figure 11.6 Segment 1. P = pitchers picking off runners at first base; R = runners taking leads and going back to first base; C = catcher blocking; P_2 = pitcher throwing to hitter; P_3 = pitcher throwing to target; 1B = first baseman working on tags for pickoffs; T = hitters hitting into sock nets off tees; C_3 = catcher catching live pitching in cage; B = batter facing live pitching.

SEGMENT 2: BLOCKING AND PICKS AT SECOND BASE COMBO

Pitchers

On one side of the floor, two pitching alleys are set up. In one pitching alley, the pitcher pitches to a hitter. In the other pitching alley, the pitcher pitches to a target. From the center of the floor, a group of pitchers work with base runners, second basemen, shortstops, and third basemen on pickoffs and rundowns between second and third base.

Base Runners

Base runners work with pitchers, second basemen, shortstops, and third basemen on pickoffs and rundowns between second and third base.

Second Basemen, Third Basemen, Shortstops

Second basemen, third basemen, and shortstops work with pitchers and base runners on pickoffs and rundowns between second and third base.

Catchers

One catcher catches live pitching in one of the pitching alleys. The other catcher practices signals for pickoffs.

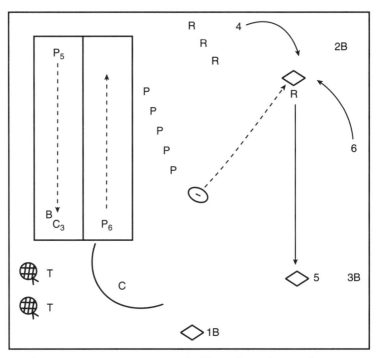

Figure 11.7 Segment 2. 5, 4, 6, P = pickoffs and rundowns between second and third base; R = runner in rundown; 1B = first baseman blocking balls in the dirt; C = catcher working on signals for pickoffs; C_3 = catcher catching live pitching in cage; P_5 = pitcher pitching to hitter; P_6 = pitcher pitching to target; T, B = outfielders hitting off tees or live.

First Basemen

First basemen practice blocking balls in the dirt.

Hitters

Outfielders are hitting. One hitter is in one of the pitching alleys, hitting off live pitching. The other outfielders hit off batting tees into sock nets.

SEGMENT 3: 20-MINUTE WORK

Pitchers

Two pitching alleys are set up on one side of the floor. In one alley, the pitcher throws to a hitter. In the other alley, the pitcher throws to a target. On the diamond, one pitcher rolls the ball to the third baseman, who practices fielding a slow roller. One pitcher throws changeups from the mound to the catcher. Another pitcher starts the double play for the second baseman and shortstop.

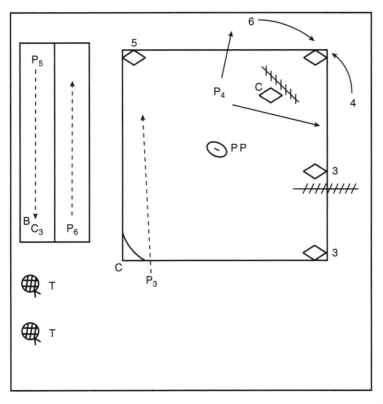

Figure 11.8 Segment 3. 4, 6, 3, P_4 = players turning 4-6-3 or 6-4-3 double play; 5 = third baseman fielding slow roller; 3 = first baseman covering bag or taking throw from third baseman (first basemen switch); C = catcher throwing to second base into screen or to other catcher; T, B = outfielders hitting off tees or live; PP = pitcher throwing changeup to catcher; C_3, P_5 = live pitching in cage; P_6 = pitcher pitching to target; P_3 = pitcher rolling slow rollers to third baseman.

(continued)

SEGMENT 3: 20-MINUTE WORK *(continued)*

First Basemen, Second Basemen, Shortstops
First basemen, second basemen, and shortstops practice turning the 4-6-3 double play.

Third Basemen
Third basemen practice fielding slow rollers off a rolled ball from the pitcher.

Catchers
One catcher catches live pitching in one of the pitching alleys. The other catcher catches the changeup from the mound and throws to second. Use a screen or another catcher to catch the throw to second since the second basemen and shortstops will be practicing the 4-6-3 double play.

Hitters
Outfielders are the hitters. One hitter stands in a pitching alley and hits off live pitching. The other hitters hit off tees into sock nets.

SEGMENT 4: THREE-LINE DRILL

Pitchers
Two pitching alleys are set up. In one pitching alley, the pitcher pitches live to a hitter. In the other pitching alley, the pitcher throws to a target. In the middle of the floor, three pitchers work on three different fielding situations. One pitcher fields a slow roller from a catcher and communicates the best play. The second pitcher fields comebackers to the mound. The third pitcher fields balls hit to the right side from a fungo hitter. Pitchers rotate into the line after each hit.

Catchers
One catcher is in the pitching alley catching live pitching. One catcher sends slow rollers to the third baseman and to one of the pitchers, communicating the best play. One catcher works with the group fielding comebackers to the mound. One catcher works with the group fielding balls hit to the right side. If there are not enough catchers, any player or manager will do.

First Basemen
First basemen practice fielding balls hit to the right side from a fungo hitter.

Second Basemen and Shortstops
Second basemen and shortstops practice fielding throws from the pitchers who are fielding comebackers to the mound.

Third Basemen
Third basemen practice fielding slow rollers and communicating the best play. No throw can be made in this line if the third baseman fields the ball.

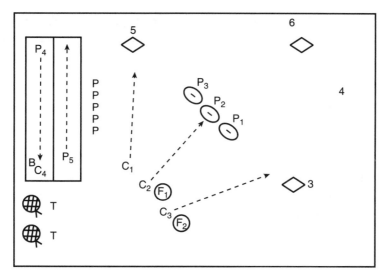

Figure 11.9 Segment 4 (three-line drill). P_3, 5, C_1 = slow rollers from C, communicate but no throw; P_2, C_2, F_1, 6, 4 = comebackers to the mound from fungo 1; P_1, C_3, F_2, 3 = balls hit to right side from fungo 2; P = pitcher who rotates in after each ball is hit; P_5 = pitcher pitching to target; P_4, C_4 = live pitching in cages, throwing to hitters; T, B = outfielders hitting off tees or live.

Hitters

Outfielders are hitting. One hitter stands in the pitching alley and hits off live pitching. The other two hitters hit off batting tees into sock nets.

SEGMENT 5: MULTIPLE-INFIELD DRILL

Pitchers

Two pitching alleys are set up. In one alley, the pitcher throws to a target. In the other alley, the pitcher pitches live to a hitter.

Catchers

One catcher catches live pitching in a pitching alley. The other catcher practices making tags at the plate.

Outfielders

Outfielders practice fielding the ball off a wall. They also stand in as hitters for live pitching.

Infielders

Infielders practice different fielding schemes. All plays in a scheme happen simultaneously.

(continued)

SEGMENT 5: MULTIPLE-INFIELD DRILL *(continued)*

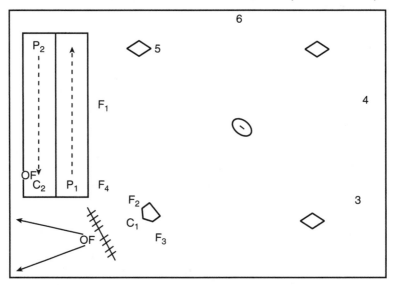

Figure 11.10 Segment 5 (multiple-infield drill). F = fungoes; C_1 = catcher making tags; OF = outfielders playing balls against the wall and hitting; C_2, P_2 = live pitching in cage; P_1 = pitcher pitching to target.

Scheme 1

F_3 to 5 to C_1: Third baseman goes to the plate.

F_2 to 6 to 4 to 3: Players turn the double play.

F_4 to 3 to F_4: First baseman takes deep ground balls and returns them to the fungo hitter; first basemen switch.

Scheme 2

F_2 to 6 to C_1: Shortstop moves to a shallow spot.

F_3 to 5 to 4 to 3: Bases are moved slightly to make room to turn the double play.

F_4 to 3_1 to F_4: First baseman takes deep ground balls and returns them to the fungo hitter; first basemen switch.

Scheme 3

F_2 to 4 to C_1: From a shallow position, the second baseman goes to the plate.

F_4 to 3 to 6 to 3: Bases are extended back for the double play.

F_3 to 5 to F_3: Third baseman fields balls to his right and returns them to the fungo hitter.

Scheme 4

F_4 to 3 to C_1: First baseman goes to the plate.

F_2 to 4 to 6 to 5: Ball is too late for double play, so shortstop fakes throw to first base then whirls and throws to third base.

Practice for Outfielders

"What do I do with the outfielders?" is a question that coaches often ask when planning indoor practices. After hitting and bunting, outfielders can have the gym floor while the infielders bunt, hit, and do tee work. The following sample schemes can be done with a gym floor.

FOUR TYPES OF GROUND BALLS

Pitchers
Pitchers fungo hit ground balls to the outfielders (two pitchers per line).

Outfielders
Outfielders field ground balls off pitchers' fungo hits. Four types of ground-ball situations are practiced. Ground ball 1 is fielded as if the play is a normal infield play. Ground ball 2 is the same as ground ball 1 except with a runner attempting an extra base. Ground ball 3 is a do-or-die play with a winning run potentially scoring. Ground ball 4 is a play on which the defense is preserving a big lead or a play on a rough field. The outfielder goes down on one knee to make the play.

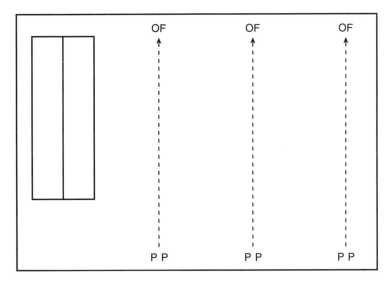

Figure 11.11 Outfielders fielding ground balls. OF = outfielders; P = pitchers fungo hitting ground balls.

OUTFIELDER'S REVERSE PIVOT

Fungo Hitters
Fungo hitters hit the ball to the bare-hand side of each outfielder.

Outfielders
Outfielders field the ball backhanded and practice the reverse pivot.

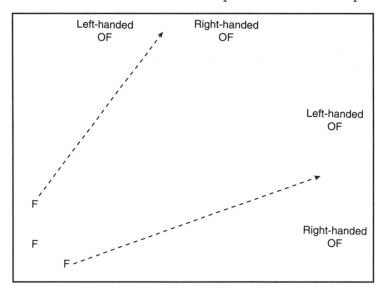

Figure 11.12   Outfielder's reverse pivot. F = fungo hitter hitting the ball to the bare-hand side for the backhand and reverse pivot; OF = outfielders.

BALL OVER HEAD AND OFF THE WALL

Coach
A coach throws the ball over the outfielder's head or shoulder.

Outfielder
Outfielders practice footwork and work on finding the wall and catching the ball.

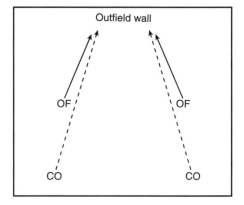

Figure 11.13   Ball over head and off the wall. CO = coach throwing the ball over the outfielder's head or shoulder; OF = outfielders.

DIVING DRILL

Because outfielders will be diving, you should place tumbling mats on the floor to prevent injury.

Coach

A coach throws a long-hanging ball over the mat.

Outfielders

Outfielders practice catching the ball while falling and rolling correctly.

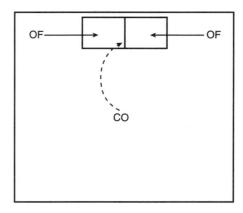

Figure 11.14 Diving drill. OF = outfielders; CO = coach.

STATIONARY BALL DRILL

Place five balls in different spots on the floor. The outfielder is told which ball to get from the floor. If space allows, an infielder can be added. The outfielder gets the ball from the floor, using both hands to field the ball, and throws to the infielder.

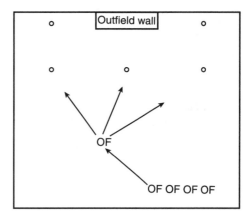

Figure 11.15 Stationary ball drill. OF = outfielder.

Small-Space Drills for the Entire Team

What does a coach do when he arrives at an indoor practice site and someone in authority says, "You have to share the gym floor today"? The following examples assume that you have a space that is 60 by 120 feet (18.3 by 36.6 m), although most can be adapted to fit smaller spaces. In each example, the players are practicing simultaneously.

SMALL-SPACE MECHANICS

Pitchers
One group of pitchers is in a corner practicing pickoff footwork to first or second base. Another group works on fielding bunts and proper communication (no throws).

Catchers
Catchers work with pitchers on pickoffs to first or second base.

Infielders
Infielders practice short hops, quick tags, double-play feeds, reverse pivots, backhands, and four-corner throws.

Outfielders
Outfielders practice crow hops.

Coaches
One coach tosses balls to the infielders. Another coach rolls balls to the outfielders. A third coach stands in as the hitter for the group fielding bunts.

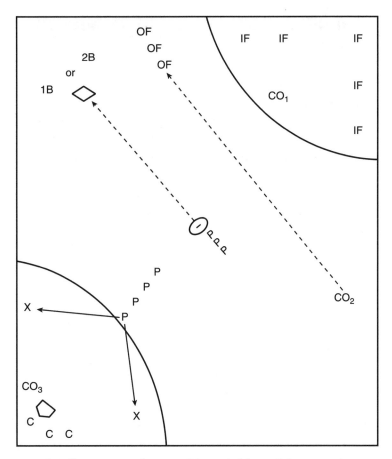

Figure 11.16 Small-space mechanics. IF = infielders; CO_1 = coach tossing balls to infielders; CO_2 = coach rolling balls to outfielders; OF = outfielders; P = pitchers working on pickoffs to second or first base; CO_3, P, C = players working on communication and bunt fielding (no throws).

Pitchers

Pitchers pitch changeups to another pitcher.

Base Runners

Runners on the same base at the same time go through different baserunning skills. Each base runner must find his pitcher if he is stealing second base. Runners rotate around the square and then start another skill.

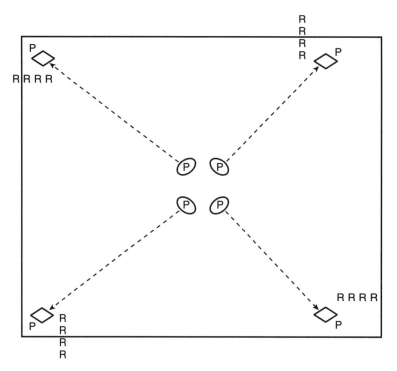

Figure 11.17 60-feet square baserunning. P = pitchers; R = base runners.

Pitchers

Pitchers practice pickoffs and rundowns at second and third base.

First Basemen

First basemen practice fielding low and high balls and using proper footwork.

Second Basemen, Shortstops, Third Basemen

Second basemen, shortstops, and third basemen practice pickoffs and run-downs at second and third base.

Base Runners

Base runners practice escaping pickoffs and rundowns at second and third base.

Hitters

Hitters bunt off a machine or live pitching.

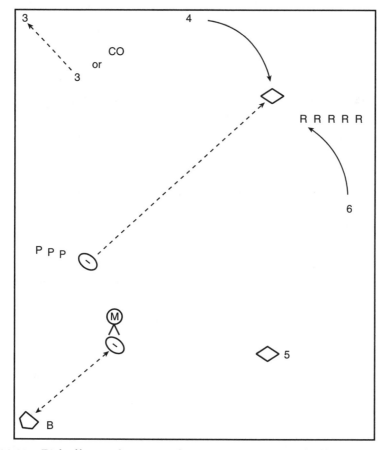

Figure 11.18 Pickoffs, rundowns, and more. 4, 6, 5, P = pickoffs and rundowns at second and third base; R = base runners; CO = coach; 3 = first baseman; B = hitters bunting off a machine or live pitching.

Indoor Practice Plan That Uses Three Gymnasium Floors or a Field House

After deciding what skills to work on and looking at the space and time available, a coach is ready to design the indoor practice plan for the upcoming day. The ideas discussed previously as well as the sample practice segments and small-space drills should be a great help in creating the plan. Remember that drill periods should be kept short and held often, thus creating a feeling of freshness with each day. Plan each practice so that it begins with a large-group activity, branches off into a small-group activity, and ends with a large-group activity. This way the day begins and ends with the team together. The following sample practice plan uses all the information covered in this chapter.

3:00 p.m.: Coaches meet with the team.

3:05 p.m.: Players circle the field house for warm-up laps and stretch.

3:20 p.m.: Players throw the length of the facility; players partner with others at their positions.

3:30 p.m.: Pitchers throw to targets and hitters or work on picks to first base (rotating to these stations). Outfielders hit and do tee work. Catchers catch pitchers and work on blocking (rotating to these stations). Infielders do throwing and fielding warm-ups.

3:50 p.m.: Pitchers throw to targets and hitters or hit fungoes to infielders. Catchers hit and catch pitchers. Infielders take ground balls at their positions and work on all plays (6 to 3, 5 to 3, 4 to 3, 3 to 5, and others).

4:10 p.m.: Pitchers continue pitching and practice fielding bunts. Catchers catch pitchers and drill with pitchers. First basemen work on communication when covering first base on balls hit to the right side. Shortstops, third basemen, and second basemen hit and do tee work. Outfielders field four types of ground balls.

4:30 p.m.: Outfielders practice diving on mats and fielding the ball against the wall. Catchers practice throws to second base (find a proper space in the gym). Pitchers, first basemen, second basemen, and shortstops work on picks and rundowns between first and second base. Third basemen practice fielding bunts and slow rollers.

4:55 p.m.: Catchers, pitchers, and third basemen work on picks and rundowns between third base and home plate. Shortstops, second basemen, and first basemen practice bunting. Outfielders work on drop steps, crow hops, and reverse pivots.

5:15 p.m.: Players work on conditioning and baserunning (done simultaneously).

5:30 p.m.: Coaches meet with the team.

5:35 p.m.: Practice ends.

Coming indoors does not have to be a detriment to a team's progress. In fact, being indoors allows a coach to take advantage of small-group instruction, which leads to more effective learning. Also, a coach can be close to everything that is taking place in his allotted practice space. Being indoors usually leads to shorter practice time for the afternoon or evening, which helps keep athletes' minds fresh and aggressive.

During indoor practice sessions, coaches must be sure not to practice against the clock. Baseball is unique in that it doesn't have a time factor during competition. If a particular drill doesn't go well and you think you need more time than was allotted for a particular practice segment, you should take the pragmatic approach. Change your plan. Every plan may look better on paper than on the gymnasium floor, so a coach must be comfortable with changing the segment or allotted time on the spot. Remember, having to come inside is not the end of the world.

chapter 12

Using Equipment and Technology

GARY PULLINS

Some baseball coaches' use of today's equipment can be compared to showing an old black-and-white classic movie instead of taking advantage of the dramatic special effects of modern films. Holding the attention of present-day moviegoers requires more than a solid script and presentation. Many baseball instructors know their lines. However, a coach needs to understand the proper use of equipment in order to hold athletes' attention and thus shorten their learning curve. When used properly, equipment can enhance the skills of baseball players, just as special effects enhance the skills of the actor.

Stagecoach to Rapid Transit

Many of us are old school when it comes to repetition. However, a coach can't simply subscribe to the practice-makes-perfect approach without taking into account the various tools available to enhance practice. Coaches should consider the use of tees, machine toss, golf-sized Wiffle balls, myriad swing-right inventions, paddle gloves for defense, bare-hand drills, towel drills, throwing dowels, and so on. The products on the market are very effective, provided that the athlete uses them with a specific purpose. For this to occur, the coach needs to assess the specificity of the skill being taught. This makes for perfect practice, which makes perfect.

Rapid-fire toss, for instance, does not promote better hitting skills. The swings taken in this drill may contribute to strength and endurance; however, these swings do not help cultivate a consistent load, a consistent approach, and dynamic balance, which should be the objectives of a hitting drill. Baseball is such an enjoyable sport to practice that we are often too easy on ourselves in practice and too hard on ourselves in the game. Optimal preparation requires that we make practice as gamelike as possible for the age group we are coaching. Each player should be encouraged to repeat the skills with intensity and pronounced definition in practice, realizing that this may not be possible on game day against challenging opponents.

Some young pitchers have experienced the frustration of knowing exactly how to pitch but still being dominated by hitters, and have rededicated themselves to their practice regimen. The attitude toward the use of instructional devices seems to be as important as the equipment itself. Specificity of training engenders improved execution.

Inquisitive coaches are always seeking instructional media that will resonate with their players. The things that have been effective for you may need refining and updating. Check out the latest equipment on the market. These tools may speak to a given athlete at just the right teaching moment. Always be on the lookout for methods and tools that will allow you to give customized instruction in various skills. Let's look at some equipment available and some unique ways that it may be used to enhance your practice.

Speed or Radar Gun

This tool was initially used by Danny Litwiler, a former major-league outfielder and longtime college coach. Many coaches have become enamored with the simple arm strength measurement that the gun affords, but Danny used the gun to determine what changes in velocity from fastball to breaking ball to changeup would be most effective for each pitcher on his club. The gun also informs the coach (through his experience) when a pitcher may be tiring.

When a speed gun is used during a bullpen session, pitchers are able to recognize at what speeds they lose control or movement on the ball. Many young pitchers overthrow and muscle their throws, resulting in poor command and excessive arm strain. By interpreting the information provided by the radar gun, the coach can objectively define ways that each pitcher may throw with less effort while maintaining velocity and enhancing command. Top-end velocity is overrated with high school and college pitchers, whereas command, movement, and change of speed are trainable skills for all pitchers. It's a nice luxury to have arms that deliver a baseball in the upper 80s to mid-90s; however, you shouldn't be deceived into thinking that velocity alone will produce a winner or that the speed gun should be relegated exclusively to building egos.

Use the gun with position players as well. This can help outfielders, infielders, and catchers learn the importance of footwork before the release. They will see a difference in accuracy as well as velocity.

Pitching Machines

Beyond the obvious benefits provided by a pitching machine—such as accuracy and stamina (allowing more swings for hitters)—these machines can enhance practice in a variety of additional ways. The use of a dual-machine station will provide hitters with the challenge of seeing a fastball from one machine and a breaking ball from another unit. Or, the hitter may be called on to hit an inside pitch and then transition to a ball away on the next delivery. Purchase several varieties of pitching machine balls, and mix different textured balls at the same station. Speeds will vary, and some machines may even be a little erratic, delivering pitches out of the zone. This simulates the experience your players will have on game day, helping them learn discipline at the plate. Any attempt to produce more gamelike conditions will help your team's offensive game.

The machines should be fed to give the hitter five or six seconds between pitches. This enables the hitter to assess his sequence and to watch his body as well as the ball. Help players avoid the temptation of simply becoming robots in the cage instead of having a plan for that specific practice station. Depending on the number of machines your program can afford, specify the hitting skill that hitters are to refine at each station. Bunting, situational hitting, breaking-ball approach, coverage of both sides of the plate, bat quickness, and vision training can all be enhanced by employing a machine.

Some coaches believe that pitching machines should not be used during the season. You need to experiment to know what works best for you. What is effective for one player may not work for another. Player attitude has a great deal to do with the effectiveness of any drill, and nothing is more diverse than the hitting game. If a player thinks hitting off the machine helps him be a better hitter, then it will. This is the real reason you want to begin using the machine during the off-season. In time, each athlete will incorporate his signature drills while facing the machine.

A coach can find machines and devices that help players improve their ability to see the ball and deliver the bat to the ball more effectively. Among the best tools are multiple-head tees, life-size video pitchers (such as ProBatter), elastic straps that eradicate casting and premature arm extension, soft-toss units that deliver more repetitions in a small space, and Wiffle ball applications for gymnasium use. Your imagination is the only limiting factor (after considering your budgetary restraints, of course).

Most baseball coaches fail to use machines to improve defensive skills. You would be wise to do so, especially for catchers and outfielders. Identify the most challenging plays for these positions. Catchers, for example, don't see enough pop-ups in practice. Equip catchers in their complete gear, and angle the machine to get backspin on the ball around home plate and toward the stands. The catcher is at the plate until you give him the word to find the ball and catch the pop-up, taking into account infield drift. Also, the catcher can use the machine to practice catching the ball in the dirt at an elevation consistent with a wild pitch or to practice firmly receiving a pitch on the periphery of the strike zone.

Outfielders can practice going back to the warning track and wall. Once calibrated for distance, the machine will be much more consistent than the best fungo hitters. These drills also free the coach to instruct the outfielder while other players feed the machine.

I realize that each coach has his own approach to the use of any machine or device. I have found that the players will provide feedback on which drills are most effective. Don't hesitate to call a drill experimental and then ask if team members think the drill will help them become better players. Remember, though, if players detest the drill, this may mean that the drill is tough but effective. You reserve the right to make the final evaluation.

Overloaded and Underloaded Bats and Balls

Coop DeRenne of the University of Hawaii has done extensive research on the benefits of using slightly overloaded and underloaded bats in tee drills and soft-toss drills. The use of a ball that is 1 ounce (28.3 g) lighter or heavier than a regulation ball in throwing exercises has also proven effective in arm conditioning. Coach DeRenne's research suggests that the use of extreme overload, such as the donut on a bat or a steel ball for throwing, does not promote speed development. In fact, the use of the weighted donut on a bat typically alters a young hitter's stroke, distancing it from what really happens in the hitting sequence. More is not better; slightly overloaded or underloaded resistances are most effective.

Some years ago, our BYU baseball team participated in a study with several other universities. The study was the brainchild of noted pitching instructor Tom House. This research project measured arm strength development using 4- and 6-ounce (113.4 and 170.1 g) baseballs and a football. Initially, pitchers were the focus group; however, because our team was confined to indoor workouts from November through February, we developed a training station where all position players rotated into the study as well. Some athletes showed improvement in throwing velocity, and some did not. But all players—both pitchers and position players—avoided that dead-arm stage that typically hit our players when we finally began playing outdoors. The use of several types of balls promoted more throwing and reduced the boredom that stems from the sameness of throwing exclusively with the official 5-ounce (141.7 g) ball. In fact, the football toss graduated into a running and throwing exercise as each player began seeing himself as a quarterback and wide receiver, all wrapped into one body.

As the coach incorporates varied practice protocols, his players find ways to improve in areas that were unanticipated. The use of technology in sport is inspired by a periodic leap of faith that is often promoted by frustration with previous failure. True success is the positive utilization of failure.

Special Effects

When many of today's veteran coaches were playing the game, some of their innovative predecessors began using super eight and multiple-shutter cameras to film hitting and pitching mechanics. At the time, these techniques were considered avant-garde technology. The next generation progressed to video and instant replay. Before this time, athletic kinematics were taught simply by demonstrating what were considered to be proper actions. Then instructors realized the following: "The hand may be quicker than the eye, but 160 frames per second can't lie." With today's technology, the astute instructor can see precisely what the athlete is doing and, through applied biomechanical adjustments, can make improvements that make the athlete more efficient.

What the best hitters and pitchers in the game do in order to be successful may not be applicable to your athletes. Indeed, attempting to model every action after one specific major leaguer could produce what we call *paralysis by analysis*. However, the ability to videotape, replay, and instruct with these mediums certainly outweighs the critical-eye-at-game-speed approach. As the highway caution signs read, "Slow Down: Construction Ahead." The highway to success in this game is always under construction. A three-dimensional approach to motion analysis (such as the model developed by Bio-Kinetics) is one of the great vehicles available today for baseball coaches. As you become familiar with one or more of the playback systems on the market, I can assure you that slowing down the motion will accelerate the learning.

Most major-league teams use some motion analysis throughout the entire season, but those of us who work with younger, less experienced players witness better results using it during the off-season when experimentation time is available. Studies conducted years ago revealed that filming and then allowing the athlete to review the tape did little to enhance the player's performance. Two fallacies applied to those findings. First, the athletes filmed were novices who knew little of correct mechanics to begin with. This would be tantamount to teaching algebra to those with no knowledge of timetables. Second, the youth of today are more savvy with technology, and thus, they are more innovative when looking at film. The instruction will not be left on the cutting room floor, provided the coach and player understand what constitutes good mechanics.

Properties of good hitting and pitching mechanics or kinematics will always be debatable because neither is an exact science. But the astute instructor can contour the principles taught so they are correct for the level of the participant. Without question, the findings of biomechanists employing three-dimensional digitized analysis reveal not just what a majority of successful athletes do but also when they do it.

Correcting hitting and pitching faults does not usually require beginning at square one. Should the problem be corrected by sermon or surgery? This is a tough question to answer. That's why you are the artist whose craft is to explore every possibility to help each willing player improve. Change should not be made simply for change's sake, but because a different approach will enhance performance.

Keep those ankles taped as we move beyond capturing video for review. Be assured that you and your athletes will enjoy analyzing athletic movement under the right circumstances. You'll need to enlist the assistance of another coach or teacher because film of actual game conditions will be far more instructive than recordings of the practice routine. The alien within shows his face when adrenaline is flowing, so get his portrait during real time. Even pitchers throwing at maximum velocity during a bullpen session will not exhibit the identical delivery that they employ under game conditions.

I have found that the less experienced the player, the greater the discrepancy between his practice and game performance. In other words, a major-league player may be more easily analyzed during practice than a youth league or high school player. The irony of this, of course, is that video analysis at the major-league level is far more easily obtained. If you coach baseball or softball in high school, college, or even the minor leagues in professional baseball, you should make every attempt to capture video in games rather than in practice. By doing so, you will have a more accurate depiction of what your athlete is doing up at the plate and on the mound.

Let's retrace a few of our steps to review some major-league averages and discuss those of importance in developing an economical and efficient hitting stroke. With respect to stride length, 4 to 6 inches (10.2 to 15.2 cm) from stance to foot strike is considered optimal and seems to reduce head and eye movement during the stride. However, the average for major-league players does include those who may have a measurement of 15 inches (38.1 cm), a figure far exceeding what most hitting instructors would advocate. Nine inches (22.8 cm) of head movement during the stride seems to be about average.

Head movement during the swing is much more complex because of what has become known as measurable movement X, Y, and Z. This is measured by the distance the head moves on a horizontal plane from catcher to pitcher. The goal should be about 1 inch (2.5 cm) forward, but the average is about 3.72 inches (9.4 cm). This constitutes the X measurement. The direction from dugout to dugout is used to measure any head lean toward or away from home plate. This is defined as the Y measurement, and it is usually a positive figure measuring (in inches) the amount of head lean toward home plate. The Z measurement is usually a negative figure because it indicates how far the head and eyes drop from stance to swing. The longer the stride, the more the head will drop in elevation as the body goes directionally from a linear to angular shift. The average Z measurement is –2 inches (–5.1 cm). The bottom-line goal in all of these measurements is head stabilization, which minimizes head and eye movement during the stride and swing.

Front-side blocking simply measures the lateral hip drift after the front foot has landed and before rotation begins in the sequence. Violent hip rotation cannot occur until blocking is completed. Similar to head movement during the swing, the lateral hip drift from catcher to pitcher needs to be minimized. This is a key link in the hitting sequence. In younger hitters, the position of the back foot is often overlooked in favor of swing content. The foot must move to a "heel-up, toe-down" position to allow full rotation. If the back heel remains in contact with the ground, the remaining aspects of the sequence (i.e., angular rotation and axis of rotation) are impeded. A poor sequence equals a poor strength base and, therefore, poor timing.

Overall kinetic link—a measurement, in degrees, of disassociation of lower body from upper body—indicates the degree to which the hips are leading the way. This will drastically affect bat speed and quickness. In other words, the lower half leads the upper half in order to deliver the bat to the ball. The movement of the upper half requires surgical, quick finesse; below the belt, there is a storm going on. One might say that the hands ride the crest of the wave that the hips create. A disassociation of 30 to 40 degrees is average for major-league hitters. Evidence shows the importance of sequential rotation: A hitter with a 15- to 20-degree disassociation generates poor bat quickness and speed.

The Science of Hitting by John Underwood and Ted Williams makes the point that the hips need to lead the way. Charlie Lau articulated the same thing but called it a *weight transfer*. This may simply be a matter of semantics. Nevertheless, angular velocity and axis of rotation depend on the inclusion of sequential rotation energized by this disassociation or separation of lower half from upper half.

Your reward for negotiating through this part of the text is a better understanding of why some hitters are simply more efficient. A more economical approach and stroke allow the hitter to see more of the ball by waiting longer to commit, thus permitting fewer mistakes. If you ask a hitter what part of the bat has to interface with the ball in order to hit the ball hard, unless the hitter is the village idiot, he will respond by pointing to the sweet spot or barrel of the bat. Unfortunately, some players allow this knowledge to create anxiety about casting the barrel prematurely to the ball.

Conversely, if a hitter maintains bat lag (or, in other words, rides rotation with the knob end of the bat), allowing the barrel to lag slightly behind, he is in a better position to generate bat quickness. This measurement, defined in hundredths of a second, is a pivotal element of the efficient hitting stroke. A major-league hitter whose quickness is 0.165 of a second is about average, whereas 0.18 to 0.20 of a second is considered poor, because pitch recognition requires approximately 0.20 of a second before initiation of the swing. For many years, we thought that bat speed was the real deal. And, admittedly, there is a correlation between bat speed and bat quickness. However, a slowpitch softball hitter who generates a swing in excess of 80 miles per hour at club head may not be sufficiently quick to catch up with a pitch in excess of 80 miles per hour. Average bat speed of major-league hitters is 72.1 miles per hour. Hence, bat quickness—measuring the time from launch to contact while hitting a ball into fair territory—is really a better measure of potential hitting success.

Rehearsal

Coaches seek to instruct players at the level they can understand. Some players simply understand the words, while others comprehend the theory behind the instruction. Most amateur players trust that the verbal training is reinforcement for the skills training that is taking place; however, they may not be connecting the two parts, and movements may not feel right. A young player will often respond favorably to a positive "Way to go!" without really knowing what he did to deserve the compliment. In this case, the coach is giving positive reinforcement for good effort but not necessarily proper execution.

Every coach should have a tool that will help the athlete learn the proper *feel* for the correct movement. Remember that making changes in throwing, hitting, or running form will take time and that these changes are best rehearsed during the off-season. However, your training sessions may not afford you this luxury, so precision in the instructional mode is very important. Don't reinvent the wheel all at once, unless injury is a risk. Making subtle rather than sweeping changes works better with older players. A more novice player may require more broad-sweeping changes, depending on the receptive nature of the athlete and your relationship with him.

Let me offer a few tricks that have worked for me during practice sessions. I have found that, regardless of the age of the players, asking them questions will stimulate their thinking. Ask the players if they have ever been to a diving or gymnastics meet. Then ask about how the athletes in those sports are scored. Most players will know that the athletes in these sports are evaluated on their form: A 9.6 score is very good; a 10 is perfect. Now introduce the idea of what players would do if the rules of baseball were changed to reflect more on how the players performed when they are throwing, hitting, fielding, or running. Would this change the way the players approached the game? I did this once with a professional minor-league affiliate when we were working on sliding. The very next game, a player performed a less-than-perfect slide while in the act of stealing second base. The fact that he was not injured was a miracle. From our team dugout came the observation, "That was a –2.5 on a scale of 10!" I was pleased that the players remembered the analogy, if not the skill.

No doubt you have some favorite toys that work for you. In hitting, any device that shortens the stride and reduces head and eye movement is practical. A strap or concept bat that prevents casting or premature arm extension is always handy. With respect to throwing, any device that teaches proper arm action and pronation after release will reduce the incidence of arm injury.

Broad-sweeping changes are only needed in the case of potential injury. In baseball, this is especially important when it comes to the throwing action and to sliding. Although sliding occurs less frequently than throwing, proper attention to that skill is equally urgent. At summer youth camps, I used to employ a Slip 'n Slide to teach sliding. The slick surface of the pad allowed anyone to slide, even if his form was not correct. For years, sliding pits filled with sand or sawdust were used by major-league teams at their spring training sites. The landing was soft, but the proper approach was not reinforced because the athlete would simply stop on contact. Purchase one of the padded fabric slides on the market, and place it on the outfield grass or pointing downhill on a grassy surface. The players will run and fall into the slide correctly after just a few repetitions. Very little instruction will be needed; the skill will practically be self-taught.

Paying attention to arm injuries is particularly important because of their frequency and the diverse schools of thought regarding the reasons for them. Many experts claim that overuse is the cause of arm injury. Others maintain that players pitch too much and throw too little. I'll leave the answers to those who are more qualified than I am. Suffice it to say, throwing as little as one inning is overuse when the athlete is using poor mechanics. Your bag of tricks should include video footage of proper throwing technique, very light dumbbells for rotator cuff exercises, tubes for stretching and underload, and lightweight balls for closely supervised warm-up drills for throwing. When your players start asking to check out some of your gadgets for overnight practice, you'll know you have arrived. They actually want to take the lab home with them.

Through the Lens

I believe that those of us who teach the game of baseball are just beginning to scratch the surface in the area of visual training. In the mid-1970s, Dr. Bill Harrison, a doctor of optometry and former college baseball player, recorded an audiotape series titled *Vision Dynamics*. After listening to the tapes, I decided to have my players' eyesight checked each year at the end of fall ball. Without fail, several athletes would require some correction in their vision.

Some players could not be fitted for contacts and would simply have their eyeglass prescriptions updated. Interestingly enough, of those players whose eyesight needed to be corrected and adjusted over the years, two were future major-league players, Vance Law and Wally Joyner. Law could not be fitted with contacts, and he found ways to succeed as a Division I basketball and baseball player while wearing glasses. During his 10-year professional baseball career, Law remained aware of the importance of visual acuity; he had annual checks of his vision to determine if any prescription upgrades were needed. In his case, he found that the use of glasses outweighed the fear of blinking at just the wrong time.

Joyner took a different approach. After his freshman year in college, he found himself playing in the very competitive Alaskan Collegiate League. That summer, I received a call from Dennis Mattingly, the general manager of the Cook Inlet Bucks, Wally's team. He was reporting on the progress of two of my players: Kevin Towers, who would become the GM of the San Diego Padres, and Wally Joyner. He ended the conversation by saying that they were both doing well, but that Joyner wasn't hitting. Well, I would have believed that Wally had missed a sign or was late for the bus, but not that he was having trouble hitting. The kid from Stone Mountain, Georgia, could hit line drives while standing on his head. I immediately called Wally in Alaska only to find out that he had been hit in the eye while playing pickup basketball and could no longer wear one of his hard contact lenses. He had been playing baseball wearing his reading glasses. He couldn't hit because he couldn't "get true meaning from what he saw." Once he could properly wear his lenses again, he was able to hit again, and he eventually spent 17 years in the big leagues. Joyner did get Lasik surgery late in his career. When he and Tony Gwynn, who was reputed to have terrific vision, were teammates with the Padres, Joyner commented that the true challenge for Gwynn would be hitting with Joyner's eyes.

The point is that you should make your athletes aware of visual training and should encourage them to integrate this into their game plan. Many athletes will be able to adjust, to a certain degree, simply because they are good athletes. However, making them aware of the importance of visual acuity—and how to gain more meaning from what they see—will encourage these players to do what is necessary to compete successfully at higher levels.

Acuity is only a small contributor to improved visual performance. The use of a tachistoscope, a device used by the military to train fighter pilots to view pictures rapidly, can be introduced into your baseball practice. The apparatus has also been adapted to train for speed-reading classes. A strobe light is set to various intervals, from multiple seconds to fractions of a second. The players view cards and experiment with their ability to see words or pictures in minimal time. Using these types of reaction units can be integrated at one of the hitting or defensive stations at practice.

Innovations in visual training are forthcoming each year. A complete sequence of a ball being released from pitcher to hitter in multiple slides has been on the market for some time now. Frozen Ropes, a performance enhancement company, is just one of the entities working to assist baseball players in making sure their strategies of visualization contribute to their success in competition.

Baseball is a game with a certain amount of intellectual elegance. That elegance is enhanced by the passion of coaches always seeking a better way. Each coach could write his own chapter for this text, combining that passion with knowledge of the game and experience. Your own creative use of special effects in teaching will contribute to a standing ovation when the curtain falls on your practice.

chapter 13

Incorporating Competitive Drills and Games

SEAN MCNALLY

One of the core values of any successful baseball program is taking pride in the effort level and competitiveness of its practice sessions. Game day is a window into how organized, disciplined, and structured the team's practices are—day in, day out. Here at Duke we take great pride in our culture of practicing at a high level and doing everything at a focus and concentration level that will prepare us to win on game day.

One of our responsibilities as a staff is to incorporate drills and games that foster the competitiveness that will be critical to our success during games. On most days, we combine a routine or a set of drills with a constant effort to come up with new ways to keep things fresh and keep the intensity high during practice. The framework that we use encompasses four areas: individual drills, positional drills, drills between positional groups, and team drills.

As a general rule, we start with individual drills, move to positional drills, then move to multiple positional drills, and finish with team drills. Sometimes we start with a team drill, but we always finish with a team drill to conclude practice. All of this drill work is important for skill development, but it is equally important in assessing each player's attitude, effort level, and concentration as he goes through practice. Winning attitudes in practice help foster a winning environment on game day. A group that does not execute well collectively in practice will struggle on game day. Keep the energy level and intensity up by using competitive drills in practice.

Individual Drills

Our competitive mind-set for practice starts when our players come through the gate and onto the field. This is easier said than done, because all players have many responsibilities in the classroom and in the community apart from baseball. During individual drills, make sure each player is engaged, attentive, and focused. Get started on a positive note every day.

Throwing Program

To jump-start this mind-set, especially during the fall practice period when the season seems so far away, we start competing during the throwing program (figure 13.1), immediately after the team stretch. We work on four facets during the throwing program:

1. Building arm strength
2. Increasing throwing accuracy
3. Preventing injuries
4. Improving communication between thrower and receiver

Position players throw at specific distances for specific times as they loosen their arms to prepare for practice. Infielders always catch the ball with two

Figure 13.1 Throwing program.

hands and drive their legs toward their target; they concentrate on hitting their partner in the chest every time. When the distance increases, infielders run through the proper footwork when receiving the ball as if they were a cutoff man or a relay man. Outfielders go through their outfield footwork once they get past 90 feet (27.4 m) away. Catchers always catch and transfer as if they were throwing out a runner at second base.

When players move back in to 90 feet after stretching out to a distance up to 180 feet (54.9 m), they compete with their partner in an accuracy game. Each time a player hits his partner in the chest, he scores a point. A hit above the shoulders or below the belt does not score, even if it is in the middle of the body. The game usually goes to 10 points (sometimes 5 points if we have less time). The reward for winning varies; sometimes the loser has to run a brisk lap around the field, get the winner a drink of water, or perform a field maintenance task at the end of practice.

Regardless of the rewards for winning, this simple drill raises the level of concentration significantly, and our players enjoy it as well. We work each day to be the most accurate throwing team in the country during the throwing program. Any time you can emphasize this goal and work toward it in a fun way, the activity is helpful. We want players to think that when they secure the ball, the difficult part is done. After that, it is a simple game of catch that we have worked at relentlessly since the start of workouts at the beginning of the school year.

The throwing game performed during the later portion of the throwing program emphasizes accuracy and concentration and also promotes communication between thrower and receiver.

Pepper Games

Another drill that players enjoy doing before the start of formal practice is the pepper game (figure 13.2). Pepper games are very beneficial to development from both offensive and defensive standpoints, yet they are often undervalued. Many players simply go through the motions when playing pepper.

Figure 13.2   Pepper game.

During pepper games, the hitter focuses on these keys:

- Use a short, direct path to the ball.
- Hit the ball squarely.
- Control the bat.

The fielders focus on these keys:

- Catch the ball in a proper fielding position.
- Move the feet correctly before throwing.
- Throw accurately.

We play pepper a certain way in order to get the most out of it, as we would with any drill that we do. In our pepper games, we have one hitter and three fielders. (If we add more than that, there is not enough action for the fielders.) We try to group infielders together if possible and let the outfielders and catchers work together. The hitter lays his glove down as a home plate, and the three fielders stand 10 to 20 feet (3.0 to 6.1 m) in front of him.

Players use one ball. The fielders are expected to field the ball cleanly and deliver a strike to the hitter. The hitter chokes up on the bat. He works on handling the bat, putting the barrel on the ball, and squaring it up. The hitter is essentially preparing to gear back and hit with two strikes in a game—but still make solid contact. The hitter tries to hit the ball to each fielder in order from left to right on one hop.

Fielders work on throwing accuracy. After fielding the ball, the fielders are required to funnel the ball to their center and move their feet in the direction of their target before they throw. Fielders must throw a strike to the hitter each time. We do not want to see players acting lazy and developing bad habits during pepper games by throwing without moving their feet or without pointing their shoulders to the target.

In our pepper game, the hitter stays in for the duration of the game. There is no set rotation between the hitter and the fielders. If the hitter is successfully hitting the ball to the fielders on one or two hops, he stays in as the hitter. Hitting seems to be the favorite thing for position players to do, so naturally our players came up with a way to rotate the hitter based on his performance and the performance of the fielders. The hitter gives up the bat for any of the following situations:

- The hitter swings and misses.
- The hitter hits a second foul tip, provided the thrower has thrown a strike.
- The fielder catches a line drive.

If the hitter swings and misses or hits a second foul tip, the hitter rotates to the spot on the far right, farthest away from hitting again; the next hitter comes from the left. If a fielder catches a line drive, that fielder becomes the hitter, regardless of his position in the line. Fielders can lose their place in line as well, because of errors in performance. If a fielder boots a ball, he goes to the end of the line. The pepper game makes both the hitter and the fielders concentrate on their respective tasks in a fun way. Everyone wants to hit.

With some of our more advanced hitters, we sometimes offset the fielders to give the hitter practice hitting the ball behind the runner. In this case, the hitter is simulating a base hit between first and second with a runner on first. We position two fielders in the hole and one fielder directly in front of the hitter. This fielder always receives the ball from the other two fielders and throws it to the hitter.

Another variation involves the middle infielders. They back up to a position 25 to 30 feet (7.6 to 9.1 m) in front of the hitter. They simulate a double-play feed before throwing the ball back to the hitter.

Pepper is part of our daily practice routine. It enables players to work on many types of critical baseball skills at a basic level. Making the pepper game competitive and requiring that it is played a certain way help ensure that we get the most beneficial result out of it. Don't waste any time, and don't create any bad habits along the way.

Positional Drills

After the throwing program and pepper game, we move to the positional drill phase of practice, which we call individual defense. By position, the infielders, outfielders, catchers, and pitchers are grouped together. As a former infielder, I coach the infielders directly here at Duke. My focus in this section will be on the competitive drills that we incorporate to make our infielders better.

Although the relationship between the catcher and pitcher is correctly considered the most critical on the field, we believe that the heart and soul of our defensive team is the infield. The infielders must provide energy and life to the club. Their play must be sharp and efficient in order to maintain tempo and energy during the ball game. Our drill work must prepare guys to play this way and to take pride in striving to handle the ball and play catch successfully each and every time.

Knee Drill Series

During an individual defense session for the infielders, we often start with a knee drill series that takes place in the outfield on the left-field line. This drill allows infielders to handle the ball many times without expending much energy. The fielders focus on these keys during the drill:

- Catch and transfer successfully on each routine play.
- Concentrate each time a ball is hit.
- Focus on the ball even when others are trying to be distractive.

Infielders, usually in a group of no more than four, are on their knees about 20 feet (6.1 m) in front of a coach with a fungo bat. The coach hits one-hop ground balls to the infielders in order from right to left. The infielders have their chest facing the coach (figure 13.3*a*). The coach is not trying to hit balls that are difficult to handle; rather, the coach tries to hit routine one hoppers that should be caught every time. If a ball is mishandled, the fielder receives a point. We usually set an elimination number at 3 points before starting the drill. A fielder who gets 3 points is eliminated and watches the rest of the drill.

Figure 13.3 Knee drill: (*a*) infielders face the fungo hitter; (*b*) infielders turn so knees and chests face home plate.

After starting the drill by hitting the one hoppers in order, the coach can mix it up and hit multiple balls to the same fielder or go in random order if he chooses. Moving in random order helps to ensure concentration each time the ball is hit, which is required in game action.

After a short period, all fielders turn so that their knees and chest face the plate (figure 13.3*b*). That puts right-handed fielders on their forehand side and left-handed fielders on their backhand side. The same sequence is followed: The coach fungo hits routine one hoppers to the fielder's forehand side in random order with a set elimination number. We then do the same drill to the backhand side; the players' knees and chest are facing the outfield wall. We emphasize concentrating and focusing on making the routine play every time.

After everyone but one fielder has been eliminated on the backhand side, we require that fielder to catch one more ground ball to win the segment for the day. The other fielders are allowed to do anything they want to distract the fielder from making the play—yelling, screening him from the ball, throwing their gloves through his line of sight. However, they are not allowed to touch the fielder in any way, just distract him. If he catches the ball, he wins and the group gets him water for the rest of the day. If he misses, then everyone is back in. On some days, this drill goes by quickly, but most days it takes awhile to eliminate everyone because the concentration level and the competitiveness between fielders are high.

Timed Drill: The Eight

We often progress from the knee drill to a timed drill that requires effort, conditioning, concentration, and execution. We call this drill "The Eight." The setup requires eight baseballs to be placed in various areas around the shortstop position (figure 13.4*a*). By making an X in the dirt, we mark a spot at standard depth to indicate where the infielder will start (figure 13.4*b*). The eight baseballs are put within the range of the shortstop, including some routine plays, some balls to the left and right, one ball deep in the hole, one ball up the middle, and a slow roller. We use The Eight as the last part of an individual defense segment because it is a tiring drill. This drill also helps to measure the ability of a particular infielder to concentrate and focus while fatigued.

During The Eight, we emphasize these points:

- Good conditioning
- Good fundamentals
- Accurate throwing
- Competitiveness

This is a good drill for seeing how hard the players will compete with each other and how they respond to adversity if they bobble the ball or throw it away. We expect to see players go harder after a miscue rather than give in and stop.

Each infielder takes a turn, and the coach times the drill. The fielder must field each of the eight balls (figure 13.4c) and throw accurately to first base (figure 13.4d), returning to the X after fielding each ball. Usually, one of the other infielders in the group stands at first base to receive the throw during the drill. The more efficient the infielder's technique is, the less fatigued he will become during the drill. Additionally, the fielder will need to have a strategy regarding the order in which he chooses to field the balls. In general, fielders work from most difficult to easiest, and they finish with the slow roller. We add 5 seconds to the final time for any throw that pulls the first baseman off the bag and for any bobble or mishandling of the ball on the transfer before the throw. We set a baseline time of 30 seconds to completion, meaning that if any fielder takes longer than 30 seconds to complete the drill, there is no winner.

Figure 13.4 The Eight: (*a*) placement of balls prior to start of drill; (*b*) an X indicates where the infielder starts the drill and where he returns after fielding a ball.

Figure 13.4 (*continued*)   (*c*) The infielder fields a ball and (*d*) throws to first.

The drill can also be done with 4 or 6 balls, depending on the intensity, conditioning, and experience of the infielders. Although we use 8 balls in the shortstop area, the number of balls and the position can be adjusted based on needs and ability level. We do variations of this drill using 6 balls at third base and 10 balls in the first-base area. The combination of competing against teammates as well as the clock elevates the level of effort and concentration. We expect infielders to be technically solid during this drill.

Other positional groups can be involved in this drill as well. Sometimes first basemen and catchers compete with middle infielders. Occasionally, we encourage the crossover of positional work with this type of drill in order to give catchers or outfielders a greater appreciation for the skill level and intensity of the work done by the infielders.

Drills Between Positional Groups

Preparing your club to play together as a team is just as important as developing individual skills and abilities. After the individual defense segment of practice, we move to defensive drills that require multiple positional groups to work together. Two examples of such drills are pitchers fielding practice (PFP) and relay throws involving outfielders and middle infielders.

Pitchers Fielding Practice (PFP)

Fielding the position and controlling the running game are two aspects of the pitcher's job that are generally underdeveloped before the college level. Many college pitchers were dominant in high school and therefore gained little experience pitching with runners on base. Additionally, they may have spent the majority of their time working on pitching and not put much time into learning the nuances of fielding.

Every day we emphasize the importance of pitchers fielding their position, and we try to involve the infielders as often as possible when the pitchers are working on fielding. Infielders need to get a feel for the athleticism of each pitcher, how well and how hard the pitcher throws to the bases, and the arm slot and movement on the ball when he delivers it to a base. For this reason, we try to incorporate both infielders and pitchers in PFP.

We start PFP with three groups of five or six pitchers in the mound area. The group on the first-base side of the mound (just off the dirt) practices regular pickoff moves to first followed by third-to-first moves, rotating through the line. For each accurate throw to first, the group is given a point. For each throw that is high or in the dirt, 2 points are deducted.

Pitchers in the second group operate from the rubber. They practice both the timing pickoff play and the daylight pickoff play with the shortstop and second baseman. The same scoring system is used. Because this is a more difficult throw for pitchers to make, the group score at this spot is usually lower.

On the third-base side of the mound, pitchers field bunts in a first-and-second situation, throwing the ball to third base for the force play. On this side, the emphasis is on footwork and accuracy. The third baseman keeps score. He deducts 3 points for a bad throw, because a bad throw in this situation would cost us a run if the ball got away.

Each group spends approximately 3 minutes at each spot. At the end of 10 minutes, points are totaled. These groups stay intact during the next portion of PFP.

For the second phase of PFP, all pitchers line up and run through all the basics of fielding the position one at a time:

- Fielding comebackers and throwing to first
- Fielding bunts and throwing to first
- Covering first base on ground balls to the first baseman
- Covering first on a double-play ball hit to the first baseman
- Fielding comebackers and throwing to second for the front half of a double play
- Fielding a bunt in a squeeze play situation and throwing to the plate

Each time any of these individual plays is completed successfully, the pitcher's group receives a point. A point is deducted for any miscue.

At the end of phase 2 (about 25 minutes), we identify the winning group. Usually, the pitchers in the winning group get one of their all-time favorite things: a chance to take some swings in batting practice. Other times we exempt the pitchers in the winning group from shagging during batting practice, which is generally one of their least favorite activities on the field.

During pitchers fielding practice, you should try to involve infielders as often as possible. This makes the drill more gamelike and provides infielders with some insight into the athleticism of the pitchers. Divide pitchers into groups to maximize repetitions, and keep score to maximize concentration. Finally, try to expose pitchers to a variety of situations in order to keep practice interesting and fresh. The reward of taking batting practice for the winning group always guarantees a high level of concentration by our pitchers here at Duke.

Relay Throws

Another defensive drill that involves multiple positional groups is relay throws. The need to relay the ball to a base in a cutoff or relay situation comes up quite often—especially if the pitcher is having a tough day—but many teams practice this play infrequently. While an extra-base hit creates momentum for the offense, a successfully executed relay will minimize the damage. A successful relay can also seize the momentum back for the defense if the batter–runner is thrown out while trying to advance. If the relay is executed poorly, not only may runs score, but the batter–runner may also move up a base. We want to minimize the damage in these situations. Having the infielders and outfielders practice relays under duress helps prepare us for success on game day.

We look for three things from outfielders during any relay situation:

1. Run as hard as possible.
2. Pick up the ball on the first try.
3. Make a strong, accurate throw to the relay man.

The relay man focuses on these points:

- Catch the ball cleanly.
- Make a strong, accurate throw to the receiver. The throw must go all the way to the bag in the air or on a long hop.

Our relay drill consists of two groups. Outfielders start near the left-field corner, and infielders are grouped in position to relay the ball to third base. Catchers receive throws at both third base and home plate—it serves them well to take as many of these throws as possible. We usually run this drill with five outfielders, five infielders, and two catchers. An outfielder is paired with an infielder, so we have five groups that compete against each other.

A coach throws a ball into the left-field corner, simulating a sure double, possible triple. The outfielder has three responsibilities: run as hard as he can to the ball, pick it up with his bare hand on the first try, and hit the relay man (the infielder) in the chest. The infielder is approximately 110 feet (33.5 m) away. The infielder catches the ball with both hands and fires the throw all the way to third base in the air or on a long hop. The infielder must never short-hop the relay throw.

After a few repetitions, we time each group. Time starts when the coach releases the ball. That way, we can measure the outfielder's speed and effort in getting to the ball in addition to the velocity and accuracy of his throw. If the infielder short-hops the catcher at third base, the time does not count. Each pair goes three times, and we count their lowest time. We then repeat the drill with the infielders relaying the ball to home plate (and we take the lowest time). Then we move the outfielders to left center field and repeat the throws to third base and home plate.

We usually hit two different spots each time we do the drill. If we do the drill twice in a week, the second time we'll put the outfielders in the right-field corner and then right center field. We spend equal time in all of the possible spots where a relay might occur. The use of the clock and the competition between groups certainly raise the level of concentration, but these factors can also decrease the execution level for certain players. This drill helps us get a feel for who can execute a critical momentum play the fastest while maintaining control and accuracy. Because the arm strength of outfielders varies, we change up pairs each time we do the drill. This also helps to emphasize to infielders that the better the outfielder's arm, the farther toward the infield they can adjust their distance. Our relay game has improved substantially through the years following the implementation of this relay drill.

Stickball

A large portion of practices at Duke consists of competitive defensive drills. We believe that if we play great fundamental defense and if pitchers throw strikes and keep the ball in the park, we have a good chance to be competitive every time. However, we do spend some time on offense, specifically hitting. One way we do this is by playing stickball. Both players and staff really enjoy this hitting game, and it has helped our offense, specifically our two-strike approach.

Many coaches at the college level played stickball in some form while growing up. However, stickball is a game that seems to have faded with the passage of time. The majority of my players (past and present) have never played stickball, and I tell them that they really missed out. Here at Duke, they get the opportunity to play stickball because it is a staple of our hitting program, especially when we are looking to change the routine.

Through stickball, we are trying to develop hitters who battle and compete when they have two strikes. Also, during stickball, we want the teams to compete with each other to win, in addition to individually competing to square up to the ball. We look for hitters to have minimal body movement during stickball. We want the hitter to have his stride foot down, use his hands, and not overswing.

We play with two teams, one in the field and one at the plate. For the strike zone, we set up a garbage can with a screen or backstop behind it (figure 13.5). Fielders face home plate. This creates a natural field and provides the opportunity for players to hit the ball out of the park for home runs. We play with a tennis ball and a dowel (wood stick) for a bat. Only the coaches throw during stickball so we don't injure the arms of players. The coach stands about 50 feet (15.2 m) away from the hitter on a batting practice ramp with a bucket of tennis balls. The fielding team retrieves balls only; there is no fielding of consequence during the game. A hard-hit ball is a single, a ball that short-hops the wall is a double, a ball that hits off the wall is a triple, and a ball that goes out of the park is a home run. Any pitched ball that hits the garbage can—even if it just nicks the can—is a strike. This is a great feature because, as much as players may want to complain, it is tough to argue with the garbage can. Four balls is a walk, and three strikes is an out, same as in the real game.

The key is the coach's ability to pitch so that hitting is difficult for the hitters. We throw fastballs, sliders, curveballs, and knuckleballs. We also try to throw from as many different arm slots as possible to make hitters really track the ball. As the coach throwing the ball increases velocity, the hitters must stay short to make contact. When the hitter gets two strikes, we really want to see him compete against the coach on the mound and find a way to put the ball in play, no matter what pitch is delivered—as long as it is in the strike zone.

Figure 13.5 Stickball.

We keep score as in a regular game. When a team gets three outs, we switch the offense and defense. Depending on time constraints, we play a five-, seven-, or nine-inning game. Some of our best competitors are revealed during stickball games, and some of the most animated conversations take place between the two teams. Anytime you can find a drill that the guys really have fun with and that is a little bit different, it can be a terrific benefit to your club. Stickball has certainly been this kind of competitive drill for us.

Team Drill

To this point, I have discussed individual drills, positional drills, drills that incorporate multiple positions, and some offensive drills. I want to finish up with a drill that incorporates our entire club. We use this drill to finish practice nearly every day. We call it 27, or Prepare to Win. It is taken from my playing experience at the professional level. Several organizations I played for used this drill. It is the best way to finish a solid practice day, and it gives you an idea about your club's ability to execute defensively over the course of a full ball game. The purpose of the drill is to go from 0 outs to 27 outs (the duration of a nine-inning ball game) without committing a physical or mental error. We time this drill, starting the clock when the first fungo is hit and stopping it when we get to 27 outs. If we make a physical or mental error, we start back at 0. A good time for our club is to get to 27 outs in around 7 minutes.

Put a defense on the field—nine players including a pitcher and a catcher. The reserve pitchers are in foul ground on the first-base side, and the reserve position players are in foul ground on the third-base side. The reserve catcher is just off to the first-base side of home plate in foul ground. A group of about five reserves puts on helmets and will run the bases during the drill.

The coach is at home plate with a fungo bat. All reserve pitchers have a ball in their back pocket. The coach calls out a situation, and the players react accordingly. For example, we usually start with no outs and nobody on base because that is how every game begins.

The pitcher on the mound goes through his windup (nobody on base), but he does not pitch to the plate. He only simulates his delivery. The coach hits any kind of ball he wants. I usually start with a ground ball to first base so the pitcher has to get over and cover the bag.

A runner is even with home plate but offset into foul ground on the first-base side to give the coach room to operate. On contact, this runner runs as hard as he can through first base. The expectation is that the first baseman will field the ball cleanly and flip it to the pitcher covering first base before the runner gets to first. If this is accomplished, this is 1 out. A new pitcher sprints out to the mound, and a new situation is given.

Usually, we stay with no outs, nobody on base for the first 5 or 6 outs before adding runners on base. Any situation that could possibly happen during a game is in play. Sometimes I script exactly what I want to cover, but most of the time, I pick a few fundamental areas to emphasize.

If a double play is turned, that counts for 2 outs. We keep a running total as we go and call the total after each situation.

Any error, big or small, resets the number of outs to 0. If a player boots the ball or misses the cutoff man, or if the pitcher forgets to back up a base or goes from the windup when runners are on base, we reset the total at 0 and start over. Therefore, the length of the drill is undetermined. It depends on how well and how crisply the team executes the fundamentals. As the total creeps closer to 27, it is amazing to watch how some players want the ball and others become more and more uncertain. This is critical information for a coach. I try to involve younger players more at the later stages of the drill to see how they respond when things are tense. I also make the situations more complicated as we go along. For example, I might call a routine double-play ball early in the drill. But later in the drill, I might call a situation in which a fast runner is on first with two outs, the runner is in motion on the pitch, and the ball is hit in the right center-field gap (a sure double, possible triple). I may be looking for the middle infielders to line up to home plate but then have them relay the ball to third because they realize as the play develops that they do not have a play at home.

We have progressively improved each year with Prepare to Win. At first, it often took an hour to get to 27 outs. Now we routinely run through it in 8 to 12 minutes, with a maximum of two or three miscues. This drill is useful in so many ways—you can reemphasize a team fundamental worked on in practice or maybe cover something you were not able to fit in the practice plan.

We try to rotate all defenders in during the drill so that everyone gets some experience making plays under pressure. We rotate catchers each time one of them makes a play. At the other positions, we rotate about every 6 to 9 outs. As mentioned, the pitchers have a ball in their pocket. If I give them a situation and tell them to pick to second base (runner on second, one out, good time to steal third), they can grab the ball out of their pocket, execute the play, and keep the drill moving.

The element of the clock really helps pitchers get on and off the field quickly. We want them in sprint mode anyway because they have to be full go when they are backing up bases.

I usually end the Prepare to Win drill the same way every time. I pick a particular play that I think will be critical, and I make sure that the same key guy makes that play to get us the last out under pressure. One year the key man was a freshman shortstop. I would hit a ball in the hole with two outs to see if he could make that throw at the end of practice with all his teammates pulling for him. This year I hit a pop-up as high as possible to our senior catcher. Before the ball was caught, I started walking to the back of the mound for the end-of-drills meeting because I knew this player would catch the ball to end the drill, the practice, and the game.

The Prepare to Win drill is our signature defensive drill at Duke, one we use because it makes us game ready. Our goal each ball game is to play nine innings without committing a mental or physical error. If we do this, we will always be competitive and have a chance to win. This drill involves the entire team and inspires the whole group to pull for each other and encourage each other to concentrate and execute. You will see how your club can bounce back from adversity when mistakes are made. When you reset the outs to 0, it is interesting to see if the energy picks up or if the club deflates. We want guys who bounce back. Base runners increase the intensity of the drill, but we make sure that we do not have any collisions at home plate. Runners veer off if they are coming to the plate. Depending on your club's skill level, you can make plays more routine or more advanced. As the season goes on, I script more tough situations that require mental effort and physical execution. Remember, as your team gets better at getting to 27 outs faster and more efficiently, your club is getting better defensively and is more ready for success on game day.

I hope you find some of these drills beneficial to the individual development of players and the collective development of your team. We use these drills daily and have found that through repetition and routine we have improved each year. The competitive aspect of the drills and games that we use raises the level of performance in practice and accelerates team growth. We try to make drills original and fun to keep things fresh. I am always tweaking drills to make them better or different, always looking for a way to make practice more creative or competitive. When you stop learning, you stop growing. I apply that notion to all parts of my life, including researching, designing, and finding new ways to teach the world's greatest game. I hope you enjoy the teaching process as much as I do. There is no greater reward than to see one of your player's hard work pay off with success on the baseball diamond.

chapter 14

Evaluating Practice Sessions

PETE DUNN AND BOB BENNETT

Practice, practice, practice. Individual and team success have never been accomplished nor have championships been won without hundreds, even thousands, of hours devoted to this segment of the game. For teams to compete at the highest level, coaches must recognize that the time practicing and the quality of practice sessions determine how teams perform on game day.

Certainly, game competition provides invaluable opportunities for player development through the experience gained by those on the field. But the repetition of required skills, fundamentals, and situations is not provided sufficiently in a game to guarantee improvement.

And, what about those team members who aren't starters or impact players but are only one or two injuries away from becoming everyday players or, at least, platooning with other bench players? Practice sessions, and especially intrasquad games, are of paramount importance to these team members.

Practice, therefore, should be designed and structured to provide the optimum degree of skill development, implementation, and integration of offensive and defensive philosophies as well as teamwork. Most important, coaches need to integrate the sense of pride, satisfaction, and enjoyment that come with a well-run practice session.

How, then, do coaches measure and evaluate the degree of success of an individual or team practice session? How do we improve as teachers and how do our players become more proficient at the game? We must have a well-designed plan, and we must have ways to monitor and assess these practice sessions. This chapter offers some practice strategies and emphasizes the importance of evaluation tools. These tools will help coaches become more efficient and help players become more skilled.

Essential to the success of the player and the coach is a consistent and efficient evaluation system. For example, you should take detailed mental or written notes on each player's performance and the team's performance for each practice and each game. Include the following in your evaluation process:

1. Analyze the performance.
2. Note the positive aspects.
3. Prioritize the issues that need attention.
4. Develop a plan to highlight the performances.
5. Develop a plan to attack each problem area.
6. Share your findings with each player and the team.
7. Incorporate the correction, maintenance work, improvement, and perfection into the daily practice schedule.
8. Follow up and make sure that the plan is carried out.

Vigilant eyes that are trained and committed to assess, correct, improve, and pursue excellence are necessary to perform these important tasks. Evaluation should be a constant process.

An efficient and consistent evaluation system is a key component of any winning program. The system should include goal-oriented practice sessions. Each session should be well organized and understood by the coaching staff and players. Each activity within each practice session should have a purpose. It is the responsibility of both coaches and players to see that the purpose is achieved. Therefore, evaluating each activity is important.

For example, when players are working on the first-and-third situation, the coach should be performing a close and ongoing assessment of the drill. Defending an attempted double steal requires timing, communication, coordination, and efficient throwing and catching. Players should run through lead-up drills before attempting drills that involve practicing the complete defense.

The player at each position needs to understand his respective duties and must be drilled on those responsibilities before the players come together as a unit. After each player is sufficiently trained to accomplish his tasks, the whole defense is ready to practice. The coach must constantly and closely scrutinize and monitor the drill. If the drill is being run efficiently, then continue. If there is a severe breakdown—such as players who have difficulty catching and throwing, poor communication, or improper timing—stop the drill and divide the team into parts. Have each part work on its respective duties. Continue to work in this manner for the rest of the allotted time or until each problem area is solved before getting the unit together again. This is where the evaluation becomes extremely important.

Continuing to work on any drill that is being poorly run or that uncovers one or more glaring weaknesses is not only frustrating but is also a waste of time. Continuing without dealing directly with the glaring weaknesses will serve little purpose. In fact, this type of practice will set the team back. Breaking the team into parts (with each group concentrating only on a designated problem) and then bringing them back together as a unit is a sound teaching technique that will produce positive results.

The next important step is to communicate the results of the evaluation. The evaluation is of little value if it is not acknowledged and understood. Therefore, how the evaluation is presented is one of the most important factors. A concise, clear, and positive assessment is the most productive procedure. Furthermore, this procedure should allow for feedback.

Assessment of skill, performance, attitude, competitive output (in drills), or results should be formulated with consideration for the ability and competence level of the players being evaluated. For example, an inexperienced player with some skill deficiencies should not be held to the same standard as a player who has confidence and experience. This is not to say that the standard should be lowered. It means that the player without confidence and experience will take longer to perform at the same level as a player with experience.

The degree of difficulty in some drills must also be taken into consideration. For example, drills that work on the first-and-third situation are much more difficult to execute than regular steal drills. A player without experience who has not yet developed throwing and catching skills requires more repetitions than an experienced player with elevated throwing and catching skills.

By adjusting to these difficulties, a coach can make practices much more efficient. The coach should draw up a plan to take care of these deficiencies. The evaluation may lead to adjustments during the practice session and should certainly lead to adjustments for subsequent practices. In other words, if it isn't working, fix it! Careful evaluations allow coaches and players to pinpoint trouble spots, highlight strengths, and create efficient and successful working conditions.

Developing a Checklist

Develop a checklist that covers offensive and defensive situations, hitting, pitching, and so on. Use this checklist as a guide for the coaching staff. The checklist will also aid the coach in developing sequential planning. A coach doesn't want to include activities that require skills that have not been covered yet in the practice schedule. It is futile to work on bunt defenses without first having worked on coverage, spacing, and communication, to say nothing of the fundamentals of bunting.

Prioritize the items on the checklist (figure 14.1). For example, make catching and throwing the top priority for defensive practice. Also include the basic fundamentals for each position as top priorities. When these basic fundamentals are accomplished, proceed through the checklist.

Checklist of Baseball Fundamentals

Catchers

____ 1. Stance
____ 2. Signals
____ 3. Footwork
____ 4. Rhythm
____ 5. Rotation
____ 6. Target (giving in game and in practice)
____ 7. Attitude
____ 8. Low pitches
____ 9. Ball reception (relax, let the ball come to you)
____ 10. Expectations on each pitch
____ 11. Pitchouts
____ 12. Strategy (setting up batters, etc.)
____ 13. Base coverage
____ 14. Field generalship (taking charge and calling plays)
____ 15. Pop flies
____ 16. Pickoffs
____ 17. Bunt fielding
____ 18. Double plays
____ 19. First and third situations
____ 20. Infield procedures
____ 21. Tag plays
____ 22. Pitcher warm up
____ 23. Practice procedures

Pitchers

____ 1. Position on rubber
____ 2. Grip
____ 3. Ball to crouch
____ 4. Knee and hip action (shoulders level)

Figure 14.1 Sample checklist of baseball fundamentals.
© Bob Bennett, *The Complete Baseball Book of Handouts,* Coaches Choice, page 170.

_____ 5. Push off rubber

_____ 6. Follow through

_____ 7. Stretch position

_____ 8. Base coverage (covering first, backing up other bases)

_____ 9. Bunt fielding

_____ 10. Adjustments to wildness (changing position on rubber)

_____ 11. Knowledge of hitters

_____ 12. Attitude toward game

_____ 13. Pitchouts

_____ 14. Run downs (running at runner)

_____ 15. Pickoffs

_____ 16. Strategy against would-be bunters

_____ 17. Squeeze plays

_____ 18. Waste pitch

_____ 19. Practice procedures

_____ 20. Targets (throwing to)

_____ 21. First and third situations (three ways of handling)

_____ 22. Double plays

_____ 23. Play to kill situation

_____ 24. Type of clothing to wear (keep arm warm)

Infielders

_____ 1. Stance (feet and hand positions)

_____ 2. Readiness

_____ 3. Position for fielding ground ball (head down, eyes on ball, knees bent, low body, low glove)

_____ 4. Footwork (coming in, fielding high hopper)

_____ 5. Positions (where and when)

_____ 6. Throwing (grip, rotation, receiving position of hands, throwing from different positions, relays)

_____ 7. Tag plays

_____ 8. Double plays (footwork, throws, when not to complete double play by way of first base)

_____ 9. Infield procedures

_____ 10. Signals from catcher (relay to outfielders)

_____ 11. Pop flies (communication, leadership, elements, situations)

_____ 12. Taking charge of plays

_____ 13. Attitude on receiving throws

_____ 14. Attitude toward ground balls

_____ 15. Watching man tag base

_____ 16. Talking to pitcher.

(continued)

Checklist of Baseball Fundamentals *(continued)*

First Basemen

___ 1. Footwork (tagging first base, position of bag)
___ 2. Positions (where and when)
___ 3. Holding runners on
___ 4. Bunt situations (play to kill, breaking off and coming in)
___ 5. Watch runner tag first and follow him to second
___ 6. Handling low throws
___ 7. Relays
___ 8. Rundowns
___ 9. Pivot (right hander)
___ 10. Stretching (when and why)
___ 11. Pickoffs
___ 12. When to play the line

Second Basemen

___ 1. Positions (when and where)
___ 2. Double plays (footwork, special types, throws, getting ball away, aiming)
___ 3. Bunts (cheating over, covering first)
___ 4. Relays (trailer)
___ 5. First and third situations
___ 6. Pickoffs
___ 7. Fielding line drive hit right at you
___ 8. Pickoff at first base
___ 9. Pop ups
___ 10. Relaying signals.

Third Basemen

___ 1. Positions (when and where)
___ 2. Double plays (where to play)
___ 3. Relays
___ 4. Bunts (play to kill, special types of bunts, drag bunts)
___ 5. Backing up pitcher (throws from first base)
___ 6. Bases-loaded situations
___ 7. Pop ups
___ 8. Playing hitters (watch hitter for giveaway of bunt, play the line when appropriate)
___ 9. Pickoffs at third
___ 10. Balls hit straight to the third baseman
___ 11. First-and-third situations
___ 12. Practice procedures

Figure 14.1 *(continued)*

Shortstops

_____ 1. Positions (when and where, special)
_____ 2. Double plays (footwork, throws, getting ball away, aiming)
_____ 3. Pickoffs (method, holding runner on, signals)
_____ 4. Bunts (where to go and base to cover)
_____ 5. First-and-third situations
_____ 6. Leadership (covering second with pitchers and second baseman, taking charge on all plays)
_____ 7. Covering third
_____ 8. Pop flies
_____ 9. Relays (trailer)
_____ 10. When to try for runner going from second to third
_____ 11. Relaying signals to outfielders
_____ 12. Playing the hitter

Outfielders

_____ 1. Stance
_____ 2. Position
_____ 3. Cross step footwork (in, back, right, and left)
_____ 4. Throwing position
_____ 5. Throwing (grip, rotation, accuracy, follow through)
_____ 6. Backing up other outfielders
_____ 7. Backing up infielders
_____ 8. Coming in and backing up a base when a runner is in a rundown
_____ 9. Fielding ground balls (when to play safe, when to go for broke)
_____ 10. Fielding high fly balls
_____ 11. Fielding foul flies
_____ 12. Checking the weather (wind, sun, rain)
_____ 13. Signals from infielders
_____ 14. Alignment of plays
_____ 15. Playing hitters (playing in, watching batter's stance)
_____ 16. Bunt situations
_____ 17. Practice procedures

Batters

_____ 1. Bat selection
_____ 2. Stance (feet, legs, weight distribution on balls of feet, balance, grip, arms, head and eyes, position at the plate, hips)
_____ 3. Getting ready to swing
_____ 4. Throwing the bat
_____ 5. Watching the ball
_____ 6. Waiting
_____ 7. Following through

(continued)

Checklist of Baseball Fundamentals   *(continued)*

____   8. Getting away from the plate

____   9. Attitude

____   10. Practice procedures

Baserunners

____   1. Sliding

____   2. Circling the bases

____   3. Rounding first (going straight down line of infield hits)

____   4. Hitting the bag

____   5. Getting back to the bag

____   6. Stance and leading off

____   7. Jump (footwork)

____   8. Leading off base (pitching move, number of steps or distance, philosophy, cross step and stance, procedure for getting back)

____   9. Stealing strategy (count, inning, overall situations)

____   10. Base coaching (runner is responsible most of the time, runner's job is to move ahead on every possible mishap, both base coach and runner must be alert 100 percent of the time, signals, stance)

____   11. Helping out other runners

____   12. Alert at all times

____   13. Eagerness to advance

____   14. Tagging on fly balls (how, when, how to get jump)

____   15. Bunt and run

____   16. Hit and run

____   17. Squeeze bunt (types and when to use)

____   18. Helping out other runners and helping out at home plate

____   19. Rundowns (what to do if you are trapped)

____   20. When to stop and make infielder tag you

____   21. Observing opponents throwing

Bunters

____   1. Stance

____   2. Purpose

____   3. Types (drag bunt, squeeze, bunt and run, push bunt, fake bunt and hit away)

Figure 14.1 *(continued)*

The following sections describe how to evaluate each type of player. This information will be helpful in the evaluation process, although this certainly isn't a comprehensive list. The coach alone knows and understands his players and can determine what direction they need.

Evaluating Hitters

For position players, more practice time is devoted to swinging the bat than to any other aspect of the game. Live on-field hitting, live cage work, soft toss, and tee work are all, in some combination, practice mainstays.

Any kind of hitting drills should be observed closely. Insist on a steady and persistent commitment to correct technique and sound fundamentals. When problems are spotted, share the criticism with the hitter immediately, keeping instruction positive and constructive. Be sure to praise good technique as well. Identify the problem, explain how to solve the problem, and incorporate a drill or activity that will correct the problem. Persistence from the coach, player, and team must be part of the follow-up.

Each practice should be carefully monitored. Expect correct technique and dedicated effort in the daily hitting sessions, which should include working on all phases of hitting as well as game situations. Careful attention to technique and effort creates a positive and productive atmosphere. Simulate game situations to help players master execution. Work on perfecting the sacrifice bunt, the hit-and-run, the push and drag bunts, and specific situations such as a runner at second base with no outs, a runner at third base with less than two outs, and so on. Steady repetition with the right kind of effort and the correct technique will produce a successful and meaningful practice.

With the structured batting practice plan, the coach and player alike can better assess the progress of the hitter in his ability to handle the bat as well as make adjustments. A practice schedule is mandatory in order for coaches and players to stay on task and stay on time. This will also add a sense of enjoyment and accomplishment in a structured practice atmosphere.

Evaluation of hitters should be ongoing. For both the coach and the player, a commitment to sound techniques, correct fundamentals, and successful execution will pay great dividends. In a sense, the coach and player are both making a detailed assessment of hitting on each swing.

Besides the hands-on and daily scrutiny of each at-bat and each drill, many other aids can be used to grade and test each hitter and each situation. Pictures, charts, videos, and point systems can be used effectively. The chart shown in figure 14.2 is designed to record individual or group performance of basic skills during live on-field batting practice. It can be used daily or on occasion at the coach's discretion. When this chart is used, an element of competition can be added by presenting an award or perk to the winning individual or group at the end of practice. It is amazing how the level of concentration rises when rivalry among teammates is included. Coaches can tailor the chart to reflect their personal hitting priorities and philosophies. A point is given only when the task is performed to the coach's or recorder's satisfaction. For example, a bunt on the ground that is bunted fairly hard back toward the pitcher would not earn a point. A ball not hit on the ground during the hit-and-run would not be rewarded.

Name	Three sacrifice, three hit-and-runs	Six opposite field	Six ground balls	Six gap to gap	Six base hits	Total
Player 1	5	6	5	3	4	23
Player 2	2	3	3	5	2	15
Player 3	5	3	3	3	2	16
Player 4	6	5	3	4	4	22
Player 5	6	6	6	5	3	26
Player 6	6	5	6	5	3	25
Player 7	4	5	4	4	5	22
Player 8	5	5	6	3	4	23
Player 9	5	3	3	3	4	18
Player 10	3	2	5	3	3	16
Player 11	3	3	3	4	3	16
Player 12	5	6	4	3	2	20
Player 13	6	5	5	6	3	25
Player 14	6	6	6	5	3	26
Player 15	5	4	4	4	1	18
Player 16	4	6	6	3	3	22
Player 17	3	4	5	5	3	20
Player 18	5	6	6	6	2	25

Figure 14.2 Recording scores for on-field batting practice.

Other charts can be used to record and evaluate performances. Each coach should select the charts or other recording methods that fit with his priorities.

If you have enough coaches, one coach should supervise and evaluate each hitting station. If your coaching staff is limited in number, you may assign a veteran player to supervise and evaluate a hitting group. Regardless of who manages the hitting stations, each player should be involved not only with his own performance in practice and games but also with the performance of his teammates. When a player is called on to evaluate a teammate's hitting and to make necessary improvements or corrections, that player will learn to pinpoint details. This will help his own hitting as well as his teammate's. In addition, his leadership skill will be enhanced.

Evaluating Base Runners

Baserunning is one of the most important parts of the offense. Sound techniques and proper strategy are critical to winning results. Therefore, coaches should pay a great deal of attention to the baserunning game. Fortunately, this part of the game is relatively easy to measure. A stopwatch reveals the actual speed of the runner and also provides insight into the runner's techniques. Poor technique is easily revealed by the stopwatch. A wide turn produces a slower time for the base runner. A short lead or a slow jump also produces a slower time.

Here is another way to evaluate and improve the leads that base runners take. Mark spots 12 feet (3.6 m) from each base to illustrate the desired minimum distance for the lead off a base. Good base runners extend the lead to 13 feet (3.9 m) or more. During intrasquad games, have a player or coach pay careful attention to the distance of each player's lead off a base. (This can be checked during regular games as well.) Record notes or make mental notes on the lead, and get the information back to each base runner. Follow through and make sure each player responds.

A player's time from home plate to first base provides valuable information and a focal point from which to teach and learn. The following times are close to the acceptable numbers used nationally, although some would debate these times:

Time From Home to First

4.2 seconds or less = fast

4.3 to 4.4 seconds = average

4.5 seconds or more = slow

Test each runner's speed and develop a practice plan to improve it. This test provides a starting point for each player, revealing what each player needs to improve. It also highlights each runner's shortcomings and assets. As far as baserunning is concerned, the player's speed indicates how he should run the bases. The base runner may be limited or may have wide latitude on the basepaths. For example, if a slow base runner is on base, the bunt or the hit-and-run would be better options than the steal for moving the base runner. A fast base runner would be able to perform well when any of these three choices are called.

Live drills and drills that use gamelike situations can also be used to measure the skills and abilities of base runners. The defensive players will be tested in these drills as well. A live drill with pitchers, catchers, and infielders to challenge the base runners as they attempt to steal bases will reveal loads of information. Coaches can evaluate leads and turns. In addition, they can study and test the decision making of each base runner. Defensive players may also reveal their strengths and weaknesses.

Virtually all aspects of the offense and defense can be evaluated in the game setting. This will be the most accurate evaluation. Coaches and players alike should develop a system for analyzing performance. The key is to develop an eye for details. Learning to pay close attention as the game unfolds is the best way to get information. Record this information, either to memory or on paper or computer. It must be clearly and specifically recalled and meticulously applied.

These notes do not need to be lengthy, but they should be specific and to the point. Consider the following example. In the last game, the coach noted that the second baseman's approach and fielding fundamentals were very sound on ground balls. However, the coach also noted that this player did not align properly on extra-base hits. Furthermore, in one instance, the second baseman threw to first base with no chance to throw out the runner during what started as a potential double play.

The coach should take the opportunity to compliment the second baseman on his ability to field ground balls and on his approach to the ball. Then he should point out the need for better alignment and the importance of holding the ball on some plays. After carefully pointing out where the infielder should be aligned on extra-base hits and getting enough feedback from the second baseman to know that he understands the importance of proper alignment, the coach has set the stage for corrections.

The next practice should include a drill on alignment with special emphasis on proper positioning. If the player has successfully made the correction after one session, then move on. If corrections have not been made, incorporate this drill into the next practice until the middle infielders understand where and how to position themselves to defend an extra-base hit.

After fielding or catching the ball, sometimes the best decision for the infielder is to stand pat and not throw the ball. Middle infielders in particular must learn when to throw and when not to throw. When it is obvious that the infielder has no chance to throw out the runner, he should hold the ball.

A good way to work on this issue is to incorporate a drill that includes live runners. This gives infielders a chance to make decisions about where and when to throw and when to hold the ball. Every play should begin as a double-play ball. When an infielder fields the ball with a runner at first base and less than two outs, he should be thinking of turning a double play. He will continue with the double-play attempt unless there is a reason not to do so, such as the ball is hit too slowly, the ball is fumbled during the initial phase of the defensive play, or the batter–runner is extremely fast and will obviously beat any throw. In any of these instances, both infielders should be involved. One fields the ball and feeds it to the other. The receiver should communicate with the fielder about where the ball should be thrown. The receiver is responsible for getting one out and attempting to get a double play, provided the proper circumstances are present.

This type of drill should be included in each practice until the middle infielders understand when to complete the double play and when to stop the attempt.

It may take several practices to accomplish this feat. This type of drill should be a part of most practice schedules. Not only is this drill important for corrections, but it is also essential for maintenance, improvement, and perfection.

Evaluating Catchers

There is no debate about the importance of the catcher to his team. The team is as good as its catcher. Championship teams usually have outstanding defensive catchers who are also leaders. Catchers are an extra coach on the field. The catcher is a counselor, a field director, and a workhorse. Catching also requires a great deal of skill that is often overlooked, especially in practice. In fact, catchers have so much to do during a practice that their skill work is often limited to the bullpen and batting practice. Many coaches are unsure of the specific skills and intricacies of catching, particularly since it is such a unique position. Catchers are members of their own fraternity. They usually work well together and share information. The following 15-minute routine will help your catcher with his skills. You may implement these drills at practice or shorten them on game day for a great warm-up. This 15-minute session is an excellent time to evaluate and teach.

Phase 1

When working together, catchers should be about 15 to 20 feet (4.5 to 6.1 m) apart for these drills.

Catchers begin by working on framing and receiving. The catcher gets in a ready position; the feet are shoulder-width apart, and the toes are pointed out toward the bases. The mitt arm is extended but not straight; the pinky and thumb are at five o'clock with the palm up. The catcher should loosen the wrist once the ball is delivered to help with receiving. He frames the strike zone and concentrates on catching the outside half of the ball. The catcher must not flip the mitt or try to steal a pitch well out of the strike zone. He must keep his head and eyes on the back of the mitt and make a good throw back to his partner.

Next, catchers move to blocking. First, the catcher establishes proper blocking position—down with the knees pointing to the bases, the mitt on the ground in front of the cup, the arms to the sides, and the throwing hand behind the mitt or to the side. The body forms the letter C. The eyes and head are down. Teach catchers to soften their bodies with a deep breath. Remember, the ball needs to be stopped then retrieved. Too many catchers try to pick the ball or push their bodies at the ball. The partner throws sidearm and skips the ball to the catcher. Later in the drill, the catcher can start from a ready position and then drive down into the proper blocking position.

Finally, catchers work on quick hands and quick feet. In this drill, the catcher works on transferring the ball from glove to hand and moving his feet. Time catchers who use various styles of footwork (jab step or pivot) and determine which works best. Arm strength is a big factor, so most catchers use the jab step. Transferring the ball can be practiced just by playing catch. The catcher starts in a ready position with a man on base. In most cases, this means the feet are slightly wider than shoulder-width apart and the throwing hand is behind the mitt. The catcher's bottom should be raised slightly. Many catchers are taught to have their seat parallel to the ground, but this may not be necessary. What's more important is to anticipate and keep the weight going forward. Partners can feed each other. The catcher should transfer, execute footwork, and freeze in the throwing position. Repeating this drill will help the catcher improve his time.

Creative coaches can put together other skill sets for catchers to work on. However, keep this phase to three skills, with 5 minutes per skill. Get a better catcher in 15 minutes.

Phase 2

Drills in this phase can be designed to work on various skills and game situations, such as the following:

- Fielding bunts and pop-ups (first-base side, third-base side, and straight up)
- Making plays at the plate (force-outs and tags) and covering wild pitches
- Picking off runners at all bases and throwing to second base

These short routines give catchers the skill work they need and also provide a setting for evaluation. One of the coach's best tools for evaluating catchers is a stopwatch. The catcher's time on throws to second base reveals a great deal about his skill level. Footwork, grip, rotation, position of the hands, and arm angle can all be tested during these drills. A fast time without accuracy is not satisfactory. A slow time with accuracy is not acceptable either. Having both speed and accuracy requires diligent, consistent, and dedicated work in all areas.

Evaluating Infielders

Playing a position in the infield requires attention to detail and a mastery of fundamentals. Excellent throwing and catching skills are absolutes for a good infielder. Good infielders are able to throw from many different angles and are able to adjust to the speed of the ball, their position on the field, the speed and actions of the runner, and the distance of the throw.

In addition to being fundamentally sound in catching and throwing, the infielder must always be aware of the situation, the score, the number of outs, the inning, and the ability of the base runner. The infielder must study the tendencies of his opponents and the skill level of each opponent.

The final test for each infielder is a game. His score is revealed after every game. He is judged on the following:

- Understands game situations
- Knows the opponent
- Can anticipate situations such as steals or the hit-and-run
- Can adjust to the hitter's speed and ability
- Is aware of the pitcher–hitter matchup
- Executes plays successfully

A good infielder knows how to position himself for each batter, understanding that correct positioning is based on the game situation and the ability of the players involved in the situation. Remember, we give up something to gain something. These positions should match up with the game situation: basic, regular depth (includes cheating with the pitch and the hitter), double-play depth, infield in (no outs or one out), halfway, hold a base runner, or cover the lines.

The infielder's general approaches to a ground ball are regular, angle backhand, dive, slow roller, ball deep to left side, back in, or double-play ball.

The following general philosophies should be adopted:

- The infielder should attack the ball in a way that gives him a chance to throw out a runner.
- The infielder should use his feet and work through the ball.
- With two outs and a runner on second base, the infielder must knock down the ball to save a run.
- The infielder should keep his fingers down and should catch the ball in the web of the glove.
- The infielder must know that a sure, accurate throw is better than a rushed, hard throw.

The following areas should be constantly graded, discussed, drilled, and perfected:

- **First baseman.** Stretching to get the ball; picking the ball in the dirt; holding a runner and getting off the bag; feeding the ball to the pitcher covering first; making the double-play feed; executing pickoffs and throws to second base; executing pickoffs and tag plays; fielding the bunt and throwing to first, second, and third; reading the ball in the four hole; coming off the bag to catch a bad throw and making the tag; communicating with the pitcher and position players; executing tandem relays and trailing the runner.

- **Shortstop and second baseman.** Executing double-play feeds; throwing underhand, backhand, and reverse; dropping to the knee; pivoting; covering on the steal and making the tag; executing pickoffs; holding the runner; communicating with the pitcher and position players; executing tandem relays; fulfilling bunt responsibilities.

- **Third baseman.** Fulfilling bunt responsibilities; feeding the ball to second base; executing pickoffs; executing tandem relays; communicating with the pitcher and position players; making tags.

To help infielders learn to get a better jump on the ball and master their inner time clock, a coach should teach the infielders these two important tips:

1. Track the ball out of the pitcher's hand on its way to the plate.
2. Read the speed of the ball by recognizing the way it is bouncing.

Evaluating Pitchers

The position most responsible for controlling the game is pitcher. Paying attention to details is extremely important for both the coach and the pitcher. Seeking and responding to these details will pay dividends for the pitcher and his team.

To be a consistent winner, the pitcher must master several areas of the game. Daily assessments of sound fundamental mechanics will help pitchers maintain and improve their skills.

Game day is always a test for the pitcher. The pitcher is judged on his total performance, including mechanics, gamesmanship, the proper use of a fastball, the bite and accuracy of breaking pitches, the movement and speed of the changeup, the ability to control base runners, and the command of all of his pitches. And, of course, he is judged on his results.

Each practice should help the pitcher prepare to be successful on the test that he faces on game day. All of the areas described in the previous paragraph should be included in the practice schedule. Set priorities and emphasize one or more of these areas in each practice. Take a methodical and persistent approach to seeing that the pitcher is grounded in all these areas and is ready for each game. Each practice, intrasquad game, and regular game provides data to be used in designing each practice schedule.

Pitcher is perhaps the easiest position to evaluate and the most difficult position to coach. Pitching is easy to evaluate because the pitcher has the ball on every pitch. No other player on the field has that responsibility. Coaches have many more opportunities to assess the performance of the pitcher. Not only is the pitcher responsible for delivering the pitch to the plate, he is also responsible for a good portion of the defense. His control, command, stuff, demeanor on the mound, and skill level at which he fields his position all contribute to the high demands placed on his performance.

The coaching staff must consider it a high priority to develop the pitching staff, regardless of age level. Because the demands on the pitcher are high, the attention that the position receives in practice should be equally high.

For a few minutes each day, isolate one or more duties for the pitchers to work on. This will help maintain and improve the pitchers' abilities. Make sure that pitchers put forth a diligent and concerted effort in each practice session and each drill. Overlooking any portion of the pitcher's duties will show on the final test—the game.

Daily observation, assessment, and follow-through by the coach and the pitcher are critical. There is no substitute for consistent and persistent evaluation. A number of other methods and tools may help measure the performance of pitchers. Charts, stopwatches, videos, pictures, competitive practice situations, and gamelike drills can contribute to the evaluation and teaching process.

The stopwatch, for example, could help the pitcher learn to defend against the base runner. If the pitcher cannot hold a runner on base and deliver the ball to home plate in 1.3 seconds or less, he will have difficulty shutting down the running game.

Use charts, such as the one shown in figure 14.3, to record anything from mechanical execution to the variation of speeds on pitches.

Pitcher Performance Chart

Pitcher _____ Date _____

Pitch Count

	Fastballs		Curveballs		Changeups			
Total pitches	Number	Strikes	Number	Strikes	Number	Strikes	Strikes	Balls
50	30	20	10	6	10	6	32	18
Percentages	66%		60%		60%		64%	36%

First-Pitch Strike

Batters faced	First-pitch strike
10	6

Hits, Walks, and Strikeouts

Hits	Base-on-balls	Strikes
3	1	3

Pitch Velocity

Best fastball velocity	Average fastball velocity	Curveball velocity	Changeup velocity
90 mph	88 mph	78 mph	80 mph

Errors

Physical errors	Mental errors
Threw wide to second base on start of 1-6-3 double play	Failed to back up third base on base hit to right field with runner on first

Figure 14.3 Sample pitcher performance chart.

The following process can be used to evaluate pitchers. The pitcher will face three batters. Two of the batters are same side, and one is opposite side. The pitcher determines the pitch selection, but the selection must be within the guidelines established by the coach (table 14.1). All pitches will be used, and locations will be count oriented. The goal is correct execution of each individual pitch one at a time to complete the inning. Make no judgments based on contact; only consider whether or not the correct pitch was made. A base on balls ends the game. Execution is all that matters.

The strike zone is an away-game strike zone. Fastballs must be thrown inside at the first chance during an inning. Well-executed 0-1 and 0-2 pitches will get a more generous call on the next pitch. Well-executed 0-2 fastballs up or curveballs down may or may not be ruled an out. The evaluator has the right to call a foul ball on all two-strike pitches.

The point of this bullpen workout is to emphasize the execution of one pitch at a time. This workout also stresses the idea that a pitcher can control his approach and execution of a pitch only. He needs to be free of result-oriented outcomes, such as contact. Learning to throw only one pitch at a time and learning to use backward patterns and off-speed pitches for strikes are the main objectives. Judge execution strictly—this makes the workout more game-like. Allow the pitcher to have some input on the selection of pitches; however, insist that all pitches be thrown somewhere during the at-bat. This will help the pitcher develop each individual pitch as well as the ability to throw each pitch at any count. Execution is what matters most. The chart shown in figure 14.4 can be used to record the results of the bullpen workout or a pitcher's output during a game.

Table 14.1 Rules of Engagement for Evaluating Pitchers

Count	Pitch selection
0-0	One fastball, one curveball to same-side hitter; one fastball to opposite-side hitter
0-1	Located fastball
1-0	Off-speed pitch: curveball to same-side hitter; changeup to opposite-side hitter
1-1	Pitch not yet thrown (fastball to other location counts as different pitch)
2-1	Off-speed pitch (different than off-speed pitch thrown at 1-0 count, if applicable)
2-0	Tight zone
0-2	Fastball out of zone; curveball down
1-2	Located fastball, curveball, or slider
2-2	Located fastball, curveball, or slider
3-1	First time in inning: fastball Second time in inning: changeup Third time in inning: curveball
3-2	Different pitch than previous pitch
3-0	Cannot follow with three consecutive fastballs

Count	Hits	Outs
0-0		
0-1		
1-0		
1-1		
2-0		
2-1		
3-1		
3-0		
0-2		
1-2		
2-2		
3-2		

Figure 14.4 Action versus pitch and count.

Evaluating the Team

Games, whether intrasquad games or regular games, tell us where we have been, where we are now, and what we need to do to be successful in the future. The more we observe, the better we will become. Either we execute properly or fail to execute properly. Vigilant, keen eyes see what works and what needs to be fixed. Games are like tests we can grade. The results of these tests should be carefully analyzed and acted on.

Intrasquad games are similar to trial tests. They provide a pretty good indication of what we've been doing and what we need to do. Regular games are like final tests. The results are final for each game, but as long as there are games left to play, we can build on our strengths and improve on our shortcomings.

Games tell us how we have been operating in practice. They reveal the effort given in practice. They also reveal the intensity level, the organization, and the overall results of practice. Poor execution on the field indicates poor execution in practice. Erratic play indicates bad practice habits. Mishandling pop flies, unsuccessfully covering bunts, and being unable to minimize the number of base runners who get in scoring position all result from poor practice habits or a failure to spend enough time and practice in those areas.

Game evaluations are extremely important. During each game, a written, recorded, or mental note should be taken on all that is taking place. After the game, those notes should be carefully scrutinized as coaches and players look for more ways to maintain or strive for excellence. For example, miscommunication on a pop fly could be the result of a simple mistake or the result of a lack of emphasis on pop-fly execution in practice. The coach notes that not enough time was spent on pop flies during practice, so his next practice sessions include work on pop flies.

Evaluations should be ongoing because they provide the information necessary to draw up each practice schedule. Drills and practice serve one of four purposes: (1) introduction, (2) improvement of skills and execution, (3) perfection of skills and execution, and (4) maintenance of skills and execution. The development of skills, techniques, and fundamentals is done in phases. Each of these four purposes represents a phase.

In the introduction phase (or learning phase), players walk through a nonlive situation. Coaches describe and explain the drill as the players walk through it, making sure that players understand the purpose of the drill. Proper spacing, sound communication, good timing, and overall execution must be fully understood before moving to the next phase.

In the improvement phase, the pace is faster and more gamelike, although the coach has leeway to slow things down if necessary. To improve, players must operate the drill as though executing the activity in a regular game. In this phase, the coach may need to have the players stop the drill, back up, and start over. It may be necessary to adjust the drill and work on only the parts of the play that need improvement. For example, if the emphasis of the drill is baserunning but players are struggling to make turns properly or they take inadequate leads, the coach needs to make adjustments. Stop the drill, review turns and leads, and then design the rest of the drill to focus on those two areas. Demand excellence in this part of the drill.

Perfecting skills and execution calls for full-speed, competitive, and gamelike performance. This type of practice requires elevated intensity, high motivation, good timing, impeccable communication, and a totally coordinated effort.

Drills for maintaining skills and execution are designed to continue the march toward excellence. High skill levels and excellent execution must be maintained. Generally, this calls for short, concentrated practice sessions that are done with high intensity and a commitment to doing things correctly.

After evaluating performance, the coach determines which one of these four phases should be used in response to the players' performance. Once the team commits to championship practices, all evaluations need attention—from evaluations of individual swings to those of team performance. If done well, skills need to be maintained. If there is room for improvement, that should be the focal point. If the team is already working at a good pace, adhering to sound fundamentals, and executing efficiently, then perfection should be the goal. Keep these four phases in mind when evaluating the team.

When evaluating the team, you should watch for and encourage the following:

- Commitment to championship-level play
- Teamwork
- Sound communication

- Proper execution
- Championship-level enthusiasm
- Attention to details
- Consistent success

Careful attention to detail, diligent observation, sound analysis, and consistent follow-through will produce good results. Evaluate individual skills, perfection at each position, team execution on pop flies, alignment during plays, bunt coverage, control of the running game, individual defensive and offensive technique and execution, team offensive execution, and gamesmanship. A careful assessment and response to these factors will provide information to help you develop a sound day-to-day practice schedule, which will in turn help you develop a successful team.

Following Up

Perhaps the most important part of the evaluation process is the follow-up. What do we do with the information once we have it? If the information is not shared with the parties involved in a meaningful way, the evaluations are a waste of time. For example, evaluating a pitcher by going through an elaborate chart system is not very useful if the pitcher is not apprised of the details involved.

Evaluation should be done in a positive, helpful way. The evaluation may be extremely good, extremely bad, or somewhere in between. Regardless, it should have a good tone, be constructive, and provide a path for improvement and hope. There is always an avenue that leads to improvement.

Evaluations are constant and ongoing. Most evaluations are taken care of instantly. How these are dealt with is critical to the success of the player, the coach, and the team. Assessments are valuable when acted on. They are of little use when ignored. For example, if players are working on baserunning but the coaches ignore their technique, the practice could be detrimental. Take action to make sure that good technique is being used. Ignoring the evaluation is not an option.

Perpetuating bad habits should not be tolerated. For example, if the catcher has been taught correct footwork but does not use that footwork in practice drills, while playing catch, while taking infield, or during games, he is perpetuating bad habits. These kinds of acts should not be tolerated. That's what is meant by being persistent in following through on what is being taught. If the coach allows these things to happen, then he is equally responsible for perpetuating bad habits.

Following through is more than announcing or telling. For example, if an evaluation pointed out that base runners were overzealous in their attempts to advance on bunts, proper follow-through would call for a clear review of leads and jumps on bunts. The coach should urgently express the need for a good and intelligent lead as well as the need for the base runner to let the bunter have the responsibility for advancing the base runner. Drills emphasizing these points should follow. During these drills, each bunt attempt and each baserunning attempt should be closely observed, and both the bunter and the base runner should be held accountable for their respective duties. Repetitions continue until execution is done correctly. This may take several sessions.

During this process, adjustments may be necessary. If the bunters are having trouble executing successful bunts, stop the drill and work only on bunting techniques and fundamentals until that end is accomplished successfully. If leads or jumps are a glaring problem, then stop the drill and devise a drill that focuses on leads and jumps.

When the points of concern are corrected, return to the original drill and repeat the drill until success is attained. Persist, adjust, and persist.

Repetitions make actions and habits permanent, not perfect. Players must practice proper techniques using sound fundamentals. Perfection, or near perfection, is the result of persistent, consistent, and fundamentally sound repetitive actions. The success of the team and the progress of each player depend to a large extent on how consistently and steadfastly the coach insists on things being done correctly. For example, an outfielder should take two and a half steps as each pitch approaches home plate. It is the outfielder's and the coach's job to see that those steps are taken on every pitch. Making consistent observations, holding the outfielder responsible, and accepting nothing less than perfection are what follow-up is all about.

One of the important tools in the evaluation toolbox is the input of the person being evaluated. Encouraging, even insisting on, feedback from the person being evaluated is a good teaching procedure. Allowing and expecting information from the player being evaluated empowers that player to take charge of his own destiny. He is responsible for assessing himself, which means he must examine, scrutinize, and seek out details that make a difference. This will pay great dividends because, in a sense, the student becomes the teacher.

The learning process is built around details. Pinpointing a detail requires a vigilant and attentive eye. Undivided interest is not only a tenet of teamwork but also an important principle of learning. The reason for pinpointing details is to use the information gathered to improve skills and enhance the learning process.

about the American Baseball Coaches Association

The **American Baseball Coaches Association (ABCA)** is the largest baseball coaching organization in the world. The association's mission is to improve the level of baseball coaching worldwide, while promoting the game of baseball and acting as a sounding board and advocate on issues concerning the game. In addition, the ABCA promotes camaraderie and communication among all baseball coaches from the amateur to the professional levels. The ABCA also gives recognition to deserving players and coaches through several special sponsorship programs. It is an organization that has grown steadily in membership, prestige, and impact in recent years. The ABCA's headquarters is located in Mount Pleasant, Michigan.

In 2002, **Bob Bennett** retired from coaching with a career record of 1,302-759 1-14, ranking him seventh in NCAA Division I history. Bennett closed his career with 26 consecutive winning seasons. In 34 years as head coach at Fresno State, his teams had 32 winning seasons, won 17 conference championships, made 21 NCAA regional championship appearances, and competed in two College World Series. During the 2000 season, he became only the 10th coach in NCAA baseball history to reach the 1,200-win plateau. More than 100 of his players have gone on to careers in professional baseball. Bennett earned conference Coach of the Year honors 14 times in addition to being named NCAA Coach of the Year by *The Sporting News*

in 1988. In 2000, he earned the prestigious Lefty Gomez Award for lifetime contributions to baseball. Bennett is a former president of the ABCA. He serves on the Hall of Fame and All-America committees within the ABCA and is a member of the ABCA Board. Bennett is a member of the Fresno State Hall of Fame, the ABCA Hall of Fame, and the Roosevelt High School Hall of Fame as a charter member. Bennett and his wife, Jane, have three children—Karen, Todd, and Brad—and eight grandchildren.

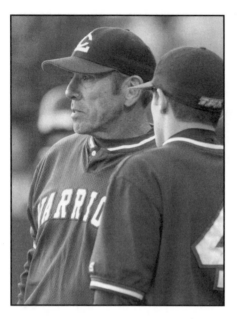

Ed Cheff, head coach at Lewis-Clark State College, has built one of the most impressive collegiate athletic teams at any level in the nation. From 1982 to 1992, the Warriors played in 11 consecutive national championship games and won 8, a feat unequalled by a collegiate team at any level in any sport. The Warriors have won 16 national titles since the early 1980s. Coach Cheff's overall record going into the 2008 season was a remarkable 1,617 wins and 410 losses. Beyond on-the-field performance, Coach Cheff's Warrior baseball team is recognized in the community for its involvement in local events, fund-raisers, and volunteer programs. Coach Cheff has been NAIA Coach of the Year eight times and was inducted into the NAIA Hall of Fame in 1994 and the ABCA Hall of Fame in 2006. In 2009, Cheff won the ABCA's Lefty Gomez Award for his lifetime contributions to amateur baseball. In 1994, Coach Cheff was the hitting and third-base coach for Team USA.

Keith Madison is the winningest coach in University of Kentucky baseball history, earning more than 730 victories in 25 years as head coach. In recognition of his contributions to Wildcat baseball, the University of Kentucky retired his jersey. In his tenure as head coach, Coach Madison was an accomplished leader and motivator. He shared his passion for the game with numerous baseball coaches and players. After retiring from coaching in 2003, Madison joined SCORE International, where he works as the national baseball director.

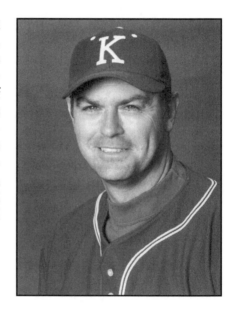

In 2008, **Terry Rooney** was named the head baseball coach of the University of Central Florida. In Rooney's first year as coach, the Knights posted a school record number of wins since joining Conference USA. Before becoming head coach at UCF, Rooney was an assistant coach at the Division I level for 12 years. He most recently served as the associate head coach at Louisiana State University. At LSU, he was the pitching coach and recruiting coordinator for two seasons. He helped guide the Tigers to the 2008 College World Series while landing the number-one-ranked recruiting class in the country. A native of Fairfax, Virginia, Rooney is considered one of the nation's premier recruiters.

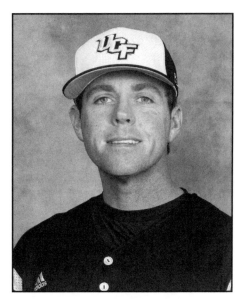

Rooney also served as the pitching coach at the University of Notre Dame, Stetson University, George Washington University, James Madison University, and Old Dominion University. Rooney has spoken at several coaching clinics throughout the country, and he authored a video titled *30 Minutes to Better Pitching: A Championship Workout*. Rooney and his wife, Shaun, were married in December of 2007.

In 2006, **Mark Johnson** became the head coach at Sam Houston State University. With a record of 989 wins, 502 losses, and 3 ties, Johnson ranks 17th in career victories among active NCAA Division I baseball head coaches. In Johnson's first three seasons at Sam Houston State University, the Bearkats earned NCAA Division I tournament berths by sweeping undefeated through the Southland Conference postseason tournaments; the team became only the second in Southland Conference history to earn three consecutive NCAA Division I regional playoff berths and win three straight Southland Conference postseason tournaments. In 2007, the Bearkats reached the NCAA Division I regional finals for the first time in school history. Johnson's Bearkats have set 18 school records, including most RBIs (457), hits (740), doubles (144), and triples (25) and best team batting average

(.335). Before coaching at Sam Houston State University, Johnson was the head coach at Texas A&M, directing the Aggies to two NCAA College World Series appearances and a record of 876 victories, 433 losses, and 3 ties in 21 years. In the summer of 1999, Johnson was the head coach for Team USA. Johnson was *Sporting News'* National Coach of the Year in 1993 and United States Olympic Committee Coach of the Year in 1999. He is a member of both the American Baseball Coaches Association (ABCA) and the Texas Baseball Halls of Fame. In 2007, Johnson was inducted into the University of New Mexico Athletic Hall of Honor, and the Fellowship of Christian Athletes presented him with the FCA Baseball Jerry Kindall Character in Coaching Award. In January 2008, Johnson was the first recipient of the ABCA's Ethics in Coaching Award. Johnson and his wife, Linda, have been married for 42 years. Both their sons, Ron and Brian, played baseball for their father at Texas A&M and were awarded Texas A&M's Student-Athlete of the Year. Mark and Linda have five grandchildren.

In 2007, **Dave Serrano** was named the head coach of Cal State Fullerton's baseball program. In his first two years as skipper and pitching coach, Serrano guided the Titans to a 88-38 record, a conference championship, two regional championships, a super regional championship, and a trip to the College World Series in 2009. Before returning to Fullerton, where he'd been a relief pitcher during his college years and an assistant coach and recruiting coordinator under George Horton, Serrano was the head coach at UC Irvine for 3 seasons, posting a 114-66-1 (.633) record. He guided the Anteaters to postseason appearances in 2006 and 2007 and their first College World Series in 2007. In 2007, he was named Baseball America's National Coach of the Year. In all, Serrano has compiled a record of 202-104-1 as a head coach and has averaged more than 40 wins a season. In 2010, Serrano will serve as the pitching coach for the U.S. Collegiate National Team. Serrano holds a bachelor's degree from Trinity College and University, and he lives in Irvine with his wife, Tracy, and their sons Kyle, Zachary, and Parker.

Gary Ward serves as the hitting coach for the New Mexico State University Aggies under his son, head coach Rocky Ward. In 2008, Gary Ward was inducted into the College Baseball Hall of Fame and the College Baseball Foundation Hall of Fame. He coached at Oklahoma State from 1978 to 1996, leading OSU to 16 straight conference titles, 17 NCAA regional appearances, and 10 trips to the College World Series while compiling a 953-313-1 record. In his first stint with New Mexico State, he led the Aggies to a Sun Belt Tournament Championship and an NCAA appearance, finishing with a career record of 1,022-361-1. In recognition of his accomplishments as an athlete, Ward was inducted into the New Mexico State University Hall of Fame. Ward has produced several baseball instructional videotapes, and he was the founder and director of the Mid-America All-Star Baseball School while at OSU. Ward and his wife, Catherine, have three children: Rocky, Roger, and Sherri.

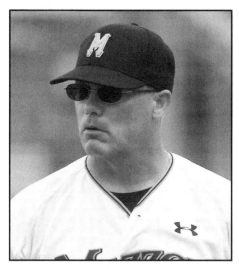

Tim Jamieson is the head coach of the University of Missouri Tigers. The second-winningest coach in Mizzou baseball history, in 2009 Jamieson led the Tigers to a 35-27 record and a third-place finish in the Big 12 Conference. He played baseball at the University of New Orleans and then spent 6 seasons on the UNO coaching staff. In 1988, he joined Coach Gene McArtor's staff and was an assistant coach for 6 seasons before becoming head coach after the 1994 season. Jamieson's Tigers have recorded at least 30 wins in 13 of the last 14 seasons. Mizzou has won at least 35 games in each of the last 7 seasons and has advanced to the NCAA tournament eight times under Jamieson. In 2008, Jamieson led the Tigers to a 39-21 record and a fourth-place finish in the Big 12 Conference. Mizzou opened the 2008 season ranked number 5 and ascended to number 2 during the year, marking its best ranking ever. In 2007, the Tigers posted a 42-18 record, which was a career best in wins for Jamieson and the fifth-winningest season in MU history. The Tigers' 19 conference victories in 2007 set a new school record. Missouri finished second in the Big 12 Conference, the team's best showing ever in the Big 12 and best league finish since winning the Big Eight Conference crown in 1996, Jamieson's second year at the helm. After the 2007 season, Jamieson was named the Big 12 Co-Coach of the Year. In 2005, Jamieson served as an assistant coach for Team USA. Jamieson and his wife, Cindy, have two sons, Mickey and Ty.

Under head coach **Steve Jaksa,** the Central Michigan University Chippewas have won a Mid-American Conference regular season title (2004), two MAC West Division crowns (2004 and 2006), and the championship round of the MAC Tournament (2005). CMU is 227-171-1 during Jaksa's tenure, the third-most victories by a head coach in program history. The Chippewas have finished either first or second in the West Division in four of the past five seasons, winning at least 17 conference games each of those four years. The Chippewas' 96 MAC victories under Jaksa are the most conference wins during the past five seasons. In 2007, the Chippewas won 21 conference games, tied for the most in the MAC. CMU finished 35-23 overall—the third straight year the team won at least 35 games—and advanced to the MAC Tournament for the fourth consecutive season. CMU was the only MAC program to finish with a team batting average above .300 (.308) and ranked second in the conference in team ERA (3.71). In 2004, Jaksa was named MAC Coach of the Year after leading the Chippewas to their first regular 1-1 season conference title since 1993. In 2000, Jaksa was inducted into the Michigan High School Baseball Coaches Association Hall of Fame. Jaksa and his wife, Patti, have four children: Stacey, Rachel, Marc, and Kelly.

Head coach since 2001, **Dave Perno** led the University of Georgia baseball team to the College World Series in 2004, 2006, and 2008. In 2008, Georgia reached the College World Series finals and earned a consensus number 2 final national ranking, the second-best finish in school history. Perno is 1 of only 12 men in NCAA history to take three teams to the CWS in his first seven years as a head coach. In 2008, Perno earned SEC Coach of the Year honors for the second time in

his career. In 2004, his third season as a head coach, Perno was named the College Coach of the Year by Baseball America. Perno and his wife, Melaney, have two children, Saidee Woodlyn and David Hayes.

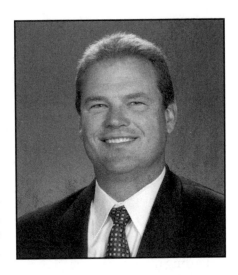

In 2005, **Dan Hartleb** was named head coach of the University of Illinois baseball team. He had served as an assistant coach under Hall of Fame coach Richard "Itch" Jones for 17 years (2 at Southern Illinois and 15 at Illinois). Hartleb guided the Illini to the Big Ten Tournament in each of his first four seasons as head coach. Illinois currently holds the second-longest active streak of reaching the Big Ten Tournament. During his tenure at Illinois, Hartleb has helped recruit and develop many top Illini players. Hartleb and his wife, Gina, have two children, Zakary David and Haley Noel.

Bob Warn was named head coach at Indiana State in 1976. Warn won an incredible 1,050 games, including seven seasons with 40 or more wins. He ranks 10th in total victories among Division I head coaches. Warn has taken seven ISU teams to NCAA championship competition, including a College World Series appearance in 1986. Warn led the Sycamores to a school-record 57 wins in 1985 and trips to the NCAA postseason tournament in 1979, 1983, 1984, 1986, 1987, 1989, and 1995. He was named Missouri Valley Conference Coach of the Year in 1979, 1983, and 1984. He has been inducted into the Iowa Western College Hall of Fame and the Indiana High School Baseball Coaches Hall of Fame. From 1997 to 1998, he was president of the ABCA after serving as vice president from 1995 to 1996. Warn was inducted into the ABCA Hall of Fame in 2003. Warn and his wife, Bonnie, have three sons—Brian, Brad, and Barry—who have all played for Warn at Indiana State.

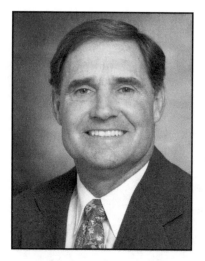

When he retired from coaching at BYU, **Gary Pullins** had compiled 913 wins, which ranked 16th among active NCAA Division I baseball coaches. Under Pullins' direction, the Cougars won 7 Western Athletic Conference titles and 15 division titles. He led the baseball team to the NCAA Regional Tournament nine times. He was inducted into the ABCA Hall of Fame and was named District Coach of the Year four times, WAC Coach of the Year nine times, and Diamond Division I Baseball Coach of the Year in 1985. In 1983, Pullins guided his team to the Cougars' only number 1 ranking in program history. After his retirement, Pullins served as the president of the ABCA for one term and coauthored *The Baseball Coaching Bible* and *Teaching the Complete Baserunner.* Pullins and his wife, Kathy, have four sons, five granddaughters, and one grandson.

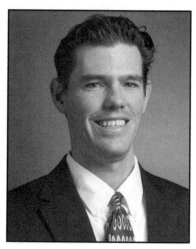

During his tenure as head coach at Duke University, **Sean McNally** has infused his teams with his philosophy of excellence in the classroom, involvement in the community, and achievement on the field. In 2000, the team posted a 3.23 GPA. The team has been awarded the ACC Top Six for Service Award for their various community service initiatives. On the field, McNally led Duke to a four-year record of 116-107-1 (.520) with back-to-back 30-win seasons in 2008 and 2009. In 2009, McNally became the fastest Duke coach to reach 100 wins when he led his alma mater to its best season in over a decade. In his fourth year at the helm, McNally guided the Blue Devils to a 35-24 overall record that included series wins over No. 1 North Carolina and No. 7 Georgia Tech. Before coaching at Duke, McNally served as the hitting coach for Cleveland Indians affiliates Burlington (A) and Akron (AA) before being promoted to manager of the Burlington Indians in 2005. McNally and his wife, Kim, have two children, Michaela and Jackson.

Pete Dunn, head coach at Stetson University, is the 8th winningest Division I coach with 1,097 wins. His winning percentage of .614 (1,097-688-3) places him 41st on the list of active Division I coaches. He was named head coach at Stetson in 1979 after serving as an assistant under Jim Ward. During Dunn's tenure, Stetson has earned 16 NCAA tournament appearances. In 2007, Stetson won the Atlantic Sun conference regular-season championship with a 21-6 conference record (42-21 overall), and Dunn was honored as the league's Coach of the Year for the fifth time in his career. Since 2000, Stetson has

averaged over 40 wins a season, advanced to seven NCAA regionals (including three regional finals), and won four conference championships. In 2001, Dunn guided the Hatters to a 43-17 record and the team's highest national ranking ever—number 7 in the country. In addition, Stetson earned its 11th overall NCAA postseason appearance and advanced to the regional finals. Stetson's 43 victories marked the third-highest single-season total in school history and the first back-to-back 40-win seasons for the Hatters. Dunn was inducted into the Stetson University Sports Hall of Fame in 1992 and received the 1996 Volusian Sportsperson of the Year award presented by the *Daytona Beach News-Journal*. In 1997, Dunn was awarded a 25-year service award by the ABCA, and in 2007 he was inducted into the Central Florida Sports Hall of Fame. Dunn also authored a chapter on catching in *The Baseball Drill Book*. Dunn and his wife, Debbie, have four children: Rayni, Marc, Taylor, and Emily.

You'll find other outstanding baseball resources at

www.HumanKinetics.com/baseball

In the U.S. call 1-800-747-4457

Australia 08 8372 0999 • Canada 1-800-465-7301
Europe +44 (0) 113 255 5665 • New Zealand 0800 222 062